MW00652848

CATHOLICISM and ZEN

CATHOLICISM and ZEN

Richard Bryan McDaniel

Foreword by Mitra Bishop-roshi

CATHOLICISM and ZEN
Richard Bryan McDaniel

Text © Richard Bryan McDaniel 2016
Cover enso © Lynette Genju Monteiro
Kwanyin and baby © JoeyPhoto, Shutterstock
All rights reserved

Book design: Karma Yönten Gyatso

Published by
The Sumeru Press Inc.
PO Box 2089, Richmond Hill, ON
Canada L4E 1A3

ISBN 978-1-896559-35-3

LIBRARY AND ARCHIVES CANADA CATALOGUING IN PUBLICATION

McDaniel, Richard Bryan, author
        Catholicism and Zen / Richard Bryan McDaniel ; foreword
by Mitra Bishop-roshi.

Includes bibliographical references.
ISBN 978-1-896559-35-3 (softcover)

        1. Zen Buddhism--Relations--Catholic Church. 2. Catholic
Church--Relations--Zen Buddhism. I. Title.

BQ9269.4.C35M33 2017   261.2'43   C2017-900024-1

For more information about The Sumeru Press
visit us at www.sumeru-books.com

To the decidedly non-Catholic members of my family:
Phil, Bob, Chris, and Andrea.

Contents

There are two types of Zen practice. The first is really strict Buddhist Zen. You have all the statues and everything else like that; you follow all the Buddhist teaching and everything. And then there is just pure Zen. You will follow that, and that will make you a better Catholic.

— Yamada Koun Roshi, speaking to Thomas Hand

Forward

Ever since Catholic priests from Portugal and Spain entered Japan in the 1500's on missions to convert the Japanese to Christianity, a quiet transformation has been taking place, beginning among those Jesuit missionaries and spreading into the present day among American and European Catholics, lay and ordained alike. As Rick McDaniel writes in this important book, in seeking to understand the Japanese mind so as to know better how to convert the Japanese to Christianity, these early – and later – priests undertook Zen practice. And, as one Japanese Jesuit who was raised Buddhist wrote,[1] in reading the Bible after attending sesshin (Zen Buddhist meditation retreats) he found he could understand it more clearly as a result.

Although there are a number of books written on Christianity and Zen, including several by Catholic clergy, this is the first to take it from its origins with the Jesuit missionaries sent to Japan, to interviews with the many contemporary Catholic clergy – priests and nuns both – who maintain their Catholic faith and practice and find it enhanced by their Zen training. Many of these men and women have done extensive Zen practice under recognized Zen masters and have become authorized themselves to teach Zen practice – and see no conflict with their Christian faith. The author himself was raised Catholic and has practiced Zen for several decades, thus having a unique background through which to explore the congruencies between the two, and his research has resulted in some fascinating insights into the accord between the two religions. Read on!

– Ven. Mitra Bishop, Abbot, Mountain Gate

---

1   J. K. Kadowaki, *Zen and the Bible*, tr. Joan Rieck (Maryknoll, NY: Orbis Books, 2002).

Overture in Montreal

Regardless of previous experience with meditation or spiritual practice, the entry point for membership in the Montreal Zen Center was attendance at an introductory workshop. So in September of 2003, I was seated with about twenty others in what is called the Lower Zendo. A Zendo is a meditation hall. The Upper and Lower Zendos were located in a small building on the Zen Center property that in former incarnations served both as an elementary school and an auto mechanic's garage. The Lower Zendo was a large open room then filled with two dozen chairs arranged theatre style before a platform. To our left was an altar to Kannon – the Bodhisattva[2] of Compassion – with a vase of freshly cut flowers from the center's extensive gardens. In the stairwell leading to the Upper Zendo, suspended by a rope, there was a large circular sawmill blade which served as the Zendo's gong and had a surprisingly sonorous and pleasing tone.

Although Albert Low, the teacher at the Montreal Zen Center, was British, the membership of the sangha (community) was predominantly francophone. As we sat waiting for the workshop to begin, soft vocal music played over the sound system. I noted as I came in that it wasn't in English and supposed it to be French, a language I don't speak, so I didn't pay much attention to it. As I sat there, however, I realized it was actually Spanish – a language I do speak – and, further, that I was familiar with the lyrics. They came from St. John of the Cross:

> One dark night, fired by love's yearnings
> – oh, happy chance! –
> I went forth unobserved, my house now being all at rest.

---

2 Roughly equivalent to a saint.

The poem describes the difficulties encountered on the path of those seeking mystical union with God.

The second part of the workshop began shortly before noon in the Zendo proper upstairs. There was a platform, called a tan, around the perimeter of the room on which were mats (zabutons) and cushions (zafus) for twenty-eight. We took our seats, faced the wall, and began our first formal sitting as Zen students. Shortly after the sitting began, I heard Angelus bells ringing from a nearby church, their sound magnified, so it seemed, by the silence around me. I had heard those bells every day of my attendance at Catholic school in Indiana, but I couldn't remember having heard them for decades. The Angelus is a devotional prayer addressed at noon to the Virgin Mary. I would later learn that in the East, Mary is often identified with the Bodhisattva Kannon. Hearing those bells gave me the feeling that I was, indeed, in the right place.

Albert Low was not a Christian, and he could be withering in his comments about the Catholic culture which permeates this now very secular city where streets are named not only after saints but popes as well. Yet at times, in his teisho (formal lectures) and dokusan (individual interviews with students), he quoted mystics like John of the Cross or Dame Julian of Norwich and the Christian poetry of T. S. Eliot. He wasn't a theist, and yet he told his students that Zen could be thought of as the practice of assenting to the admonition from the Lord's Prayer, "Thy will be done."

Although there is little in common between Buddhism and Christianity as they are commonly understood, at some level both the Zen experience and the experience of certain Christian mystics intersect. This, I would learn, is something a number of committed Catholics had discovered. There has been a Japanese-style meditation hall – a zendo – at the Franciscan Abbey in Dietfurt, Germany, since the 1970s. It was established with the aid of a Jesuit priest, Hugo Enomiya-Lassalle, who was also an authorized teacher in the Sanbo Zen[3] tradition. In Dallas, Texas, the Maria Kannon Zen Center is located in rented space on the second floor of a building owned by the Methodist church. It, too, has the appearance of a traditional zendo except that its altar is graced not with the familiar seated Buddha but with a standing female figure which simultaneously represents Kannon and the Virgin Mary.[4] The Center's founder, Ruben Habito, is now a layman but had been, like Lassalle, a Jesuit and remains both a practicing Catholic and a Zen teacher. The first Canadian to receive transmission – or authorization to teach Zen – is a Roman Catholic nun, Elaine MacInnes, who was awarded the Order of Canada for following the Christian prescription to minister to those in prison. And in Wrentham, Massachusetts, the Zen teacher at the Day Star Sangha is a Trappist monk, Father Kevin Hunt, who once told me that all he had ever wanted in life was to see God. "And Zen has provided

---

3   Formerly Sanbo Kyodan.

4   Buddhist images of Kannon as "Loving Mother" are at times portrayed holding a child.

the best way for me to do it."[5] Each of these individuals has been able to bring two disparate spiritual traditions together in a way that many Christians and Buddhists still disapprove of but which evidently works for them. It was a union I became aware of while writing a book on contemporary American Zen – *Cypress Trees in the Garden* – and determined to look at more closely.

North American Zen adherents inevitably come from non-Buddhist backgrounds; there were very few Asian Buddhists in the early Zen communities established in San Francisco or Los Angeles, although local Buddhist "churches" at the time frequently had substantial ethnic congregations. The membership of the early centers – as today – was largely made up of occidentals who questioned or wholly rejected the faith traditions in which they had been raised. It is intriguing, however, how frequently Catholics retained affiliation with their church even as they committed themselves, often with fervor, to Zen practice. Nor were these Catholic inquirers necessarily disaffected church members. Loyal clergymen and women religious took up Zen practice, encouraged others to do so as well, and at times went on to acquire authorization to teach. They, in effect, earned the right be considered Zen Masters.

As I noted in *Cypress Trees in the Garden,* the term "Master" used in this context refers to one who has mastered a particular practice. In Japan, where the term originated, there are masters of the tea ceremony, master flower arrangers, and master swordsmen. There could also be master carpenters, master piano tuners, and master electricians. "Zen Master" is an unofficial term for one who has not only attained a certain degree of spiritual insight – the stated aim of Zen practice – but who also has demonstrated an ability and an inclination to help others attain similar or deeper insight.

It is a rigorous process. In institutional Zen only a very few receive formal recognition – transmission or *inka shomei* – of such attainment. When I was writing *Cypress Trees,* the American Zen Teachers' Association [AZTA] had only 224 members, which included teachers in Canada and Mexico as well as the United States. Given the sparse number of authorized teachers, the fact that any at all are also Catholic priests or nuns is noteworthy.

The more I delved into the subject the richer it revealed itself to be. The relationship between Zen and Catholicism is synergetic. While Zen helped certain Catholics recapture elements of a mystical tradition in church teaching which had fallen into abeyance, Catholic enthusiasts like Thomas Merton – especially in the 1950s and '60s when the first practice centers were being established in North America – helped Zen acquire an intellectual credibility in the West long unrivaled by other Asian disciplines.

---

5 Richard Bryan McDaniel, *Cypress Trees in the Garden* (Richmond Hill, ON: Sumeru Press, 2015), p. 320.

This book does not have a thesis as such. I am merely chronicling a phenomenon I find significant and interesting. I am Roman Catholic by birth and heritage and a Zen practitioner by nature and temperament, so it is a natural subject for me. Regardless of one's heritage or temperament, however, the topic of Catholic engagement in Zen is an intriguing one for many reasons, not the least of which is that the initial encounter between Zen and the West was fraught with misunderstanding and hostility on both sides.

CHAPTER ONE

Beginnings

FRANCIS XAVIER
COSME DE TORRES
ALESSANDRO VALIGNANO
CHRISTOVAO FERREIRA

1

The two dominant colonizing powers of the late 15th century were Spain and Portugal. In order to lessen the squabbling between the two over who got where first and thus could claim control over what, Pope Alexander VI drew a line down the center of a map and declared that all new territories discovered east of the line would be subject to Portugal and those west of the line to Spain. This gave what is now Brazil to Portugal along with the so-called East Indies, which included the Indian sub-continent and South-East Asia; Spain acquired the rest of the Americas, including the Caribbean, as well as the Philippines. The agreement, codified in the Treaty of Tordesillas of 1494, did not, however, take into consideration that the earth is a globe, and the two nations would eventually find themselves at odds about whether the islands of Japan were in the western-most territory deeded to Spain or the eastern-most deeded to Portugal. When other European powers mounted their own colonizing efforts, they – and the peoples living in the lands Europeans were seeking to colonize – ignored the terms of the treaty entirely. By 1540, however, Spain and Portugal still did not yet have any serious rivals.

In that year, King John of Portugal asked the Pope to authorize missionaries to spread the gospel in his Asian possessions, and it was decided that the newly formed Society of Jesus – or Jesuits – would be given this responsibility. The founder of the order, Ignatius of Loyola, assigned the mission to two men who had been with him since the establishment of the order, Simao Rodrigues and Nicholas Bobadilla. Bobadilla, however, fell ill before the party set off, and another original member, Francis Xavier, was chosen to replace him.

Although not Loyola's first choice, Francis had a successful career in the Indies. He converted tens of thousands to Christianity and established forty churches along the west coast of India. In his reports back to Europe, he enthusiastically recounts the satisfaction he found not only in baptizing "heathens" but in then burning their shrines. "I could never come to an end describing to you the great consolation which fills my soul when I see idols being destroyed by the hands of those who had been idolaters."

His perspective was one with which few would find sympathy today – and which is no longer supported by the Catholic Church – but it is unreasonable to expect an individual to be able to see beyond the cultural conditionings of his time and place. For Xavier and the other missionaries, no work was more laudable than saving the unbaptized from eternal perdition. Their confidence in the tenets of their faith, however, prevented them from making just assessments of the cultural heritages of the societies they sought to save.

Francis was based in Goa and, from there, extended his missionary work to Ceylon (Sri Lanka), Malacca, and the Maluku Islands in present day Indonesia. In Malacca he met a young samurai named Anjiro[6] who had had to flee his native Japan after killing a man. Anjiro is the first known Japanese convert to Christianity, and Francis was fascinated by his description of his homeland. Xavier asked Anjiro if he thought the people of Japan would be receptive to Christianity. Anjiro told him that conversions would not be immediate; however, the people of Japan would inquire deeply into Christian teaching and observe the conduct of the Europeans. If they saw that the behaviour of the missionaries was in accord with their teachings, then doubtless the leaders of the country would be drawn to the faith, and no more than six months later – by his estimate – the majority of the population would follow, because Japan was a land "guided by reason."

Anjiro also reported that there was a meditation sect in the land in which monks were challenged by their teacher to reflect, "When a man is dying and cannot speak, since the soul is being separated from the body, if it could then speak in such a separation and withdrawal of the soul, what things would the soul say to the body?"[7]

---

6   His name is also recorded as "Yajiro." His Christian name, after baptism, was Paulo de Santa Fe.

7   quoted in Stephen Batchelor, *The Awakening of the West* (Williamsville, VT: Echo Point Books, 2011), p. 165.

Anjiro may have been describing a Zen teacher's commentary on the 35th case in the koan collection known as *The Gateless Gate*. Koans are enigmatic anecdotes which Zen practitioners use as meditation subjects. A koan is usually posed in the form of a question which needs to be resolved through intuition rather than reason. This particular koan refers to a popular Chinese ghost story in which a young woman, Sei, runs away with her lover. Years later, the pair returns to the girl's parents' home to discover that her body had remained in a coma on her bed all that time. At the end of the story, the two Seis come together into one. The koan asks: "Sei's soul was separate from her body. Which was the real Sei?"

Hearing Anjiro's report, Francis assumed that the monks were being instructed to contemplate a philosophical question, as Jesuits were trained to do, and that this inclination toward spiritual reflection was something upon which he would be able to build.

He set off for Japan in the summer of 1549 along with Father Cosme de Torres and a lay brother, Juan Fernandez. The country was not immediately welcoming. The Jesuits were refused entry to Japanese ports until, on August 15, they came to Kagoshima, Anjiro's home town on the island of Kyusho. There is no Japanese record of what followed; we have only Francis's and his companions' descriptions of the events. There are, however, contemporary Japanese accounts of their first contact with Portuguese traders and seaman, and these are not flattering. The foreigners were said to lack refinement and proper decorum; they ate with their fingers rather than using chopsticks; they lacked restraint in showing emotion, and they exhibited behavior which the Japanese considered boorish.

Francis, on the other hand, was impressed by the elegance of Japanese society and culture. According to his report, when the Jesuits arrived in Kagoshima they were received hospitably by local authorities and were accepted as guests in the house of Anjiro's mother, where the samurai's wife and daughter had been staying. The family arranged for the Jesuits to meet the local daimyo,[8] Shimazu Takahisa, who understood the missionaries to be envoys from the king of Portugal. Believing that Anjiro could be useful in helping him establish a trading relationship with the Portuguese, the daimyo welcomed him back to his homeland.

According to Xavier, the daimyo received the missionaries with enthusiasm. He was particularly delighted with a portrait of the Virgin and Christ Child which, when presented to him, he knelt before and paid reverence to. The Jesuits had brought portraits of Mary because they realized that the more traditional depictions of the crucifixion would scandalize the Japanese. Shimazu's mother was so impressed by the painting that she asked for a copy of it as well as a full description of the teachings of the Christian church, which Anjiro undertook to provide her.

---

8   Lord.

Xavier noted that the daimyo's coat of arms represented a cross within a circle. In addition, the Buddhist clergy made use of bells and rosaries and "prayed" with folded hands. The veneration they exhibited for bodhisattvas appeared similar to the veneration of the saints. The monks lived in communities which came together at regular intervals during the day to "pray." From these coincidences – and misleading information about the Buddha and Buddhism he received from Anjiro – Xavier came to wonder if at some time in the past Christianity had been brought to Japan, possibly by the apostle Thomas, and had then been corrupted over time because of lack of contact with other Christian nations.

During a second audience with the daimyo, Xavier presented him with an illustrated Bible and explained that the laws of the Christian faith were found therein. Shimazu replied that such a book should be treated with great care because if the teachings of Jesus were true, then the Devil must be displeased by them. He readily agreed to allow the missionaries to preach the gospel in his land and issued an edict allowing his subjects to become members of the new sect if they chose, and, indeed, several members of his household accepted baptism.

This is the manner in which the initial encounter between the Jesuits and the Japanese is usually described; however, the Swiss historian, Urs App, has pointed out that these events might have appeared differently had they been reported from a Japanese perspective:[9] The daimyo, whose family "crest had the shape of a round bit-piece of a horse with its cross-like shape in the middle," learned of the arrival of a group of foreign priests whom he would have assumed to be Buddhists since they had come from Tenjiku (India), the homeland of the Buddha Shakyamuni.[10] There were several competing Buddhist sects in Japan at the time – the Nichiren, Shingon, Tendai, and Zen – and the foreigners appeared to represent yet another. In addition, "They had apparently brought along all sorts of interesting things that nobody had ever seen – maybe even some of those firearms that were creating such a stir among rival daimyos." They were accompanied by a Japanese who spoke their language, could read their writing, and was able to explain the new Buddhist teachings they'd brought.

> So the ruler invited Anjiro to his castle to learn what all the fuss was about. He questioned him about his travels and wanted to see some of those fascinating objects everybody raved about. Having foreseen this, Anjiro obliged by showing him an image of the Virgin with child... Sitting on his knees in the formal posture and leaning

9   Urs App, "Saint Francis Xavier's Discovery of Japanese Buddhism," *The Eastern Buddhist* XXX: 1, 1997. pp. 53-76. http://universitymedia.org/downloads/app_francis_xavier_123.pdf.

10   Siddhartha Gautama, the Buddha of "Buddhism," is just one of many Buddhas (or "awakened ones") who have lived. The title "Shakyamuni" refers to his clan of origin and means "Sage of the Sakyas."

forward to see the object up close, as one does for example when admiring a precious tea bowl, the ruler was stunned: though this was a picture painted on wood, it looked so very real!

The daimyo's mother assumed the painting to be a portrait of Kannon, the Bodhisattva of Compassion, and requested a copy of it as well as a summary of the teachings of the foreign monks. Anjiro explained that they taught of Dainichi, the Japanese name for Vairocana Buddha revered by Shingon Buddhists, who was the creator of all things and had proclaimed a moral law for humankind. Further, all persons – regardless of gender or social class – had an eternal spirit (*tamashii*) which would be judged after death and then sent either to the Pure Land or to Hell where it would be tortured by demons (*tengu*) for all of eternity.

When Xavier himself came to the court, this misunderstanding would have been strengthened:

> The foreign bonzes [priests/monks] from Tenjiku, the homeland of Shaka [Buddha], wore long black robes, had partly shaved heads, were said to have no intercourse with women, refrained from eating animal meat and kept speaking of the very things Buddhist priests were so fond of … So why should he [Shimazu] not allow them to spread their buppo [version of Buddhism] and let both his vassals and his family profit from the merits of the new transmission?

Based on these fundamental misunderstandings, the Jesuits' relations with the Buddhist clergy were easy at first. Since Xavier thought Buddhism was possibly a degraded form of Christianity, he believed that if he were able to win the support of the local Buddhist clergy their congregations would follow. To that end, he made a point of trying to meet the leading Buddhist figures in the community and entered into debate with them about the existence of a God external to and responsible for Creation, which was a foreign and bewildering concept to the Buddhists. Jesuits found the Buddhist beliefs not only equally incomprehensible but bleak. One of the Jesuits who came to Japan after Xavier, Padre Luis Frois, summed up his understanding of Zen in this way: "The sect believes there is nothing more than birth and death, that there is no later life, nor a creator who governs the universe." It was difficult for the Jesuits to imagine how such an arid doctrine qualified as a religion.

Shortly after their arrival in Kagoshima, however, Xavier met and formed a friendship with the abbot of Fukushoji, a Soto Zen monastery. The abbot's name is recorded as Ninshitsu, which, in his reports back to India, Xavier said meant "Heart of Truth." Xavier describes Ninshitsu in fulsome terms, asserting that he was the equivalent of a bishop and "an amazingly good friend. Both the laity and the bonzes," Xavier writes proudly, "are delighted with us, astonished that we have traveled from lands as far away as Portugal – more than 6000 leagues – for the sole purpose of speaking of the things of God."

He discussed the concept of an immortal soul with Ninshitsu but had to report that the Zen Master was "hesitant and unable to decide whether our soul is immortal or if it dies along with the body. At times, he has said that it is immortal, at others that it is not. I am afraid that it is the same with the other scholars."

Cultural misunderstanding colored Xavier's interpretation of Zen practice. He observed the monks at Ninshitsu's temple spending long periods of time in seated meditation. What he did not grasp was that Buddhist meditation was a process of clearing the mind rather than, as in the Ignation system, reflecting on a topic or scriptural passage. When he asked Ninshitsu what the meditators were thinking about, he assumed it would be a passage from the Buddhist sutras or an edifying concept. Instead, the abbot told him: "Some, no doubt, are thinking about the income generated by their temples, others are thinking about clothing and food; still others about various pastimes and festivals. In other words, about nothing of any importance." Xavier would have missed the irony in this description of the endless train of thought that passes through the mind and which Zen practice seeks to still.

Although Xavier counted Ninshitsu a friend, he was unable to convert him, and eventually the Buddhist community understood that what Xavier was presenting was not a new form of Buddhism but a rival faith, and one which denied the validity of all other points of view. At that point they became less welcoming. There were, however, conversions. One of the appeals of the Christian doctrine was the possibility of salvation after death and a righting of wrongs in the world to come. To a populace weary of war and turmoil, these were attractive concepts. So there were baptisms, although nothing like the number the Jesuits had had in India.

Shimazu also became disenchanted with the visitors when it was clear they were not interested in helping him establish trade relations – particularly for firearms – with Portuguese merchants. As Buddhist hostility to the missionaries grew, Shimazu withdrew his support and forbade further conversions under the penalty of death.

Xavier would maintain that had it not been for the interference of the Buddhist clergy and the daimyo's edict, a majority of the city's population would have been baptized. Leaving Anjiro to care for the small Christian community that had been established in Kagoshima, Xavier and the rest of his party proceeded to Hirado, where he was received by Shimazu's rival, Matsura Takanobu, who was also more interested in trade opportunities than in spiritual endeavors.

From Hirado, Xavier and his companions set off for the capital, Kyoto, some 800 kilometers away. They began their journey in October, not a felicitous time of year to undertake such an arduous trek. By the time they arrived in the city of Yamaguchi on the island of Honshu, they were exhausted. In emulation of the poverty of Christ, Xavier had gone barefoot and in a simple robe that became increasing threadbare as the trip proceeded.

They stayed in Yamaguchi for a while, preaching on street corners, where children made fun of them. Xavier did not speak Japanese so while his interpreters spoke he stood by in prayer, making him an easy target for schoolboy jibes. The Christian forbearance with which they met this treatment eventually won a handful of converts, but Anjiro's predictions about the readiness of the Japanese to respond to the reasoned arguments of the Jesuits had yet to be realized.

Shortly after Christmas – during the worst of the winter season – the party continued on to Kyoto, wading at times through knee-high snow drifts and fording nearly frozen streams on foot.

The Jesuits were the first foreigners to enter what was then both the political and spiritual capital of Japan. It had been Xavier's hope to have audiences with both the Emperor Go-Nara and the Shogun, Yoshiteru Ashikaga, but his appearance played against him, and neither of these meetings came about. Nor was he able to gain access to the Buddhist monastery on Mount Hiei where he had imagined entering into reasoned debate with the monks residing there.

He realized that the Japanese dismissed him in part because of his apparent poverty; if he were to have an impact in Japan, he needed to make a greater display and come prepared with the kind of gifts the nobility expected. He also now understood that the Emperor no longer had any real power and that, since the collapse of the Kamakura Shogunate, even the shoguns lacked the ability to unify the land. Real power lay with the local feudal leaders, daimyos like Shimazu and Matsura Takanobu.

Francis returned to Hirado, gathered a number of gifts originally intended for the Emperor – including another portrait of the Madonna, a three-barrel musket, two telescopes, and a clock – then sailed back to Yamaguchi. This time when he sought an audience with the local daimyo, Ouchi Yoshitaka, he did so in the guise of an ambassador from the Portuguese governor of India wearing a silk cassock, surplice, and stole and attended by a retinue of converts and servants, all appropriately dressed. The daimyo, impressed by the gifts, gave the missionaries an abandoned monastery for their use and guaranteed them his protection as they sought to spread the gospel in his area. By September 1550, the Jesuits claimed to have baptized 500 new Christians.

Once the community seemed well-established, Xavier left it under the leadership of Father de Torres and made plans to return to India. He had spent two years in Japan and was never to return. He died a year later while trying to reach China.

2

Cosme de Torres, more than Xavier, was tasked with finding a way to make Christian doctrine accessible to a people he and Xavier recognized as highly sophisticated and intellectually advanced. Conversion was not going to come about as a result of an appeal to emotion but rather, in their opinion, through rational argument. So they petitioned their superiors to send linguists to the mission fields who could learn the language and study Buddhist texts in order to better be able to refute them.

The Jesuits took it for granted that, regarded objectively, the tenets of the Catholic faith were rational and self-evident. However, their catechesis was based on Aristotelian principles of logic with which the Japanese were unfamiliar. One of the proofs they asserted for the existence of God, for example, was Thomas Aquinas's argument for the necessity of a Prime Mover. Nothing which is not itself living (animate) can move without an external cause for that motion. The sun and the moon are not living things, consequently there must be an external power (a Prime Mover) responsible for their movements. Although the missionaries were able to provide evidence, to the astonishment of the Japanese, that the Earth was a globe, they were not, themselves, aware that the planet revolved around the sun, so assumed it was the motion of the sun that needed to be explained. Regardless, the Japanese were not swayed by the argument.

The idea of an external creator remained foreign to Buddhist thought. After trying to explain the necessary existence of a Supreme Being to a Zen abbot, the Buddhist's response both puzzled and frustrated de Torres. The abbot dismissed the idea of God and, instead, outlined the concept of *sunyata*, the Void or Emptiness, which de Torres interpreted as a "great Nothingness." In his perplexed report to his superiors, de Torres explained that after

> – the great Nothingness has entered existence, it can do nothing than
> to return to the same Nothingness ... This is a principle from which
> all things proceed, whether human beings, animals, or plants. Every
> created thing contains this principle in itself, and when humans or
> animals die, the four elements revert into that which they had been
> at first, and this principle returns to that which it is ... This prin-
> ciple is neither good nor evil. It possesses neither bliss nor pain. It
> neither dies nor lives, so that it is truly a Nothingness.[11]

11   quoted in Heinrich Dumoulin, *Zen Buddhism: A History – Japan* (Bloomington, IN: World Wisdom, 2005), p. 267. The Buddhist concept of the Void [*Ku* in Japanese] is easily misunderstood. Essentially, it refers to that which is beyond all possibility of human conception, beyond all duality (including the duality of being or non-being); it is that from which all things arise and to which they return.

Likewise, the notion of an eternal soul conflicted with the Buddhist perspective, which Jesuits considered nihilistic and contradictory because at times it appeared to claim there was no enduring self and, at others, to assert that the soul has successive reincarnated lives. The Christian concept of a soul, on the other hand – which though created and thus had a beginning but is then somehow eternal – made little sense to the Japanese clergy.

In spite of the opposition of the Buddhist leadership, de Torres did acquire the support of Daimyo Sorin Otomo, who became a convert, and a small Christian community began to develop in his fiefdom.

3

De Torres remained the Mission Superior in Japan until his death in 1570, after which disagreements arose within the Jesuit order about the appropriate way to continue their work. De Torres's successor, Francisco Cabral, for example, forbade all accommodation to Japanese culture, an approach contested by the more pragmatic Alessandro Valignano who eventually forced Cabral to surrender his office. Valignano sought to establish a Christian practice and form suitable to Japanese sensibilities. The model he took for ceremonial matters was the elegant Zen school

> – since this one "was considered at the time to be the most important of all religious communities in Japan and was in touch with all classes of Japanese society." The difficulty in practicing this ceremonial pattern lay in the problem of determining a hierarchy within the missionary staff, with corresponding titles and forms of courtesy. Valignano solved this problem by assigning the missionaries to ranks similar to those in the Zen community. The head of the mission for all Japan became equivalent to the abbot of Nanzen-ji, while the heads of the missionary districts of Shimo, Bungo, and Miyaki were accorded the dignity of the abbot in one of the Five Mountains [central temples] of Kyoto. The priests became the counterparts of the head of a temple (*choro* or *todo*). The Japanese brothers, who bore a great deal of the actual work of the mission, were placed on the level of the overseer or guide of *zazen* (*shuza*); novices were on the level of treasurers (*zosu*); and neophytes and catechists were ranked as tonsured novices (*jisha*) in the Zen school. Through this ingenious and bold arrangement of the visitator, the Christian missionaries attained high standing in Japanese society ...

In every mission house a tea room was to be set up near the entrance, where tea was to be served Japanese style. Guests of whatever class were to be received in a manner appropriate to their station, so that all of them might acquire sympathy and esteem for the Christian mission. Indeed, the Jesuits have been accused of addressing themselves too exclusively to the upper classes of old Japan, at the expense of the common people. However this may have been, their impact on the upper classes were extraordinary. Numerous daimyo and members of the high nobility as well as samurai and monks became Christians. At times Christianity was in the forefront. Portuguese dress became stylish in the capital and all things European were admired.[12]

Valignano's success naturally stoked the ire of the Buddhist establishment and provoked the suspicion of the Chancellor of the Realm, Toyotomi Hideyoshi, who was, in all but name, Shogun and was determined to unify the Japanese people under a single authority. He considered Christians a potential political threat. So, in 1587, he issued an edict ordering the missionaries out of the country. The edict was not enforced and, indeed, a second missionary order – Franciscans from Spain – arrived to contest the hegemony of the Jesuits and Portugal's claim on the Japanese islands under the terms of the Treaty of Tordesillas.

In 1596, Spain and Portugal came into conflict over which country, according to the treaty, had salvage rights for the cargo of a wrecked merchant vessel. To preclude the involvement of the Japanese in the dispute, the Spanish governor (in the words of Christian historian, Paul Johnson)

> – sent a threatening note to the Japanese tyrant, Hideyoshi, pointing out with unbelievable ineptitude that missionaries preceded *conquistadors*; and in response Hideyoshi promptly crucified six Franciscans, three Jesuit lay-brothers, and nineteen Japanese neophytes.[13]

Having flexed his muscles, Hideyoshi felt he had made his point and tacitly allowed the missions to continue. He died the following year, 1598, to be succeeded by Ieyasu Tokugawa, the first Shogun of the dynasty which would control Japan for the next two and a half centuries.

In addition to Jesuits and Franciscans, Protestant missionaries had made their way to the country. Ieyasu valued the trade relationship with the Dutch but was leery

---

12   Dumoulin, p. 269-70.

13   Paul Johnson, *A History of Christianity* (New York, Atheneum, 1977), p. 418.

of Christians, who were now fighting one another for the souls of the Japanese. Like Hideyoshi, Ieyasu was intent upon unifying Japan both politically and culturally. Catholicism, in particular, was viewed as a subversive teaching which might draw the loyalty of the people from the Emperor to a foreign Pope, and, for that reason, Ieyasu ordered all foreign Christians expelled from the islands in 1614. Although most complied with the edict, a group of Jesuits went underground in order to minister to a native Japanese Catholic population which has been variously estimated to have then been between 250,000 and 750,000 persons. One of the Jesuits who remained in Japan was Christovao Ferreira.

4

The story of the first Western convert to Zen Buddhism is not an edifying one from the perspective of either Europe or Japan.

Ferreira arrived in Japan in 1609 and quickly rose to prominence in the order. He was a linguist of the type de Torres and Xavier had hoped to bring to the islands, and he acquired fluency in the Japanese language. Within three years of his arrival, he was designated an assistant superior at the Jesuit residence in Kyoto and, while in hiding, was appointed Procurator of the order in 1619.

Once he went underground, he was still able to smuggle letters to his superiors in Macao in which he described the persecution in the country, emphasizing the courageous way in which both captured clergy and laity suffered torture and martyrdom on behalf of their faith.

Ferreira was finally apprehended by the authorities in September 1633. Stephen Batchelor, in his *Awakening of the West,* describes what then followed:

> By this time the Tokugawa authorities had realized that in crucifying Christians or burning them at the stake, they automatically created martyrs and thereby strengthened the faith of the underground Church. They now sought to force Christians to apostatize, issue a formal denunciation of their faith, and convert to Buddhism. In this way, especially if the apostate was a priest, the confidence of the Church would be undermined. Persuasion started softly with reasoned argument and, if that failed, proceeded to torture, the most feared of which was the *anatsurushi.* This entailed suspending the tightly bound victim upside down in a pit filled with excrement. To prolong the ordeal the temple was slit to prevent cerebral haemorrhage and the obnoxious fumes were such to induce partial anaesthesia, thus maximizing pain while delaying death. One hand was left unbound to allow the victim to signal apostasy ...

At the time of Ferreira's arrest, not a single priest had yet denounced his faith. Most died after two or three days of agony; although one young woman endured the punishment for two weeks before expiring. Less than a month after his capture, Ferreira was subjected to the pit. After a mere six hours the Vice-Provincial raised his hand and apostatized.

This was a devastating blow to the Christian community in Japan and the Jesuits in Macao and Europe. Worse still, Ferreira agreed to co-operate with his torturers in eradicating Christianity. He assumed a Japanese name, Sawano Chuan, and signed himself:

> the resident of the country of Portugal,
> Chief Bateren (priest) of Japan and Macao,
> Christovao Ferreira,
> reformed in religion and turned
> an adherent of Zen[14]

As Batchelor notes, it isn't possible to determine to what extent Ferreira actually practiced his new religion. He did, however, marry a Japanese woman and spent the remainder of his days in the country, dying there in 1650. By that time, Iemitsu Tokugawa had cut off all contact with Europe save for the Dutch merchants who had lent naval support to the shogun's forces during the battle for Nara Castle during the Catholic Shimabara Rebellion, although even they were only tolerated on an artificial island constructed in Nagasaki Bay and were not permitted on the mainland. It became a capital crime for Japanese citizens to leave the country. Europeans and children of mixed European-Japanese parentage were expelled. The foreign missions came to an end, and Japan was isolated from the rest of the world for the next two hundred years.

---

14   Batchelor, op. cit, pp. 179-81.

CHAPTER TWO

Hugo Enomiya-Lassalle & Koun Yamada

1

Two hundred and twenty years after Japan closed its ports to foreign vessels, the United States took measures to reverse that decision. Prompted by concern for the safety of American whaling vessels in the area and a desire to ensure that trade routes between North America and the Asian mainland remained open, President Millard Fillmore assigned Commodore Matthew Perry the task of gaining right of entry to Japanese ports by any means necessary. In July 1853, Perry entered Tokyo Harbor with a fleet of four gunships. After a modest initial resistance, Japan capitulated; the inability of the Tokugawa Shogunate to repel the invaders was one of the factors contributing to its eventual downfall.

Once foreigners regained the right to reside in Japan, both Catholic and Protestant missionaries rushed in although direct proselytization remained prohibited. Seven years after the missionaries returned, Father Bernard Petitjean of the French Société des Missions Etrangères learned of the existence of a number of "Kirishitans" in Nagasaki who had practiced their faith in secret since the closing of the country two centuries prior. Because Catholic iconography had been forbidden, their altars were hidden in what appeared to be Buddhist shrines, and the traditional figure of the Bodhisattva Kannon was venerated as a representation of the Virgin Mary. The pope of the day declared the survival of this community a miracle and authorized the construction of a cathedral in the city.

Once again, the Society of Jesus was among the most active orders in the country. In 1913, German Jesuits established Sophia University in Tokyo. The order still believed that the validity of Catholic doctrine could be demonstrated by rational argument, but they were also pragmatists; the university, consequently, offered courses in both philosophy and commerce.

∾

Jesuits at the turn of the 19th and 20th centuries were better informed about Buddhism than their predecessors had been but were no less bewildered by doctrines founded on premises so radically different from their own. It was difficult for them to understand how Buddhism qualified to be a religion at all. To begin with, as Francis Xavier and Cosme de Torres had learned, the concept of a creator God external to the universe was not self-evident to the Japanese, and the idea of an eternal soul was in stark contrast with the Buddhist teaching of *anatta* or "no permanent self."

The Buddha was not a god or supernatural being but rather an "enlightened" teacher. The word "Buddha" is a title rather than a name, meaning the "Enlightened" or the "Awakened One," usually – but not always – referring to Siddhartha Gautama who flourished five hundred years before the birth of Christ. Buddhism, as a doctrine, is the body of teachings – the Dharma – attributed to him. These teachings, originally received and passed on orally, were not written down until more than 400 years after the Buddha's death, and over time, as his followers reflected on these written scriptures – sutras – new interpretations evolved. Sometimes these interpretations were also composed as sutras which were attributed to the Buddha even centuries later. This resulted in a proliferation of schools of Buddhism, one of which was Zen.

The word *zen* is the Japanese way of pronouncing the Chinese character 禪 (*chan*), generally translated as "meditation." So Chan or Zen is the meditation school of Buddhism. Buddhism as it had developed in India took the Hindu concept of successive lives for granted and focused on escaping the suffering associated with the endless cycle of birth-and-death or Samsara. The goal of early Buddhist practice was to attain Nirvana, which means to "blow out" or "extinguish," as a candle is blown out. Nirvana was viewed as a state wherein all sense of "self" was burned away, a state beyond desire and the suffering that necessarily ensues from desire, as a result of which there is nothing left to be reborn. When Buddhism came to China, however, the people there did not see any particular need to escape from a supposed round of birth-and-death, consequently a very different understanding of Buddhism evolved. The Indian teaching blended with Chinese Daoism which emphasized the Way – Dao – or natural flow of the rhythms of nature. Chan was the result of the interplay between these two traditions.

A poem attributed to Bodhidharma – the legendary 6th century Indian missionary credited with bringing Chan to China – sums up the Zen perspective in four lines:

A special transmission outside the scriptures;
Not dependent on words or letters;

By direct pointing to the mind of man,
Seeing into one's true nature and attaining Buddhahood.

The signature feature of Zen is the emphasis placed on the practice of seated meditation (*zazen*) and the achievement of "awakening" (*kensho* or *satori* in Japanese[15]).
With "awakening," it is held that the Zen practitioner acquires the same insight and
perception that Siddhartha Gautama attained when he achieved enlightenment, an
awareness that one's fundamental nature is no different from that of all existence.
Although Zen practice emphasizes – as did earlier forms of Buddhism – the need for
a loss of "self," this is not so much in order to escape the round of Samsara as it is to
realize one's intimate relationship with all of Being.

By the end of the 9th Century, there were Five Houses of Chan in China, each
of which traced its lineage back to a particular group of teachers. The two most
prominent of these schools were known in Japanese as the Rinzai and the Soto. The
first Rinzai temple in Japan was established in 1191. The Soto School of Zen arrived
thirty-five years later. Because Rinzai temples were also centers for academic and artistic instruction for the upper classes, Zen sensibility came to infuse many aspects of
Japanese culture including the visual, literary, and even military arts.

Both the Rinzai and Soto schools view awakening as a goal, although not necessarily the culmination, of Zen practice. The traditional methods by which they
seek to guide the practitioner to this end, however, differ. In China, Rinzai teachers
developed the use of *koans* – such as the question concerning the story of Sei – as a
means by which the student could be led to awakening and later to the deepening
and integration of that awakening into all aspects of their life. In contrast, the Soto
student is usually taught a subjectless form of meditation known in Japanese as *shikan
taza* or "just sitting." The meditator sits alert without focusing attention on anything
in particular. These practice techniques are not exclusive. The Soto School makes
occasional use of koans, and Rinzai students may be advised to do shikan taza. What
they share is the belief that Buddhahood – awakening – is achieved not through study
of scripture or philosophical reasoning but through direct spiritual experience. It is a
perspective which thwarted Jesuit attempts to argue against the doctrine.

The urgency early European missionaries had felt in imposing Christianity on other
lands was based on a belief in a supernatural battle between truth and error. This held
that there is a single true path revealed by and leading to God; all other paths are

---

15   Although, especially in Catholic writing on Zen, the terms kensho and satori are sometimes treated
      as if they were interchangeable, there is usually a distinction made between kensho, the initial expe-
      rience of awakening, and satori, the deeper and more profound awakening to which kensho leads.

delusions wrought by Satan. It is a perspective some Christian fundamentalists continue to maintain and which explains why Francis Xavier found righteous satisfaction in destroying heathen shrines. The missionaries also believed there is a defined moral code associated with the true path. It is not enough to profess correct belief, one must also behave in a way prescribed by God and in accordance with his will. To fail to do so is to sin, which leads to damnation.

The Japanese perspective was very different. While popular imagination hoped in the existence of supernatural beings which could respond to human prayer and entreaty, the idea of "sin" as such was absent. The Buddha's Eight-Fold path,[16] for example, is not a list of moral prohibitions but a description of a healthy way of living. Nor is there a single correct way of relating to gods, spirits (*kami*), buddhas, and bodhisattvas. The point is made in a popular subject for artists in which the Buddha, Confucius, and the Daoist Laozi are portrayed drinking from a single pot of wine.[17] The Japanese perspective finds no difficulty in recognizing that multiple religious traditions can be valid. To think otherwise would be narrow-minded. So one might follow Confucius in the ordering of one's household, seek to align oneself with the way of nature (Daoism), pay reverence to local kami (Shinto), and undertake Zen practice to discover one's true nature and liberation from the world of illusion.

The immense differences between Eastern and Western perspectives, in particular the fact that the Japanese were not open to the concept of religious exclusivity, made it difficult for missionaries to make much headway in Japan, and, in the end, Zen probably had a greater impact on the Jesuits than the other way around.

2

Hugo Lassalle was born in Germany on November 11, 1898. While still in his teens, he was conscripted into military service during the First World War – a long, bleak, and ultimately futile endeavor for the German people. He was wounded in battle and, while in hospital, happened upon the biography of another wounded soldier, Ignatius of Loyola. In it he found inspiration to follow a new direction in life.

The war ended on Lassalle's 20th birthday. Five months later, he entered the Jesuit college at s'Heerenberge in Holland. The Jesuit formation process is slow, careful, and arduous. After completing the novitiate in 1921, Lassalle became a Scholastic, taking vows of poverty, chastity, and obedience. This second phase prepares the candidate for ordination – which for Lassalle didn't take place until 1927 – and includes a demanding course of study in philosophy and theology. After ordination, Jesuits enter a third period of training called the Tertianship. This includes an examination

---

16   Right View, Right Intention, Right Speech, Right Action, Right Livelihood, Right Effort, Right Mindfulness, and Right Meditation.

17   These images are often referred to as "The Vinegar Tasters."

of the history of Christian mysticism, which introduced Lassalle to the works of John of the Cross and Teresa de Avila as well as Thomas a Kempis's *The Imitation of Christ*, works in which he and others would later find intriguing correspondences with Zen.

It had been his hope to be posted to Africa after ordination, but instead his superiors sent him to Sophia University in Japan.

The Japan Lassalle encountered was very different from the feudal and largely agricultural nation that Perry had opened to the west. It had evolved into a modern industrialized state with expansionist ambitions. As commonly happens when an economy moves from an agricultural to an industrial base, many rural workers moved into the cities seeking employment and crowded into low rent districts where few facilities were available.

Although Lassalle's primary responsibility was the university, the objective of the Jesuit mission was to find effective ways of bringing the Christian message to the populace. Inspired by the Social Gospel Movement in North America – which applied Christian teachings to economic and other social justice issues – Lassalle chose to reside in one of these poorer neighborhoods; he organized university students to offer free education to the children, and he established a medical clinic.

In 1935, he was appointed Mission Superior and relocated to Hiroshima. There, professors at Bunrika University convinced him that to understand the character of the Japanese people he needed to understand Zen Buddhism, and he began what was at first a fairly superficial and academic study.

The global situation was once again dire. Two years prior, the Nazi Party had won a majority of seats in the German Reichstag and enacted legislation leading to the establishment of a totalitarian state under the leadership of Adolf Hitler. A few years later, Germany would once again be engaged in a war it was doomed to lose, this time allied with Japan which sought to expand its sphere of influence in Asia and justified its actions as a necessary defensive response to western imperialism. In spite of the political situation, Lassalle remained in sympathy with the Japanese people who endured enormous sufferings during the war. In particular, he admired the strength of character Zen monks and lay people exhibited in the face of those hardships and wondered if the mental and physical discipline of Zen had the potential of deepening his own spiritual life.

In the spring of 1943 – as the War in the Pacific raged on and the toll it took on the people of Japan became increasingly more arduous – Lassalle attended sesshin for the first time at Eimyoji[18] under the direction of Shimada Roshi.[19] This was in no way a conversion to Buddhism – Lassalle remained a committed Jesuit throughout his

---

18 "Ji" is a Japanese suffix meaning "temple." Eimyo Temple is located in the town of Tsuwano outside Hiroshima.

19 "Roshi" is an honorary title given senior Zen teachers. Literally, it means "old teacher."

life – but rather an experiment to discern whether Zen as a discipline had potential application beyond Buddhism. It was, however, a significant step in the development of Western Zen. There had been a handful of Zen students in the west already,[20] but they practiced as Buddhists. Lassalle's unique contribution was to question – if it were "a special transmission outside the scriptures" – could Zen be a practice available to people who did not also subscribe to doctrinaire Buddhism?

☙

On August 6, 1945, Lassalle and other Jesuits, including Father Wilhelm Kleinsorge, were in Hiroshima when the atom bomb fell. Kleinsorge's story was one of the six recounted in John Hersey's best-selling book on the event. An estimated third of the population of the city, nearly 80,000 persons, were either killed immediately by the blast or in the firestorm that followed. The priests' residence was among the thousands of buildings destroyed, and Lassalle was seriously injured. The scope of the devastation wrought by the nuclear explosion, its impact on civilians as well as the military population, deepened Lassalle's sense of solidarity with the Japanese people and became a factor in his decision to become a naturalized citizen after the war. He did so in 1948, taking the Japanese name Makibi Enomiya. "Enomiya" was the name of a Shinto shrine in Hiroshima, and Kibi no Makibi had been a Japanese reformer who brought new cultural influences – including Buddhist texts – to the country from China in the 8th century. For the remainder of his life, the Jesuit signed his name "Hugo M. Enomiya-Lassalle."

After the humiliation of military defeat, large numbers of Japanese turned away from the political, cultural, and religious structures – including Buddhism – they blamed for involving them in the war. Because the Shinto gods and Confucian principles had failed them, they sought new foundations for ethical behavior. Enomiya-Lassalle recognized that this provided a unique opportunity for Christianity and encouraged Jesuits from other regions to come to Japan to help with the reconstruction of the country.

Because it was recognized that the governing structures established in the country during the US occupation were based on Western principles, the Jesuit mission was called upon to explain both Christian philosophy and democratic institutions. Enomiya-Lassalle also conducted a series of lectures with the Soto abbot, Genshu Watanabe, on the shared ethical visions of Buddhism and Christianity.

In addition, Enomiya-Lassalle led the cause to have a cathedral built in Hiroshima dedicated to World Peace. With the support of Pope Pius XII, construction began on August 6, 1950, the fifth anniversary of the bombing. Donations came from

---

20   See Richard Bryan McDaniel, *The Third Step East: Zen Masters of America* (Richmond Hill, ON: The Sumeru Press, 2015), Chapters Two and Three.

around the globe. The architect, Togo Murano, used bricks made of clay taken from the blast site in constructing the cathedral. The Peace Bells in the tower alongside the cathedral, donated by Germany, were made of steel from melted-down weapons and bear the inscription: "The arms of war now sound the call to peace." The structure was completed on August 6, 1954.

∾

Enomiya-Lassalle persisted in his Zen practice. Although he had not yet had a kensho experience, he theorized – from what he had learned from others – that it might be what Catholic theology identified as a "natural" rather than "supernatural" experience of God. The church did not deny that genuine experiences of God – mystical experiences – were possible outside the faith, but it made a distinction between these "natural religions" and the "supernatural religion" which is Christianity. Enomiya-Lassalle both in his own life and his teaching presented Zen practice as a natural methodology capable of leading persons to supernatural achievement.

Watanabe suggested that Enomiya-Lassalle should continue his practice under the guidance of Daiun Sogaku Harada Roshi, the abbot of Hossinji in Obama. Zazen was primarily a monastic practice, but Harada welcomed lay people and insisted that awakening was as available to them as to monks.

Already seasoned by Jesuit training, Enomiya-Lassalle was better prepared for the rigours of the strict Zen regime favored by Harada than other Europeans would prove to be. He celebrated daily mass privately throughout his attendance at sesshin and was already contemplating the possibility of offering retreats which combined Christian and Zen elements.

In 1958, although he still had not attained kensho, he published *Zen: A Way to Enlightenment* in which he described what he believed Zen could contribute to Catholicism. The book had the approval of the Jesuit Provincial in Japan, Pedro Arrupe. Arrupe had also been a survivor of the atomic attack on Hiroshima and would go on to become the Superior General of the Jesuit Order. Enomiya-Lassalle was now studying with Harada's heir, Hakuun Yasutani, who authorized him to give introductory instruction in Zen to others. Father Arrupe supported the idea, although he felt such instruction was only appropriate for Jesuits who were in the later stages of their training.

Enomiya-Lassalle's experiments with Zen, however, were less favorably viewed outside of Japan, and, in 1961, Vatican authorities prevented further printings of *Zen: A Way to Enlightenment* and forbade Enomiya-Lassalle from promoting Zen practice. He had been censored and officially "silenced."

∾

The Catholic church of the 1950s and early '60s was a conservative institution which took seriously its responsibility to protect its members from falling into error. In order to ensure that church teaching not be misrepresented, individual Catholic clergy and even lay people writing about religious matters had to have their writing approved by church authorities. Before publication, works required a *Nihil Obstat*, a Latin term meaning "there is no obstruction." This was an official declaration that the book contained nothing harmful to the faith or morals of the reader. After the *Nihil Obstat* had been obtained, the book still needed an *Imprimatur* (permission to be printed) by a bishop. Books on Catholicism or dealing with religion or morality routinely included these approvals on the copyright page. Lassalle had realized his book would undergo this procedure and, as a consequence, had taken care how he expressed himself, but his effort proved insufficient.

Lassalle was censored in part because the church of the day had taken an entrenched position in the face of challenges from multiple directions. Science called many church doctrines into question; the church had lost most of its political influence; changes in society challenged the strict moral code it advocated; and familiarity with other cultures called into question the notion of a single divine manifestation of truth. For more and more people, especially those with higher education, religion was considered not only irrelevant but an impediment to the advancement of knowledge, a violator of human rights, and the cause of internecine conflict and cultural genocide. Humankind may have continued to feel the need for a spiritual dimension in their lives, but for many the church as an institution was losing credibility.

Then in 1962, the newly elected pope, John XXIII, called together a general ecumenical council to examine the role of the church in contemporary society. Because it was the second such council to be held in the Vatican State, it was known as the Second Vatican Council, although, in fact, there had been some twenty prior ecumenical councils. In opening the Council, Pope John declared that the church should "throw open the windows and let the fresh air of the spirit blow through." Nothing was off the table; all aspects of Church teaching were open to new reflection and consideration.

Pope John died the following year, and his more conservative successor, Paul VI, presided over the Council until its completion in 1965. Even with the moderating influence of Pope Paul, the Council wrought changes through all aspects of the church, not least in its declared relation to other religious traditions. While not surrendering its claim to be the fullest expression of God's will, it no longer demonized other faith traditions and even opened the door to dialogue with them.

Enomiya-Lassalle – who had been consulted by the Council on new forms of pastoral care and culturally appropriate ways of adapting liturgy outside of Europe – was free to re-release *Zen: A Way to Enlightenment* and to be more frank about his Zen studies in future books.

3

The Catholic Church was not the only institution undergoing change at this time.

Like Genshu Watanabe, Daiun Harada had been a priest in the Soto Zen tradition, but, dissatisfied with the level of insight he had acquired from traditional Soto practice, he studied with several Rinzai masters, eventually attaining awakening under their guidance. He became an advocate of the koan system more commonly associated with Rinzai Zen and combined elements of both traditions in his teaching. When he died in 1961, his heir – Hakuun Yasutani – formally broke with the Soto establishment and initiated an independent school, the Sanbo Kyodan, or the Fellowship of the Three Treasures,[21] modeled on Harada Roshi's approach. Both Yasutani and Harada feared that Zen was on the wane in Japan and that monasteries were falling into ritualism. Consequently Yasutani decided to focus on lay practitioners – including foreigners – rather than monks. Although Sanbo Zen, as it is now known, remains a relatively small sect in Japan, it has had a profound impact on the spread of Zen teaching and practice in North America and Europe. Yasutani's Dharma successor, Koun Yamada, in particular, welcomed Christian students.

Unlike Harada and Yasutani, Yamada was a layman. In *The Three Pillars of Zen*, Philip Kapleau identifies him as a "Japanese Executive."[22] His interest in Zen began with his friendship with Motoi Nakagawa who would become a major contributor to the development of Zen in the West.[23] The two met in high school and later attended the Imperial University in Tokyo together, where Nakagawa loaned Yamada books on Zen. They met again when they were both in Manchuria during the Japanese occupation. By that time, Nakagawa had become a monk and taken the Buddhist name, Soen. Yamada had continued his reading and was interested in discussing his ideas with Nakagawa. After a bit, however, Nakagawa challenged him, "Instead of arguing Zen, why don't you take up practice?" It was enough of a nudge that Yamada sought out his first teacher while still in Manchuria. After the war, he continued his Zen training first with Asahina Sogen then later with Hakuun Yasutani, whose Dharma heir he eventually became.

Once authorized as a teacher, Yamada built a small zendo in his yard and developed a teaching style which Europeans and Americans found attractive. Yasutani and Harada had been known for a samurai style of Zen, characterized by shouting and

---

21   The Three Treasures (or Jewels) are the Buddha, his teaching (the Dharma), and the community of his followers (Sangha).

22   Yamada's kensho experience is given as the first enlightenment story in Kapleau's book. See also fnt. 131, p. 99 below.

23   Cf. *The Third Step East*, Chapter Eight.

liberal use of the kyosaku or "encouragement stick."[24] Yamada's manner was milder. Elaine MacInnes tells of overhearing a student who came into his dokusan room with the martial attitude common to many Zen students and announced his koan by shouting at full volume, "*Muji ni sanjite orimasu!*" ("I am working on Mu!")[25]

> The Roshi was rubbing his face and eyes in that vigorous way he did when he was tired, and the disciple, who was obviously in desperation shouted again, "*Sanjite orimasu!*" The Roshi finished his massaging, took his hands away from his face, looked at the disciple directly and kindly, and said very gently, "What did you say?"[26]

Yamada continued, like his teachers, to focus on lay people. When Westerners, including priests and nuns, asked Lassalle about Zen, he directed them to Yamada's zendo. Yamada routinely told them that he had no intention in converting them to Buddhism but that he believed Zen could make them better Christians.

4

Even before the Second Vatican Council opened new opportunities for greater interfaith activity, Enomiya-Lassalle had established *Shinmeikutsu*, or the "Cave of Divine Darkness," a zendo for Christians in the Kabe district of Hiroshima. And although kensho continued to elude him, he acquired a reputation in Christian circles for being an expert on Zen. The concept he promoted – that Zen as a practice had application outside its Buddhist roots – was becoming more generally accepted. After the war, D. T. Suzuki – the man primarily responsible for introducing Zen to the west[27] – presented Zen insight as an example of a universal spiritual experience which found expression in the mystic tradition of Christianity as well as in Buddhism.

Enomiya-Lassalle's books on Zen were almost as well-known in Europe as those of Alan Watts – Suzuki's populariser – were in the US. He received invitations to lead Zen retreats in Germany which were attended by Christians and non-Christians alike. He was awarded an honorary doctorate from the University of Mainz. He was equally respected in Japan, where he was given the key to the city of Hiroshima.

On the 31st of July, 1973, he at last had a breakthrough experience which Yamada acknowledged as kensho. He then began a lengthy koan practice which

---

24   The kyosaku, or "Encouragement Stick," is a wooden rod flattened at one end used by monitors during zazen to encourage (or wake up) meditators by striking them on the back of the shoulder.

25   See fnt. 36, page 44 below.

26   Elaine MacInnes, *The Flowing Bridge* (Boston: Wisdom Publications, 2007), p. 6.

27   Cf. *The Third Step East*, Chapter One.

culminated five years later, after which Yamada gave him full transmission, recognizing Enomiya-Lassalle as an awakened Zen teacher – a Zen Master – and a Dharma heir in the Sanbo Kyodan tradition.

ㄨ

Following the changes brought about by Vatican II and bolstered by his official transmission as a Zen teacher, Enomiya-Lassalle was free to write more openly and authoritatively about Zen than previously. In 1987, he released a new book – *The Practice of Zen Meditation* – based on talks he gave during sesshin[28] which he conducted in Europe.

He began those retreats – and the book – with the assertion that because "Zen is not bound to any particular ideology, it can have a liberating effect for anyone and be useful in all situations of daily life."[29] He then quotes Yamada Roshi, who said:

> I am often asked by Christians, especially by Catholics, whether it is possible to practise Zen and still remain true to their Christian faith. To this question I usually reply that Zen is not a religion in the sense that Christianity is religion. Therefore there is no reason why *Zazen* and Christianity should not coexist. The outer garment is of a different form and colour, but what is underneath, the heart, remains the same. And this heart, this experience is not embellished with any thoughts or philosophies. It is a pure fact, an experienced fact, in the same way that tasting tea is a fact. A cup of tea has no thoughts, no ideas, no philosophy. It tastes the same to Buddhists as it does to Christians. There is not the slightest difference there.[30]

There is a basic teaching in Christianity that God dwells within us; we are not aware of this, however, because he is veiled by our sense of being a "self." Buddhists speak of one's True Nature – one's Buddha Nature – which is also veiled by that sense of self. But whereas the traditional route to Christian faith, especially as presented by the Jesuits, was through prayer, study, reflection, and reason, the route to Buddhist awareness was through direct perception. Awakening, Enomiya-Lassalle explained, was not something that could be reasoned to but was something that had to be experienced.

The first step in the process is to achieve concentrated mental stillness, and the initial practice given to Zen students to aid in developing this is counting the breaths,

---

28   Other than when referring to persons, there is no plural form in Japanese. "Sesshin" is both singular and plural.

29   Hugo M. Enomiya-Lassalle, *The Practice of Zen Meditation* (London: Thorsons, 1990), p. 8.

30   Ibid.

one to ten, over and over again. Although a preliminary exercise, Enomiya-Lassalle notes that as "one penetrates deeper and deeper into meditation through counting the breath, it is possible to achieve enlightenment through this exercise alone."[31]

In most cases, however, something further is needed. From his personal experience, Enomiya-Lassalle knew how difficult it was for people of the West "to let go of reason, will and memory, in order to find a way to absolute stillness."[32] After the student achieves some stability in his or her practice by focusing on the breath, they may be assigned a koan, usually Mu. Because koans are resolved through intuition rather than intellect, they are an effective way of overcoming dependence on the reasoning mind.

When presented with a koan, the student tends to try to find a logical solution to it. When each of these solutions is rejected by the teacher in dokusan, the student comes to recognize the futility of attempting to use reason, only then

> – does the correct work with the *koan* begin. He now no longer actually thinks about the *koan*, but he has it on his mind constantly, day and night. An intense inner dilemma then arises, in which he can neither find an answer nor any longer drop the *koan*. If he now continues working on the *koan* with great intensity, he will arrive at a point where he becomes one with the *koan* …
>
> In this situation the entire consciousness has become filled with the *koan*. Still he perseveres and continues to practise until the *koan* suddenly disappears from his consciousness. At this instant the consciousness has become completely emptied and not even *satori*, enlightenment, the aspired goal can penetrate it. Now he is very near to enlightenment.
>
> He must, however, continue practising with the utmost effort – without any reflection – and without directing his attention to any specific object. The consciousness must remain 'totally empty', otherwise the opportunity passes by. If he succeeds, then only a small spur will be necessary to open up the spirit to the new seeing, in which enlightenment takes place. Thus *satori* is generally precipitated by a sense perception, a sound that pierces the ear or an object that catches the eye, maybe even an emotion. This presupposes that such realization occurs completely unexpectedly and independent of meditation. Control on the part is of the subject is not possible.[33]

---

31 Ibid., p. 17.

32 Ibid., p. 20.

33 Ibid., p. 21.

Regular and persistent Zen practice, Enomiya-Lassalle assured his students, "leads man into the realm of the pure spirit. The pure spirit, which knows neither psyche nor body, is God. The long journey of Zen meditation leads to that place."[34]

This is not, Enomiya-Lassalle is careful to note, a new teaching for Christians. The Zen approach has much in common with the Catholic mystic tradition. With awakening, what one encounters

> – is the ground from which all things spring, the very mystery our longing draws us towards, that which supports our life and on which everything rests; that which moves us deeply; which illuminates all the senses and all beauty. This is often described as an existential experience, which it truly is. In studying the writings of the mystics, we will find that Christian mysticism is a way towards divine experience and beyond that to a divine *union with God* and the entire way will be seen to have many similarities with Zen.[35]

---

34 Ibid., p. 33.

35 Ibid., pp. 36-37.

CHAPTER THREE

William Johnston &
Thomas Merton

1

B y the time of Hugo Enomiya-Lassalle's death in 1990, Zen concepts – although
at times misunderstood and misrepresented – had acquired a degree of credibility
in Western thought and even within Catholicism that would have seemed unlikely
in the 1940s when Lassalle participated in his first Zen retreat. During the years
between, it was natural that a number of other Jesuits at Sophia University became
interested in Zen as well, if not as a practice, at least as a subject for inquiry.

Heinrich Dumoulin – like Lassalle, a German – joined the Japanese mission
in 1935. He made a study of the history of Zen. His first book on the subject was
released in 1959 and was translated into English shortly after. A longer and more
ambitious two volume history was published in 1985. Although now accepted as a
standard reference work, *Zen Buddhism: A History* was originally criticized not for
having a Catholic bias but rather for depending too heavily upon a romanticized
vision of history promulgated within the Zen establishment itself. Dumoulin also
became the first director of the Nanzan Institute for Religion and Culture – now part
of Nanzan University – which promotes interfaith dialogue between East and West.

William Johnston was an Irish Jesuit also committed to East-West dialogue and
just as interested in Zen from an academic perspective. The focus of his study was
religious experience. His graduate work had been on the 14th century English text,
The Cloud of Unknowing, which describes a form of prayer that consists of focusing
on a single word – such as "God" – with all of one's attentive powers. Johnston noted
that in a similar manner Zen students working with koans might be given a *wato* or
"head word" upon which to concentrate. The best known wato is "Mu!"which comes

from the koan most commonly assigned to beginning Zen students.[36] Further, both Christian writers like John of the Cross and Zen teachers emphasized the value of placing oneself in a receptive state of silence.

Noting these parallels, Johnston became interested in the similarities and differences between Zen and Christian mysticism. In the Catholic tradition, mysticism specifically refers to a spiritual orientation – primarily associated with monasticism – which leads to unitive knowledge of God. While Zen does not presuppose the existence of God, the kensho experience can be described as a unitive experience of Being. In that sense, the two are analogous if not identical.

Like Dumoulin, Johnston recognized that Catholics could profit from dialogue with Buddhists, but he made no pretense that his study was neutral. He begins his 1970 book, *The Still Point*, with the frank admission that it was his belief

> – that salvation is from the Jews – that theirs is the splendor of the divine presence, theirs the covenant, and that from them, in natural descent, sprang the Messiah. Yet this belief does not prevent me from having the highest esteem for the Buddha and the long tradition that stems from his enlightenment. This is a tradition that has enriched the East incalculably, and I sincerely hope that it will equally enrich the West.[37]

The issue he examined in *The Still Point* was whether the phenomenological experiences derived from the meditative activity of Christians and Buddhists were different in kind or merely in interpretation. He concluded that while Zen awakening (kensho) and the mystic experience may have certain things in common, they are essentially different. "Zen meditation," he wrote, "is a process of unification in which the whole personality is harmonized in a oneness which reaches its climax with a complete

---

36   In the koan, a monk asks the Tang Dynasty master, Joshu Jushin, whether or not a dog has Buddha Nature. In spite of the general teaching that all beings have Buddha Nature, Joshu responds by saying "Mu!" – a word which can mean "no" or "not" or function as a negative prefix similar to "un-" or "non-" in English.

Buddha Nature is a being's essential self, unfettered by the delusive self; in Johnston's words, "a self more universal than the narrow empirical ego." The monk who put the question to Joshu would have been aware that in theory all creatures have Buddha Nature, but he is looking for reassurance. Because he has not yet realized his own Buddha Nature, he may have begun to wonder whether Buddha Nature was innate or if it were something to be acquired through technique. His question, therefore, is sly. Instead of asking about his own condition, he asks whether even a dog – a despised animal in Chinese culture – has Buddha Nature. On one level, Joshu's sharp response is a refutation of the question; on another, it is a rejection of conceptual thought.

37   William Johnston, *The Still Point* (New York: Harper and Row, 1970), p. xv.

absence of subject-object consciousness in *satori*."[38] It is, in other words, essentially a psychological state, a natural phenomenon, and, as such, one not limited to Zen practitioners; it can and does occur spontaneously. Johnston cites Enomiya-Lassalle on the matter: " – enlightenment has been attained to, not only by great figures like Plotinus, but by simple and unsuspecting persons who work in the fields ... – the triumph of Zen Buddhism is to have found a system for inducing something which others have only stumbled upon."[39]

The experience of the Christian contemplative or mystic, on the other hand, is a gift of supernatural grace grounded in reflection on scripture and on the life of Jesus within a supportive ecclesiastical tradition which guides the individual and guards him from falling into error. Many theologians, Johnston points out,

> – hold that Christian mysticism is no more than an intensification of the ordinary Christian life. Reflecting against the view that mysticism is an esoteric phenomenon ... they insist it is just deepening of that faith and love that every true Christian possesses.[40]

Whereas Buddhist practice is grounded in the desire to escape the suffering which, in the Four Noble Truths,[41] the Buddha posited as the natural condition of existence, Christian mysticism is driven by the "flame of love" which is the

> – very center and core of Christian mysticism. It is precisely to foster this that reasoning and thinking are abandoned; it is to make way for this that images and desires are trampled down beneath the cloud of forgetting. Indeed, it is the vehemence of this love that impedes reasoning, causing the sense of helplessness which the mystics speak about: for all love (whether human or divine, temporal or eternal) is intolerant of reasoned discourse; it goes to its object with intuitive directness, abandoning roundabout paths of any kind. Hence mystical love eschews thinking; it rests in contemplative silence. And this stirring is, moreover, nothing else than a deeply experiential expression of that charity which Christ taught

---

38   Ibid., p. 4.

39   Ibid., p. 63.

40   Ibid., p. 28.

41   The Four Noble Truths are the most basic of the Buddha's teachings: 1) All of existence is characterized by suffering (dukkha); 2) Suffering is caused by craving; 3) Suffering can be ameliorated by overcoming craving; 4) Craving can be overcome by following the Noble Eightfold path. Cf. fnt. 16, page 32 above.

to be the whole essence of His message ... [42]

If, Johnston wrote, the Zen practice of shikan taza is described as meditation without an object, Christian meditation is meditation without a subject. The distinction is not "merely one of semantics. To forget self so that only God remains is different from forgetting everything until only self remains."[43]

Johnston respected the Zen tradition sufficiently to recognize that the pre-Vatican II distinction – to which Enomiya-Lassalle had adhered – between natural mysticism (such as Zen) and supernatural (Christian) mysticism must necessarily be irritating to non-Christians, as if by making such a distinction "Christians are claiming a phenomenological superiority for their mysticism, as though it were something much more psychologically profound than what is found in other religions."[44] He notes that in the post-council church, the former

> – reluctance to admit that non-Christians have grace and are helped
> by God has given place to an attitude which sees the working of the
> Holy Spirit in all religions... That non-Christians may have grace
> no one will now deny; that in consequence their mysticism may in
> some sense be supernatural can now be maintained.[45]

One suspects that non-Christians would find this attitude only slightly less condescending than the former. Certainly Zen would see the assumption of the existence of grace as an operative force to be as superfluous as the assumption of the existence of a Supreme Creator.

Johnston has no difficulty recognizing that the Zen experience is, in some sense, mystical and so on a par with Christian mysticism. Still he holds that a real difference exists between the two:

> – namely, mysticism which arises from, and culminates in, love of
> God in Christ is Christian; that which does not (but yet remains a
> simple intuition of the truth) is non-Christian. Nor does the Chris-
> tian claim that his experiences are deeper, more soul-stirring, more
> phenomenologically extraordinary than those of his non-Christian
> brother.[46]

---

42   Ibid., pp. 32-33.
43   Ibid., p. 41.
44   Ibid., p. 137
45   Ibid.
46   Ibid., p. 136.

While kensho might not be the same as the encounter with the "living flame of love" of the Christian mystics, still the Zen technique, Johnston decides, is one which Christians might be able to make use of. It "can teach the Christian how to relax, how to be calm, how to think in a deeper way, how to dispose himself to receive God's love, how to conceive the truths of faith not only in his brain but in his whole body."[47] The experience of the Christian taking up such a practice, however, must necessarily differ from that of the Buddhist:

> For, in the last analysis, Christians and Buddhists agree that meditation is not totally divorced from one's philosophy of life. Even though it is sometimes said "It doesn't matter what you believe: just sit!" one must sit ... on a philosophy of life. One, of course, is detached from the words and concepts and images in which this philosophy is couched: but it is there ... The Christian contemplative and the Zen monk have each his own philosophy: they sit on different *zabutons*.[48]

2

Although they admired Zen, Johnston and Dumoulin looked at it from without. Their approach was similar to that of other writers and thinkers of the time who admired Zen. The psychologists C. G. Jung – who provided an introduction to D. T. Suzuki's *An Introduction to Zen Buddhism* – and Erich Fromm, for example, found parallels between Zen thought and their perspectives but refrained from suggesting it was an appropriate practice for Westerners. Their work, however – as well as books like *Zen Catholicism: A Suggestion* by the Benedictine Dom Aelred Graham – contributed to a growing awareness of and appreciation for Zen thought in the West in the years following the Second World War.

During the 1950s, Western engagement in Zen was largely literary. The books of Zen scholar D. T. Suzuki and Alan Watts presented a new and appealing way of looking at the world. Zen was understood not so much as a practice as an attitude marked by spontaneity and freedom from social convention. It was not until a small number of Western students travelled to Japan and underwent traditional monastic training that North Americans realized how demanding a practice Zen actually was. One of the curious ironies of the 1960s was that members of the counter-culture youth movement, who rejected the authority of their elders and government institutions, willingly submitted to the authority and rigorous discipline of Zen teachers who by the late '60s had established centers in Honolulu, San Francisco, Los Angeles,

---

47 Ibid., p. 180.

48 Ibid., p. 185.

New York City, and Rochester. The membership of these centers was almost entirely made up of young people.

When these youth began to experiment with actual Zen practice, mainstream society and Christian commentators reacted predictably. Thomas Merton, however – one of the most influential Catholic figures of the time – noted that the critics who dismissed Zen as "a mixture of incomprehensible myths, superstitions, and self-hypnotic rites, all of it without serious importance"[49] did so because they lacked a genuine understanding of it.

In Catholic circles, the ecumenical spirit which followed the Second Vatican Council did not apply to non-Christian religions. While the church recognized that Christian denominations could profit from dialogue as a means for seeking some form of reunification, no similar process was envisioned for non-Christian faiths, not even with the other two Abrahamic religions – Judaism and Islam – much less the religions of Asia with which the Church did not share a common heritage. Dialogue was permitted, even encouraged, but the concept of any form of eclectic spiritual concord was dismissed out of hand.

What is more, the progressive elements in the post-councilior church tended to view Christianity as very much a call to action on social justice, political, and economic matters; therefore, any form of other-worldly mysticism – Western or Asian – was disparaged.

And yet there were Catholics, like Merton, who sought to dispel the misconceptions their co-religionists had about Asian religions in general and Zen in particular. "Though much has been said, written, and published in the West about Zen," Merton wrote, "the general reader is probably not much the wiser for most of it."[50]

Thomas Merton was a convert to Catholicism who became a Trappist monk at the Abbey of Our Lady of Gethsemani in Kentucky. The Cistercians of the Strict Observance, or Trappists, are a cloistered monastic order. Those taking full vows write a will signifying that they are dead to the world and now dedicate themselves to a life of prayer, labor, and stability. Stability means to be committed to spending the remainder of one's life in one particular monastic community. It is a life of anonymous service to God and certainly not one in which fame or notoriety is expected, and yet one of the most best known Catholics of the 20th century was a Trappist living in a monastery in rural Kentucky.

Merton initially rose to fame with the 1948 publication of his autobiography, *The Seven Storey Mountain*, which became an international best seller. The book recounts

49   Thomas Merton, *Mystics and Zen Masters* (New York: Dell Publishing, 1969). p. 8.

50   Thomas Merton, *Zen and the Birds of Appetite* (New York: New Directions, 1968), p. 3.

his conversion and decision to enter monastic life. It also identified some of the factors which would lead to his later interest in Zen Buddhism.

American interest in Asian spirituality in the post-war years was not a new phenomenon. A romanticized view of Asian wisdom had been promulgated by the Theosophical Society since the last decades of the 19th century, and Indian teachers like Paramahansa Yogananda had established large followings in America in the years between the wars. The post-Darwinian perspective had cast doubt on traditional Christian teachings for many who looked for other belief systems, largely from the East, which they hoped might be more in accord with the findings of natural science. In *The Seven Storey Mountain*, Merton describes meeting a young Hindu monk named Bramachari while at Colombia University. Merton had acquired an interest in Asian mysticism as a result of his reading and spoke to Bramachari about the topic. Bramachari advised him not to concern himself with Asian texts but to read the mystical literature of the west, such as Thomas a Kempis's *The Imitation of Christ*.

After his conversion to Catholicism and entrance into Trappist life, Merton went through a phase during which he was focused entirely on orthodox Catholic thought and showed little interest in or respect for other spiritual traditions. But as he became more familiar with the apophatic[51] tradition in Catholic mysticism, represented by people like St. John of the Cross, he could not ignore its parallels with Buddhist teaching.

In the 1960s, the United States was in a period of social turmoil. Young people were challenging many aspects of their society: its inherent racism, the marginalization of minorities, and the underlying greed which powered the capitalist system. The protracted military involvement in Vietnam had polarized the generations. Traditional gender roles and sexual mores were being questioned. Although supposedly "dead to the world," Merton, in keeping with other progressive thinkers in the church, was concerned about these issues. Although in sympathy with the progressive movement, he was disturbed by the violence that often accompanied social protest and advocated instead the approach of the Hindu, Mahatma Gandhi, whose policy of non-violent engagement with the British had successfully resulted in India obtaining self-rule shortly after the end of the Second World War. Gandhian principles were also espoused by Martin Luther King in the American civil rights movement. While these matters were very far away from the secluded life of the monastery, they became subjects Merton felt compelled to write about. Books like *Conjectures of a Guilty Bystander* and *Seeds of Destruction* brought him to the attention of a new audience which viewed him less as a spiritual than as a social writer.

---

51   Apophatic ("to deny") theology stresses that nothing can be said about God because God is wholly beyond human conception. God may be encountered, but God cannot be described. The closest one can come to describing God is through negative language, stating what God is not. Apophatic theology is contrasted with Cataphatic theology, that derives from the terms cata ("to descend") and femi ("to speak"), in other words, to find a way to speak about God. Cf. p. 144 below.

Ironically, his fame – and in particular the popularity of *The Seven Storey Mountain* – not only hindered him from becoming as socially engaged as he might have chosen to be, it also prevented him from seeking a deeper spiritual solitude. During the '60s, he felt drawn to greater seclusion than he found at the Abbey of Our Lady of Gethsemani and petitioned to be allowed to move to the Carthusians, an eremitic order. His request was denied by his superiors in the order and by the church hierarchy for fear of the scandal that would ensue if it were discovered that one who had written so movingly about taking on Trappist vows had abandoned them.

Eventually a compromise was found, and he was allowed to build a small hermitage on the monastery grounds; he also had greater freedom to communicate with the outside world than most Trappists had or desired. He maintained correspondences with some of the major literary and intellectual figures of the day including Boris Pasternak, Aldous Huxley, Lawrence Ferlinghetti, and D. T. Suzuki.

Although – unlike the Jesuits in Japan – Merton had no access to a Zen teacher, he read as much as he could about the subject and found parallels between the insights of Zen monks and his own monastic experience. Possibly to the consternation of his religious superiors, his books *Mystics and Zen Masters* (1967) and *Zen and the Birds of Appetite* (1968) contributed to the growing interest in Zen in North America.

He published some thirty-six books during his lifetime, and almost that many works were released posthumously. His personal favorite among these works was *The Way of Chuang Tzu,* a rendering of key passages in the classic Daoist text. The depth of his sensitivity to both Daoism and Zen is attested to by Burton Watson, who, in the introduction to his own translation of Chuang Tzu[52] wrote:

> Readers interested in the literary qualities of the text should also look at the "imitations" of passages in the *Chuang Tzu* prepared by Thomas Merton on the basis of existing translations in Western languages … They give a fine sense of the liveliness and poetry of Chuang Tzu's style, and are actually almost as close to the original as the translations upon which they are based.[53]

Merton admitted that "studied as *structures*, as *systems*, and as *religions*, Zen and Catholicism don't mix any better than oil and water."[54] But he looked at Zen as

---

52   Zhuang Zhou.

53   Burton Watson, *The Complete Works of Chuang Tzu* (New York: Columbia University Press, 1968), p. 28.

54   Thomas Merton, *Zen and the Birds of Appetite* (New York: New Directions, 1968), p. 3.

something outside religious categories, as something closer to the universal spiritual principle D. T. Suzuki had portrayed it to be in his later work. It is not surprising that Merton shared Suzuki's perspective, because much of what he understood about Zen came from reading and corresponding with Suzuki.

> Zen is consciousness unstructured by particular form or particular system, a trans-cultural, trans-religious, trans-formed consciousness ... – to regard Zen *merely* and *exclusively* as Zen Buddhism is to falsify it ...[55]

Which is not to deny, he adds, that there are Zen Buddhists, "but these surely will realize... the difference between their Buddhism and their Zen – even while admitting that for them their Zen is in fact the purest expression of Buddhism."[56]

For Merton, the common ground between Zen and Catholicism is the importance both place on self-noughting. In Zen, it is by seeing beyond the personal ego that one discovers one's face before one's parents' births. Individual Christians, on the other hand, following the example of Jesus – "Who, being in the form of God, did not count equality with God something to be grasped. But he emptied himself, taking the form of a slave"[57] – are called to a similar self-noughting so that they can claim, as did Paul, that "I live, now not I but Christ lives within me."[58] Both the Pauline vision and the Buddhist are examples of an awareness prior to the development of the subjective point of view by which individual persons recognize themselves as distinct from all else. As Merton put it, "Underlying the subjective experience of the individual self there is an immediate experience of Being"[59] – a pure awareness rather than an awareness *of* something distinct from one's self.

Merton concludes from this that Zen

> – is pointed to by ... the revealed message of Christianity ...
> Thus with all due deference to the vast doctrinal differences between Buddhism and Christianity, and preserving intact all respect for the claims of the different religions: in no way mixing up the Christian "vision of God" with Buddhist "enlightenment," we can nevertheless say that the two have ... [a] psychic "limitlessness" in common."[60]

---

55 Ibid., p. 4.
56 Ibid.
57 Philippians 2:6-7.
58 Galatians 2:20.
59 Merton, *Zen and the Birds of Appetite*, p. 23.
60 Ibid., p. 8.

Monastic vows limited Merton's ability to travel, but in 1964 he was given permission to meet D. T. Suzuki in New York, during the Japanese scholar's last visit to the United States. Merton wrote that in meeting Suzuki

> – one seemed to meet that "True Man of No Title" that Chuang Tzu and the Zen Masters speak of. And of course this is the man one really wants to meet. Who else is there? In meeting Dr. Suzuki and drinking a cup of tea with him I felt I had met this one man. It was like finally arriving at one's own home.[61]

Merton went on to note that as a result of this brief meeting "Buddhism finally became for me completely comprehensible, whereas before it had been a very mysterious and confusing jumble of words, images, doctrines, legends, rituals, buildings and so forth."[62] In meeting the True Man of No Rank, one experiences Zen as it is lived rather than as it is expressed.

In 1968, Merton was given permission to make a more extensive journey to Asia, in order to take part in a conference on Christian and non-Christian monasticism in Bangkok. The similarities between Eastern and Western forms of contemplation was a topic in which he had a great deal of interest. En route to the conference, he was also able to visit India, where he met with the Dalai Lama.

During one of the breaks at the Thailand conference, Merton took a shower and apparently moved an electric fan while still wet. There was a short in the fan, and the jolt of electricity he received killed him on December 10.

Merton described the Western approach to understanding as being based on a "dialectical transaction involving the reduction of fact to logical statement and the reflective verification of statement by fact."[63] Even while affirming that this is not the appropriate way to try to understand Zen, it was essentially the route he fell back on as he attempted to present Zen to the West – an irony he must have been fully aware of:

---

61   Merton, *Mystics and Zen Masters*, p. 60.
62   Ibid., p. 61.
63   Ibid., p. 36.

> For Zen, from the moment fact is transferred to a statement it is
> falsified. One ceases to grasp the naked reality of experience and
> one grasps a form of words instead.[64]

No matter how sympathetic writers like Jung, Johnston, Merton and others were to Zen, their interest remained essentially theoretical rather than practical. What they wrote about Zen was intended to demonstrate its value logically. Hugo Enomiya-Lassalle, on the other hand, and those inspired by him were less interested in understanding Zen than they were in experiencing it directly.

---

64 Ibid.

CHAPTER FOUR

Thomas Hand

In the 1950s, the number of North Americans or Europeans drawn to become engaged in the discipline of Zen training was miniscule, and those who did – like the poet Gary Snyder or future American Zen teachers such as Robert Aitken and Philip Kapleau – had to go to Japan in order to do so. These individuals naturally considered themselves pioneers, and at least one – the Dutch writer Janwillem van de Wetering – expressed surprise to discover he had been preceded in this venture by Jesuits like Enomiya-Lassalle.

Thomas Hand was another Jesuit in Japan who sought to learn what Zen had to offer by experiencing it from within. This perspective yields very different results than the approach taken by Johnston or Merton. For Johnston, in particular, Zen was a potentially useful tool for deepening the Christian experience. Those who actually undertook Zen practice, on the other hand, discovered it had the capacity to transform radically their understanding of their faith.

Hand arrived in Japan in 1953 and remained there for nearly thirty years. During that time, he came to view the West's encounter with Buddhism as a major factor in "the advance and evolutionary revitalization of Christian spirituality."[65] In this, he went a step further than Enomiya-Lassalle and in later life did not hesitate to call himself a Buddhist-Christian.

He had been raised in rural California and felt drawn to religious life while very young. He had given thought to becoming a Trappist monk while in high school but was unsure how to go about doing that, so instead entered a nearby Jesuit preparatory

---

65   Chwen Jiuan A. Lee and Thomas Hand, *A Taste of Water* (New York: Paulist Press, 1990), p. 67. Cf., the suggestion of the British historian, Arnold Toynbee, that "The coming of Buddhism to the West may well prove to be the most important event of the twentieth century."

school – Bellarmine – where some of his elementary school classmates were already enrolled. He admitted that to some extent he had just been following his friends, but it proved to be a good fit.

After the fifteen year long process of Jesuit formation, he was ordained and sent to Japan. There he was tasked with helping establish a junior and senior high school in Hiroshima. Almost as soon as he arrived, he recognized that he was in a country where people not only spoke a different language and had different cultural institutions but seemed to him to have a different consciousness as well. For a long while, however, he had a difficult time defining where that difference lay.

Although he was an effective teacher, he didn't feel the classroom was his true calling, and, after a dozen years in Japan, he discussed the matter with the Provincial – the regional superior in the country – and was reassigned to the Kamakura language school where he was appointed to be the students' spiritual director.

Hand had read Enomiya-Lassalle's *Zen: A Way to Enlightenment* and wondered if Zen training might help him get a better feeling for the unique consciousness he sensed in Japan. Enomiya-Lassalle's teacher, Koun Yamada, lived in Kamakura, and Hand made his way to the small zendo, San-un, attached to Yamada's house. It was not a rash decision on his part; he had been in Japan for more than fifteen years before he took this step.

Beginning Zen students did not have immediate access to the teacher. First they were required to attend a number of introductory lectures and demonstrate commitment to the practice by regular attendance at scheduled sittings. Once this trial period was over, the applicant took part in a ceremony called *shoken* – which means to "see one another" – the first formal interview between student and teacher. It is a ceremonial occasion during which the student is asked to present his aspiration in taking up Zen practice. When Yamada put that question to Hand, the American admitted he wasn't entirely sure. He was, he explained, a Roman Catholic priest and – at the time – had no intention of becoming Buddhist or changing his vocation. Yamada smiled and told him that was quite all right. There were two types of Zen practice, Yamada said. "The first is really strict Buddhist Zen. You have all the statues and everything else like that; you follow all the Buddhist teaching and everything. And then there is just pure Zen. You will follow that, and that will make you a better Catholic." For Hand, this would prove to be true.

Zazen wasn't easy for him. He found the sitting painful; he never looked forward to going to the zendo. He was shy about being in groups, and he didn't have a strong enough command of the language to always be able to understand what was going on. But he felt it was important to go, and he persisted for seven years. It was not a pleasant experience, but it proved to be rewarding. Whereas the long, careful Jesuit training had focused on academic studies – had been, as Hand expressed it, head-oriented – Zen practice brought one down to the gut, to the primacy of experience.

When he began sitting with Yamada, Hand was the only professed religious in the group; over time, however, other priests and nuns joined, as did lay people from Europe and America, a significant number of whom were Catholic. Hand encouraged students at the language school to consider Zen practice as a means of deepening their spiritual lives.

As it turned out, he returned to the United States before completing his Zen training and was never formally authorized as a Zen teacher. In 1984, he joined the staff at the Mercy Center Institute of Contemporary Spirituality in Burlingame, California, where for the next twenty years he served as a retreat director and spiritual guide.

Japanese words end either in a vowel or in "n"; therefore, it had not been easy for his Japanese students to pronounce Hand's family name. It came out as "Hando," which, felicitously, was written with the characters for "han" – to accompany – and "do" – to cross, as over a bridge. It was a happy coincidence for Hand, who saw his mission, after returning to the United States, as building a bridge between Eastern and Western forms of spirituality.

What he provided in the East-West Meditation Program that he established at the Mercy Center was more than meditation instruction. Buddhism speaks of "upayas," the variety of "skillful means" by which the Dharma can be presented. Zazen – seated meditation – is one upaya, but there are others.

Hand had been fascinated with haiku while in Japan, and, in the language courses he taught, he'd had his Japanese students compose haiku in English as a means of improving their command of the language. In California, he taught his Christian retreatants to compose haiku as a spiritual activity. Traditional Japanese haiku consist of three lines of five, seven, and five syllables respectively. The brevity does not allow for the development of intellectual concepts, but it does allow the poet to present, effectively and often beautifully, a concrete experience. Hand told his students that good haiku were "direct experience directly expressed."

In a video interview on the Mercy Center website,[66] Hand provides an example from Japan's master of the form, Matsuo Basho:

> Oh, the stillness
> Into the rocks it pierces
> The cry of the cicada[67]

---

66   http://www.mercy-center.org/Resources/HandoVideo.html.

67   Translations of koans do not always adhere to the 17 syllable form.

For Hand, these three lines more elegantly express the concept of the interdependence of being than any reasoned analysis of non-duality could.

In addition to seated meditation, Zen students do walking meditation, a practice which demonstrates that focused attention is not to be limited to the time spent on the cushion but can and should extend to all activity in which one is engaged. On the grounds of the language school in Kamakura, Hand had cleared a walking trail through a forested region. He designed and cleared trails at the Mercy Center as well.

Seated meditation (zazen), walking meditation, and haiku composition were all intended to promote mindfulness. The more mindful one is of one's activity and surroundings – including those other persons with whom one interacts – the less one is conscious of the personal self. The less that sense of self intrudes, the more one is aware of one's interconnectedness with the totality of Being. As Hand puts it, "– Zen is primarily concerned with the self/Self. We are to forget the self, come to the Self and ultimately to the self/Self."[68]

The term "self/Self" is Hand's awkward attempt to emphasize that the "essential Self" is not just another category opposed to the "individual self."

> If the one Self is just an "other" category, then it is distinct from the phenomenal self and our separation is only compounded. The Self is not some thing or some one that is in opposition to our self. Each one of us is simply self/Self.[69]

Although the contrast with traditional Christian spirituality is obvious – the focus of western spirituality is on seeking not the Self but God – Hand insists that "it comes to the very same process."[70]

Even in a country as ethnocentric as Japan, there is not a single universal consciousness shared by all of its citizens. There is as wide a variety of perspectives found in Japan as in any other nation. What Hand had recognized as a different consciousness in the land he'd been sent to was based on the dissimilarity in fundamental premises that had bewildered Francis Xavier. But where Xavier had felt it was his responsibility to show the people of Asia the errors of their perspective, Hand was open to learning if that perspective had anything to teach him. Like William Johnston, he did not do so with an entirely open mind. By his own admission, he was less interested in Zen for its own sake than for "the vivifying light" it and other "eastern

---

68   Lee and Hand, op. cit., p. 22.

69   Ibid., p. 25.

70   Ibid., p. 22.

philosophies and eastern practices can shed on Jesus Christ and his teaching."[71] But he was open enough to that light that his understanding of his faith was deeply affected by it.

He was not a naïve cultural enthusiast. Like Merton, he understood that in many ways Buddhism and Christianity are irreconcilable. He also recognized that there was more Christian interest in Zen than there was Buddhist interest in Christianity. While in his experience – and that of Father Enomiya-Lassalle – Zen seemed to offer a means by which Christians could more fully encounter God, he understood that Japanese Buddhism did not assume the existence of God. Nor was it clear how the centrality of Jesus to the Christian faith – "the preeminent and all-embracing place of Christ Jesus and the Christian's entrustment to His influence and His power as a living power right now" – could be incorporated into the Zen context.

> That is one of the greatest problems that arises and will continue to be a problem because Zen in its way is to seek for the true self within yourself, your own self, whereas the Christian path is to seek for the true self within Christ Jesus, so you look at and learn of Christ and find yourself. In Zen you look at yourself and find yourself. There is a kind of fundamental difference in approach to finding your own true being, finding reality.[72]

What allowed Hand to incorporate Zen practice and Zen insight into the Christian retreats he directed in California was the distinction Yamada Roshi had made between Buddhist Zen and Zen per se.

By the time he returned to the United States, Hand's time in Japan had transformed his understanding of his Catholic faith. He noted three elements in particular. First, his loyalty to the church was no longer determined by his loyalty to canon law. Second, his loyalty to Christ was not dependent on loyalty to Church dogma. And finally, his understanding of God had so changed that he could no longer think of God as a person in the way God is generally portrayed in Christian doctrine. To identify God as a person, Hand now believed, amounted to limiting God to a particular category of being.

In the late 1980s, Hand co-wrote a book entitled *A Taste of Water* with Chwen Jiuan Lee.[73] Lee was a Chinese convert to Catholicism who had become a nun in

71 Ibid., p. 1.

72 Ibid.

73 Lee and Hand admit that their book is "organized in a very western way. The ideas and explanations have been put first and the practice last. As is so often the case, the east is the other way around. In the classical Zen pattern, an aspirant is taught how to sit, to chant, to work. Then, only after some real level of insight-experience is reached, is the inner theory of Buddhism explored." Ibid., p. 190.

the order of the Sisters Missionary of the Immaculate Conception, where she was known as Sister Agnes. In the book, Hand recounts a moment after he had begun his Zen training – and "the whole Zen world, which was still so full of enigma to me, had begun its powerful impact on my consciousness"[74] – when it suddenly occurred to him very powerfully that "God was different," by which he meant that God was different from whatever one imagined God to be. There is no category which could be applied to God, including the fundamental concept of "other." Even to consider God as an entity – for lack of a better word – of an entirely different order than the universe was inadequate:

> – when we conceive of an *actual* distinction and relationship be-
> tween God and creatures, we are in effect putting God into a *cat-*
> *egory* separate from the creature category. To separate the formless
> and forms (its manifestations) into two is to place the formless into
> a category. True, God's category is called "infinite" and "absolute,"
> but nonetheless it is a category. We have given boundaries to the
> boundless. The east would say that such a conception of God is a
> product of relational experience. That it does not spring from the
> ultimate experience of the actual God. The real God is different
> from all such categorization. In the final experience of God there
> is no question of separation, distinction or relationship. The dis-
> tinguishing intellect is useless and gives way to that intuitive seeing
> which is best described as being.

> – in the western spiritual traditions, especially in their popular form,
> there is a strong tendency to conceptualize God. These concepts
> become dogmas and take on paramount importance. It is the opin-
> ion of most eastern masters that this conceptualizing, dogmatizing
> tendency, although somewhat helpful, is actually dangerous and can
> easily create real obstacles to the experience of God.[75]

For Hand and Sister Agnes, God is not "a separate reality 'out there.' Rather... God [is] the absolute commonality found in all relationship, person to person, person to thing, thing to thing."[76] In this understanding, individual persons – in Sister Agnes's words – are "manifestation[s] of unrestricted being" which is the true or essential Self one is unaware of because of one's sense of being an individual.

---

74 Ibid., p. 11

75 Ibid., pp. 12-13.

76 Ibid., p. 68.

The concept that anything one says about God necessarily falls short of God's reality certainly remains within traditional church teaching. But it also leads to a problem: if God is beyond anything one can imagine, how is it possible to know God? For Catholics, this problem is resolved through the person of Jesus through whose incarnation God's nature is manifested.

This problem doesn't arise in Buddhism because it is agnostic. If Buddhism does not posit a Supreme Being neither does it specifically deny one. When asked questions about metaphysical matters, the Buddha refused to express an opinion. And yet the whole point of his teaching, certainly as expressed in Zen practice, was to bring people to an experience which – as William Johnston had recognized – was undoubtedly religious.

The significant point here for Hand is that the East chooses "not to conceptualize the absolute."[77] Nor does it insist upon a defined statement of doctrine – such as the Nicene Creed – which adherents of a particular belief system are required to subscribe to on pain of ostracism or worse. "There are no eternal dogmas that must be preserved against all heretical opponents."[78] In fact, such a statement of belief would be considered an impediment to genuine spiritual insight. "For an easterner a conceptual framework is only a tool to be used on the path to that knowing which is beyond all concepts."[79] The idea that one particular expression of belief was uniquely true in some manner is preposterous from such a perspective.

Buddhism teaches that wisdom comes not from looking outward, not from study and analysis, but from turning inward. This perspective is succinctly expressed by the 13th century Japanese Zen pioneer, Dogen Kigen, in a short verse which Hand and Sister Agnes rendered into English:

> To learn the path (of Buddha) is to learn the self.
> To learn the self is to forget self.
> To forget self is to perceive self as all things.[80]

In other words, the sense of being a personal self – with all of the conditioning factors forming it – impedes our awareness of the essential Self which is beyond all categories, what Zen refers to as one's face before one's parents were born.

Kensho, the direct experience of one's interdependence with all of being, is – Hand says –

---

77 Ibid., p. 9.

78 Ibid., pp. 9-10.

79 Ibid., p. 10.

80 Ibid., p. 23.

– direct experience. In it the human mind does not abstract an idea and know the object through this idea. In fact, that which is known is not seen as an object at all. The self does not stand back and know something as an object. Rather, the knower, the act of knowing, and that which is known are all one.[81]

Sister Agnes notes that a similar point is made in the Book of Genesis. The Biblical story tells of a time before Adam and Eve ate the fruit of the tree which gave them knowledge of good and evil – i.e., a time before distinctions were made – and it is said that in that earlier time they had walked and talked directly with God. It was only when they learned to distinguish, to compare and judge, that they were cast out of Eden.

The value of differentiated consciousness and being able to distinguish qualities is obvious – both to Buddhists and Christians – but something is lost in attaining it. Nor is awakening simply a matter of returning to an infantile state prior to differentiated consciousness. It is not a matter of one instead of the other, but of being able to maintain both – as described in the famous analogy of Qingyuan Weixin:

"Before I began the study of Zen, mountains were mountains and waters were waters. When I first achieved some insight into the truth of Zen through the benevolence of my teacher, mountains were no longer mountains and waters no longer waters. But now that I've attained to full enlightenment, I'm at rest, and mountains are once again mountains and waters are waters."

Zazen – which Hand described as concentrated training in mindfulness in contrast to study and analysis – was specifically intended to bring the practitioner to kensho. The unique Eastern perspective Hand had intuited when he first arrived in Japan was the emphasis placed not on understanding but on experience. Religious truth was not something to be reasoned to but something to be directly encountered.

Thomas Hand died in 2005, shortly before what would have been his 85th birthday. The East-West Meditation Program at the Mercy Center, however, survived his passing and continues to use Zen as an upaya for deepening Christian spirituality, although it is no longer unique. It is now only one of several such centers in North America.

---

81   Ibid., p. 33.

CHAPTER FIVE

Ruben Habito

Ruben Habito is a Dharma heir of Koun Yamada Roshi and the resident teacher of the Maria Kannon Zen Center in Dallas, Texas. He is also a former Jesuit introduced to Zen by Thomas Hand. Unwavering in his commitment to his Catholic heritage, Ruben has earned the respect of the Zen community for his insight, compassion, and ability as a teacher. While I was writing *Cypress Trees in the Garden,* he was frequently cited to me as an example of someone who successfully merged Zen practice and insight with a Christian life, and so he was the first person I arranged to interview for this book. Although he has a slightly formal way of speaking, his personal manner is relaxed and gently humorous. I had two extended conversations with him in the summer of 2015, and the issues that arose set the pattern for later interviews.

He had been born in the Philippines in 1947, when the country was still recovering from the impact of the Second World War. "My father had many recollections of the Japanese occupation," he tells me. "When he was young, he was part of the student resistance, and so he had many tales of horror of what had been done by the Japanese to the Filipinos during the war. He came from a poor farming family, then got a scholarship to go to college. He worked hard, got good marks, and excelled. So he was given a scholarship to go onto graduate school, which he did, in the United States. He got a doctorate in agricultural education at the University of Minnesota. He took me along, when I was in fourth grade and fifth grade, together with my mother, younger sister, younger brother, and then a baby sister was born in Minnesota. We lived there for two years."

When they returned to the Philippines, Ruben's father taught at the state university in Los Baños on the other end of Laguna de Bay from Manila. "We were culturally blessed with many things that we had access to; we were acquainted with classical music that my father loved, enjoyed the finer things of a cultured middle class life, and so in that regard I had a very blessed family life."

He was aware, however, that most people in the country lived very differently, and he recognized that he viewed those conditions from a position of privilege. "Because I did not suffer the hunger or the deprivation or the discrimination or illness or the things that many of the people in my country had to – and still have to – undergo, I had the inner leeway, you could say, to reflect on these things, rather than being caught up in trying to overcome such difficulties, like those who had to work two or three jobs, or struggle a lot to keep their family fed and sheltered. And I had access to the things that I needed, unlike many of my contemporaries. You could say there was a sense of empathy with the persons who did have such situations of difficulty and struggle in their lives."

The enormous economic disparities he saw led him to wonder how, if God existed, he could allow such suffering for some while others lived in comparative luxury. Then, at the University of the Philippines in Quezon City, he met others who thought along similar lines.

"I had some friends who got me asking those questions of 'What is the point of it all? What's the meaning of it all? Is there a God after all?' I was born and raised in a devout Catholic family – and I am grateful to my parents and my siblings for that atmosphere – but when I was on my own, I started questioning all of that. And these friends were also reading the books of existential writers, so that influenced me as well. And that kind of conversation made me just look and see that, yes, there is so much injustice in the world, so much unfairness and so much suffering. And how can this be allowed if God is all-powerful and all-loving? And so the basic question of whether God did exist or not became very acute for me."

"Did you ever resolve those questions?"

"Uh…the jury's still out on that one," he tells me with a smile. Then, after a moment's reflection, "Let me correct myself. I've struggled with this throughout my life, and in a sense still do. Through all these years somehow I've come to terms with it for myself, but I don't want to impose my answer on anyone else. It's a kind of questioning that each one of us has to grapple with for ourselves, and how we resolve it, one way or another, determines how we live our life."

This questioning redirected his attention from his original course of study. "Rather than doing my math homework for my physics degree, I was poring over philosophy books – Sartre and Camus – and most of my time was, if not doing that kind of reading and thinking about those questions, spent hanging out with friends at the Student Catholic Action. And there were several who were also very astute in their philosophical questionings with whom I would get engaged in conversation. So that somehow prepared the ground for me to see that a life in pursuit of these questions and in helping others pursue these questions was something I was called to.

"And then – through some fortuitous occasion – I met a Jesuit, Father Benigno Mayo, who presented to me what a Jesuit life was all about, a lot of study, philosophy and theology, precisely to be able to help people in their spiritual search. That really clicked for me, so I applied, got through the application process, and found myself in the Jesuit novitiate instead of going to my second year of my studies in physics. I was set on a new course of life from that point on."

I ask what Jesuit training was like.

"Well, in the novitiate year it was training in prayer and meditation and living a rhythm of life that was semi-monastic and so on. And, well, Latin and Greek and some basic Bible studies using historico-critical methods of that time. But mostly it was living a life that is in accordance with God's will. Not according to my will but, as Saint Ignatius writes in his Spiritual Exercise, to live so that one's life is totally dedicated to the greater glory of God."

As many Jesuits did, Ruben might have gone onto teach in one of their universities in the Philippines had it not been for a chance encounter with an American missionary returning from Japan to the United States. The young priest was Robert Kennedy, who – by his own admission – had had no interest in Zen during his posting to Japan, although years later he would return there to become a student of Yamada Roshi.

"He was going back to the United States but was taking a round-about visit of different places in Asia. And so he came to the Philippines and gave a talk to the novices about how Japan was a very challenging place for Christians, because they were less than one percent of the population – half of them Catholic, half spread among different Protestant denominations – and that it was a country that was gradually becoming secularized and losing its spiritual heritage and so on. And so he told us that the Jesuit Province of Japan was inviting Jesuits from all over the world to come and help in the work there, to learn Japanese and be part of the team that shared the Gospel with the people of Japan. Somehow that stirred something up in me. So I sent a letter to the Father General in Rome, and they wrote back saying, 'Well, finish your studies first and let's see and apply again.' And so I did so after I finished my philosophical studies, and I was sent to Japan in 1970."

At this point he was in the stage of Jesuit training – called the regency – which precedes final preparations for ordination. His first assignment was to learn to speak Japanese. "I was in the language school in Kamakura with about 12 to 15 other seminarians or some of them were already newly ordained young priests from not just the Jesuits but from other congregations like the Society for the Divine Word or the Guadalupe Missionaries from Mexico. These were young men dedicated to giving their lives in service to the Japanese people as missionaries of the Catholic Church, and our spiritual director happened to be Father Thomas Hand who had already started practicing Zen for some years before I arrived. And he advised me, 'To deepen your spiritual life, and also to really deepen your knowledge of Japanese culture, why don't you come with me and join me in sitting in Zen with this group.'" The group was Koun Yamada's San-un Zendo.

Ruben's time in Japan also coincided with that of William Johnston, Heinrich Dumoulin, and Hugh Enomiya-Lassalle. "Father Lassalle lived in the same Jesuit house as I did. He was a very inspiring spiritual teacher already in the 1940s. He became one of my mentors. There was also a Japanese Jesuit, Father Kakichi Kadowaki, who studied for a while with Yamada Koun and then transferred to another teacher, Omori Sogen, a well-known Rinzai teacher, and Kadowaki practiced with him for many years until he also became a Zen Master in the Rinzai tradition. So there were several Jesuits who were practicing Zen and integrating it with Jesuit spirituality."

With their encouragement, Ruben became a student of Yamada and regularly attended sesshin at San-un.

∾

"You completed your Jesuit training in Japan?" I ask.

"Yes. I was ordained in 1976 in Tokyo. And then I continued graduate school in Buddhist studies another couple of years and then started teaching at Sophia University in 1978, in the Philosophy and Theology Departments."

"And you kept up your Zen studies at the same time?"

"Yes. I would go to Kamakura twice a month and then also to visit with Yamada Koun Roshi in Tokyo, in his office there. When I was first introduced to Yamada Roshi, I was given the koan called 'Mu,' so just letting that koan be the focus of my sitting led to an opening of something that gave me a very deep and profound experience of ecstatic joy. It was a sudden experience of merging into everything, and of realizing every moment as sacred. I cannot describe it fully in words, but it was so overwhelming that, the moment it hit me, I literally jumped up in joy from my seat and excitedly started running up the stairs and knocked on the door of Father Hand, saying, with a beaming smile, 'I got it! I got it!' He looked at me with some surprise and suggested I go to the master to have it checked. And so I did. So after a couple of such meetings of being examined with the usual checking questions, I was confirmed in what is called a Zen kensho experience, an experience of seeing one's true nature. And so from there, from that point on, I was presented with the curriculum of 500 or so koans that we go through in our Sanbo Zen lineage, and it takes a good number of years to go through them one by one with the direction of the master in one-on-one consultation or a face-to-face encounter until one completes the curriculum."

"Why do you think there was so much interest in Zen among the Jesuits at that time?" I ask.

"First of all it was to learn from Asian spiritual wellsprings as a way of deepening Christian spirituality. It was also to connect with Japanese culture and religion in a way that can open avenues for Christians to engage in a spiritual encounter with Japanese Buddhists. So those are two ways in which one can describe the understanding of the Jesuits who were practicing Zen at the time: to deepen their own spirituality, which was based on Ignatian Exercises, now receiving a very powerful booster in this very methodical practice of Zen."

"In what way? How did Zen enhance Jesuit practice?"

"Let me go into my own story in that regard. So when I came to Zen practice in my early 20s, we were just given simple instructions on the basic principles of taking a proper seated posture conducive to stillness and then of being aware of the breath, then allowing the mind to be calm and focused in the here and now. And so I found that very nourishing and direct. And I discovered it was a way of really arriving at the very place that Ignatius leads an exercitant who goes through his Spiritual Exercises."

The Ignatian exercises begin with an examination of the problematic nature of the human condition – which it identifies as "sin" – leading to a recognition of the elements of one's life that need to be straightened out or purified.

"In the next phase," Ruben continues, "we begin to set aside the discursive mind and are led to a more simple contemplative practice. We are now instructed to just behold the words and actions of Jesus, to contemplate this looming figure of Jesus with a view to putting on the mind of Christ in one's own life and way of being. The point of this is to become one with Jesus through listening to his words, watching his actions, and absorbing all of that into one's own being. In going through these contemplative exercises, one comes to understand that to follow Jesus does not simply mean imitating Jesus in a way that one looks at a model of behavior from a distance. Rather, all this leads one to embody the mind and heart of Jesus in one's own life, to become an *alter Christus*[82] in all the dimensions of one's own human life, infused with Divine Grace of course."

In the next stage, one dies to the egoistic self. "Dies with Jesus on the cross as it were. This is the stage wherein one experiences the newness of life in the Risen Christ. To be one with Jesus in the Risen Life is to behold the Divine Glory permeating the entire universe. This is referred to as the stage of union, wherein one's life is seen in the full light of Divine Grace and is lived in union with the Divine Will. So that final stage – the summit of the exercises, called the Contemplation on Divine Love – consists in simply resting in Divine Love, beholding everything in the light of this Love.[83]

---

82 Another Christ.

83 In reviewing the transcript of this interview, Ruben requested the capitalizations used in this paragraph.

"Now that is exactly what I found most directly and intimately in this practice of Zen. It is simply a practice of just sitting there, breathing in and breathing out, without any need for any kind of discursive or mental efforts, but a practice of just allowing unconditional Love to permeate through one's entire being. It is allowing oneself to be immersed in that unconditional Love, sitting there opening one's entire being to allow that to happen. That's where I found the point of convergence between Zen and the Spiritual Exercises."

❧

Ruben completed the koan curriculum in 1988, just one year before Yamada Roshi died. "He had an accident; he slipped while he was coming down an escalator in a department store. And so he was hospitalized for medical examinations for a few days, and that just led to his deterioration. He was not able to come back with the kind of physical health that was needed to continue teaching. So in any case, I was able to finish my koan curriculum just as he was, himself, ending his own teaching career. So I had that big blessing of having done that."

There were other changes taking place in Ruben's life. He had met a young German woman, Maria Reis, who was in Japan writing a doctoral dissertation on Guanyin – the Chinese incarnation of the Bodhisattva of Compassion – and who had taken part in Zen sesshin in Germany under the direction of Enomiya-Lassalle.

"We became good friends from the moment we met, continuing to correspond by letter from a geographical distance. She lived in Kyoto, and I was in Tokyo teaching at the Jesuit-run Sophia University. And that deepening friendship led me to a point where I needed to make a discernment, whether to remain in my celibate life as a Jesuit, or whether this was something new that was being placed before me that I had to reconsider, as to whether a new vocation was emerging. So I went through a period of discernment and reflection about what scenarios lay ahead for me. So to make a long story short, in 1989, I came to peace with the fact that I now needed to leave the Society of Jesus and seek new horizons."

He found a post at the Perkins School of Theology in Dallas, Texas. Because he had just taken up his position at the school, he was unable to attend the memorial service held for Yamada Roshi in Kamakura. During that rite, a ceremony was conducted in which a number of Yamada's senior students were authorized to teach Zen on their own. "It seems Yamada Roshi himself had seen to this before he died and had made the formal appointments by putting his seal on scrolls with the names of those students he had in mind, and even gave each of us an appropriate Zen Master's name. My name was included among those formally appointed Zen Teacher. And I have a sealed and signed certificate from him authorizing me, with about twelve or thirteen others, to be one of his successors in the Dharma with the Zen name Keiun

Ken, Grace Cloud Lineage."

When people at Perkins learned that he had been authorized to teach Zen, some sought him out. "They asked, 'Can we sit together? Could you help us in our own Zen path?'"

"That's how you began teaching?"

"Correct."

"What's that been like? Being a Zen teacher?"

"It's still a learning experience. I continue to learn from people with whom I sit. And it's also very rewarding and very gratifying to walk with people in this journey and especially to be a witness to people who undergo a breakthrough experience. In our Zen training, we get to learn the checking questions, how to check whether somebody has had a genuine experience or whether it is just an intellectual insight, or whether it is just on the level of some spiritual/devotional experience that is not yet the kind that we are looking for. What is crucial is to guide practitioners toward a transformative experience that changes one's whole outlook and attitude toward yourself, toward the world, toward reality itself. So being a witness to such events in peoples' lives is a great source of joy, seeing how things do happen to people when they just give themselves the leeway to sit and be still and be aware. That can change their entire outlook in life. And it is not because I did anything to make it happen. I'm just someone like a midwife who comes and helps in giving birth to this new life that is coming out, seeing through the process as they open their eyes, as they open their hearts to the fullness of the reality that they are."

"You remain a practicing Catholic?"

"Yes, I do."

"So, when you're teaching, are you teaching Zen or are you teaching Buddhism?"

He pauses for a moment, then says, "Neither. I don't teach anything. I just sit there with them and allow Zen to happen. Allow the breath to do its work."

"Do you introduce people to basic Buddhist concepts such as the Four Noble Truths?"

"Yes, I have recourse to all of those teachings that the Buddha entrusted to his followers, those concepts that give us a map of the terrain of the path of awakening. Concepts can be like fingers pointing to the moon. They are taken precisely as pointers for persons to see for themselves, as if to say 'Ah! Look!' When they do turn their heads and take a look, or as they open their hearts and minds to that which is being pointed to, then it is no longer a concept but something that hits a person directly when they undergo that wondrous experience. So all we can do as so-called 'teachers' is just make use of those pointers in the best way we can. And, of course, I bring in

Christian texts also, the scriptures or Christian doctrines. In fact, that's what I'm engaged in now. I've been re-editing some of the transcribed talks that I had given during some Zen retreats in which many Christians were participating, using gospel texts as the words that would be pointers to that experience."[84]

"There are many people – even some in the Sanbo Zen tradition – who would argue that you cannot separate Zen from Buddhism."

"In a sense I would agree, and, in a sense, I would also say you need to go beyond Buddhism. Zen *does* come from Buddhism, and the vocabulary that it uses is thoroughly Buddhist. That needs to be acknowledged with appropriate understanding and with gratitude. And yet, my own teacher, Yamada Roshi, emphasized that one of the four marks of Zen is that it is beyond words and concepts. So it is beyond any -isms or systems of thought or beliefs that human beings need as their props or as scaffolding. Those are not his words. I'm paraphrasing, but I am echoing his message that the heart of Zen is beyond words and concepts. So if you have really undergone and soaked yourself in that experience that is truly ineffable, beyond words and concepts, and have embodied that in your own life and are really living in that light, you appreciate that Zen can never be adequately contained in words or concepts or doctrines, Buddhism or what have you. Yamada Roshi told those of us practicing under his guidance who came from Christian backgrounds: 'As you go back to your own Christian communities, by all means, take the words and concepts your communities are familiar with, take your scriptures, take your doctrines that your community will understand for you to be able to point to that reality that is beyond words.' So he gave us that mandate, in fact, to go beyond Buddhism as such, to explore that realm that Zen opens to us through Buddhism, through Zen Buddhism, in a way that we go beyond Buddhism."

∾

"How would you explain koan training to another Jesuit – or any Catholic – who didn't know anything about Zen?"

"A koan is a way of letting the discursive mind come to face a blank wall and somehow pull it to a stop so that your intuitive mind might open up and allow you to experience reality directly without the mediation of the logical or discursive mind."

"Is that a process congruent with Christian thinking?"

"I would say so, because it invites us to be still and allow that part of us that rests totally in God to just open up, to not think about it but just be there in awe with an open heart."

"So is it a form of prayer or is it something entirely different from prayer?"

---

84   The book – entitled, *Be Still and Know: Zen and the Bible* – is scheduled to be released by Orbis Books in 2017.

"It is a way of rendering oneself totally open to God, so it is a very distinctive form of prayer in itself. I understand prayer as communion with God, and it is certainly that. Now from God's side, God is always in communion with us humans. Sitting in Zen is launching oneself in a process that opens one's heart to a way of seeing things as they are, to the wisdom of seeing things as they are, the wisdom that enables you to see one's interconnectedness with everything, with every living being, with everything there is. So at the same time it opens up your heart in compassion because you realize you are one with all and are enabled to share in the pain of all beings as well as the joy of all beings. I remember Yamada Koun Roshi saying that with Zen practice one's heart goes out to the world and that one would want to be an instrument of peace in the world. When he talked of such things, it showed how his heart embraced the whole world in a heart of compassion."

The traditional image of that compassion in Zen and other forms of Buddhism is the Bodhisattva Guanyin or Kannon.

"Your group in Dallas is called the Maria Kannon Zen Center," I note. "So you're deliberately identifying the Virgin Mary and Guanyin."

"Yes. Very deliberately. The image of compassion in Buddhism is Kannon, of course, and, in the Christian West, it's Mary, the mother of Jesus. Also Maria Kannon is a figure from the period in Japanese history when the Christians were persecuted and could no longer profess their faith openly, so they had to destroy or hide all their images of Jesus or the Holy Family or of the Virgin Mother that were of Western origin. So they found this feminine image of compassion in the Buddhist figure of Kannon, and they put it up on their altar and would recite the rosary before it. For them, it was Mary, the Mother of Jesus, but it was Kannon in the eyes of Japanese authorities then.

"It's the Mary who stood at the foot of the cross of Jesus. The Stabat Mater is a celebrated scene, also made into a hymn, that presents the image of Mary's compassion, bearing the wounds of her own son who bears the wounds of the world. So that compassion, of bearing the wounds of the world, is what is seen as the place of intersection with Kannon in the Buddhist tradition. So there is the hope and aspiration we have, that those who sit in Zen are able to activate that seed of compassion in them symbolized by Mary and by Kannon."

❧

"So let's imagine," I suggest, "that one of the students here at Perkins hears about you and wonders what you're doing. And they come to your office and ask, 'What's this all about? What does Zen do?' How would you respond?"

"It's about paying attention and opening your heart to the riches of what is and what you are."

"And what would I get out of it?"

"A sense of total peace within yourself. A sense of recognizing your interconnectedness with the whole universe, and a way of life that gushes forth in compassion."

"Okay. So let's say this student is a Catholic seminarian. Would your answer be any different?"

"No."

"And then the seminarian might ask, 'What does Zen have to offer Catholics that the church doesn't already offer?'"

Again, there is a slight pause before he answers. "It offers Catholics a very methodical way of arriving at that which we are seeking as the ultimate longing of our hearts."

"Which is?"

"The ultimate longing that lies deep in our hearts, in our Catholic understanding, is to find union with God in all eternity and to be in communion with all those that God has created out of love. This is what is called the Beatific Vision, basking in the divine presence and in the presence of the communion of saints, all embraced in Unconditional Love. So I can tell a Catholic that Zen is a way of life that gives us a foretaste and opens us to that Beatific Vision, and also opens us to the reality of Divine love in which we are totally immersed every moment of our lives, the love which empowers us to live a life empowered by that love for all beings."

"You knew William Johnston."

"Correct."

"Who, in addition to the books he wrote about Zen, also wrote about medieval Christian spirituality and released an edition of *The Cloud of Unknowing*."

"Yes. That was the subject of his doctoral thesis."

"How does the approach that *The Cloud of Unknowing* takes, focusing on a short mantra-like prayer – I think it even suggests a one syllable prayer – how is that different from working with Mu?"

"Well, it may help a person who finds that a phrase leads them to a deeper experience, into a realm that would enable them to go beyond that phrase. So there are a good number of persons who I feel can be helped with a more... How would you put it? A more Christian... No. Let me backtrack. There are persons who, because of their background and because of what they bring to practice, could be helped in deepening their spirituality in and through those Christian terms and phrases they may be familiar with.

"For example, someone who may have worked with Mu for a time and finds no headway in it may come to me and say, 'I don't know what to do. Should I just stop this?' Sometimes I say, 'Okay, instead of Mu, just breathe in and breathe out and let that out-breath be accompanied by "I am." It is the "I am" that Jesus uttered when he was asked about his origins. "Before Abraham was, I am." It is the "I am" beyond time and space, the "I am" that Moses heard when he asked, "Who is this that is sending me to my people?" "I am." So, don't philosophize about it, just be one with that "I am" and let yourself experience that "I am."' So that is one way I could also guide a person in a way that does not use Mu."

"I understand that, but the question is how, from your perspective, working with Mu differs from more traditional Christian practices, even though they may have fallen out of use, like the one described in *The Cloud of Unknowing*? Or do they differ?"

"I need to look more closely at *The Cloud of Unknowing* again in terms of its potential for Zen guidance, but as far as I see it is leading to precisely that same place that is verbalized as 'the cloud of *unknowing*,' that place where subject-object knowledge is no longer applicable. And it is precisely that place beyond words that somehow resonates with a kind of place that Zen vocabulary is also pointing to."

"Like John of the Cross's *nada*?"[85]

"Sure, yes. The '*nada, nada*.' To strip away everything you know, or think you know, precisely so you can reach that big 'nothing.'"

"So, there are similarities in the spiritual practices of two very, very distinct traditions that – until recently – had little communication with one another. As an academic, how would you explain that?"

"That it's uncanny, isn't it?" he says with a laugh. "I would say, 'Well, you see, the Holy Spirit breathes where it wills, and so we cannot determine in what way the same Holy Spirit that we recognize in our Triune God has been acting throughout all creation. So that's a sign that we need to explore these traditions more precisely to recover or discover the work of the God that we worship in our own Christian tradition.' That is how I would invite Christians to see the rationale of that, to enable them to find that. So that's connected to the traditional theological interest of faith seeking understanding, a search which has to be articulated in language, yet with the full appreciation that we are dealing with matters that simply are beyond language and beyond our intellectual capacities to fully fathom."

---

85 Cf. p. 177 below.

CHAPTER SIX

Willigis Jäger

"Many can argue whether a Christian can validly do or teach Zen or not," the German Benedictine, Willigis Jäger, declared. "The fact is, I am doing it."

Koun Yamada Roshi gave Dharma transmission to twelve Catholic religious, many of whom – like Ruben Habito – would help establish Zen practice in North America. Jäger, another Yamada heir, had an equally significant impact on the development of European Zen.

Jäger viewed Zen less as a foray into an exotic foreign practice than as a means of recovering a Catholic tradition which, as he put it, had "fallen into obscurity."

> Christianity usually teaches oral and meditative prayer, a certain moral behavior, and social commitment. But this isn't much more than the grammar school of a religion, and so many Christians remain stuck in an infantile state.[86]

Of course, he adds, many Buddhists never get beyond an infantile form of their faith either. Zen is a vehicle for cultivating maturity in Buddhism and reinvigorating the mystical perspective in Catholicism.

In addition to being a transmitted Zen teacher and a Catholic priest, Jäger is also a scholar, a student of the anthropology of religion, and an authority on the subject of mysticism. His teaching focuses on the way in which Zen has the potential to enhance Catholic spirituality and on the universal elements he believes unites the two traditions. Not surprisingly, his perspective is controversial. As his writings and public presentations attained a degree of popularity, especially in Germany, they caught the attention of the Vatican's Congregation for the Doctrine of the Faith which eventually

---

86 Willigis Jäger, *Search for the Meaning of Life*, trans. by Peter Heinegg (Liguori, MO: Liguori Publications, 2005) e-edition. Location 1319.

ordered him to stop publishing and refrain from giving lectures and courses.

ᕲ

Jäger was born in Hosbach, Germany, in 1925 to a devout family. He records that his first taste of mysticism occurred while attending a Perpetual Adoration[87] service at church with his mother when he was only five years old. The sound of a group of women reciting the rosary entranced him and roused in him the feeling that there was a level of experience which lay beyond normal understanding.

He attended the boarding school attached to Munsterschwarzach Abbey, the Benedictine monastery near Würzburg and, after graduation, remained at the abbey as a novice. During the course of his training, he came upon classic works of Christian mysticism as well as a treatise on mysticism by another Benedictine, Alois Mager. Trying to follow the instruction he found in those texts, he experienced a deepening of his prayer life; however, there was no spiritual advisor to whom he could turn for guidance, and there was a general suspicion about mysticism in the monastery, so it was an interest he had to pursue covertly.

He was ordained in 1952, and for the next twelve years served as a teacher in the boarding school. Then in 1960 he became engaged in the church's Mission and Development program which provided him an opportunity to visit a number of developing countries in Asia where he first encountered Buddhism.

When, in 1972, Hugo Enomiya-Lassalle arranged for Koun Yamada Roshi to lead a sesshin in Munich, Jäger was one of the attendees. His first encounter with Yamada was transformative. Shortly after this, the Benedictines founded a new monastery in Kamakura where Yamada lived, and Jäger – now 50 – applied to be sent there. He spent six years in Japan studying with Yamada. When the Benedictine foundation moved to Tokyo, Jäger received permission to remain in Kamakura in order to dedicate himself more fully to koan study.

After Jäger completed the Sanbo Kyodan koan curriculum, Yamada gave him permission to teach, and, in 1985, he returned to Germany where he established a zendo in a wing of what had been the abbey boarding school in Würzburg. The project had the assistance and support of both Yamada and the abbot of Münsterschwarzbach, Fidelis Rupport. Jäger had not lost his interest in Christian mysticism, and, in addition to Zen training, he offered courses in traditional Christian contemplative prayer.[88] His programs were surprisingly popular, and his daily Zen sittings had as many as 150 persons in attendance.

---

87 A service during which the consecrated host is displayed on the altar for the adoration of the congregation.

88 "Contemplation" is the medieval term for prayer that has "no concrete object." [*Search for the Meaning of Life*, location 1407] It is a form of prayer "possible only when reason, memory, and will have come to rest." [Ibid., location 1414]

In 1996, Ji'un Kubota Roshi, Yamada's immediate heir, gave Jäger full transmission — *inka shomei* — recognizing that he was a direct successor, through 86 predecessors, of the Buddha. He also later received transmission in the Chinese Chan tradition.

There was, however, a conservative element in the Diocese of Würzburg which was suspicious of Jäger's teaching, particularly its connections to Buddhism, and complaints were sent to Rome. These came to the attention of the Congregation of the Doctrine of the Faith, and, in 2002 Jäger was censured for emphasizing "mystical experience above doctrinal truth." Personal experience, the Congregation declared, must be subordinate to church teaching.

The director of the Congregation at the time was then-Cardinal Joseph Ratzinger,[89] known to have concerns about "the doctrinal consequences of dialogue between Christianity and Buddhism." In 1989, Ratzinger had issued a warning on Catholic engagement in Eastern meditative practices which needed to be "subjected to a thoroughgoing examination so as to avoid the danger of falling into syncretism."

Jäger at first complied with the terms of the censure and undertook a period of silence at an abbey in Einsiedelei. Then, although he had the support of the abbot and the Benedictine Community, he took leave from the order — a process known as exclaustration — and resumed his prior activities. In 2007, he established the Willigis Jäger Foundation for Western-Eastern Wisdom and, in 2009, a new Zen lineage called "Leere Wolke" — the German equivalent of his Buddhist name, Kyo-un or "Empty Cloud" — dedicated to providing Zen instruction to Christians and people of Western heritage. His approach to spiritual direction seeks to address the needs of people who no longer feel at home in the Christian milieu as it is usually proclaimed and who are looking for an expression more in keeping with a contemporary understanding of the nature of the universe.

He told Christoph Quarch that the inquirers who came to his courses usually did so because they had a "crisis of meaning":

> Suddenly they find themselves confronted with questions they can't answer on their own: What am I living for? Where am I going? Why did this happen to me? Religions have always attempted to give answers to those questions. But the answers no longer satisfy many people of our times. It's as if the ground suddenly vanished from under their feet, and a tremendous feeling of insecurity takes its place. It's at this point that I pick these people up, so to speak. I try to show them what an opportunity they have for a new start, whether within their religion or outside of it.[90]

---

89   Later Pope Benedict XVI.

90   *Mysticism for Modern Times*, p. 33.

❧

Jäger's understanding of spirituality derives not from academic study but from the experiential insight he terms "mystic" found in both Buddhism and Christianity. As a result of many years of Zen practice, he came to believe "that Christian mysticism teaches the same thing as Zen. It was only by way of a 'detour' through Japan that I was able to realize and value the treasures in my own Christian tradition."[91]

Mystical awareness is not a logical premise to which one gives intellectual consent. It cannot be transmitted through language. Jäger's justification for his own extensive writing and lecturing on the topic is that language can, however, lure one onto the path. As Jäger defines it, the mystical experience opens one to "transpersonal consciousness," which

> – involves an experience of emptiness, of God without a predicate. On this level we experience "pure existence," the source from which all things issue ... The mystical experience is an experience of the oneness of form and emptiness,[92] an experience of the unity of our own identity with the primary reality. This state of consciousness is the goal of the spiritual path.[93]

Mystical experience can only be attained by transcending the culturally conditioned ego which is the storehouse not only of memory but of prejudice, grievance, and conditioning as well. What we think of as our "self," the ideas and the perspective we identify as "ours," is actually the construct of a range of conditioning influences over which we have no control: the family in which we were raised, the education system we attended, the broader social and political environment, the language we speak, the people with whom we interact, contemporary popular culture. These all contribute to forming our sense of self and our way of viewing the world – our point of view. Although we take this point of view for granted, it is not in any sense objective. Had any of these influences been different, our point of view would have been different as well.

In transpersonal consciousness, one identifies not with the transient physical body or the culturally conditioned perceptions and reflections of one's thoughts but with something "beyond the concept of God."[94] This, Jäger argues, is the consciousness of

---

91 Ibid., p. 36.

92 Cf., the *Heart Sutra*: "Form here is only emptiness, emptiness only form. / Form is no other than emptiness. / Emptiness no other than form." *The Heart Sutra* is a brief summation of Mahayana Buddhist teachings regularly chanted in Zen temples.

93 *Mysticism for Modern Times*, p. 4.

94 *Search for the Meaning of Life*, location 126.

Jesus and the consciousness to which Jesus calls his disciples.[95] Although it has fallen into abeyance, mysticism is not, he argues, a marginal aspect of Christianity but is, rather, central to its purpose.

∾

Jäger rediscovered the importance of mysticism through Zen, then dedicated his career to trying to revive the mystical tradition within the church so that others could encounter in their native heritage what he had to first discover outside of it. In order to achieve that – although it seems strained at times – he seeks to articulate what amounts to a Zen-based theology.

Religious language is metaphorical. It is also inevitably the product of a particular culture and era and the general knowledge common to those. Jäger stresses that, in order to remain vital and effective, the religious models used to understand the world must be modified as the scope of human knowledge expands. Twenty six hundred years ago, when the book of Genesis was composed, the story of the tower of Babel might have seemed a reasonable theory for the diversity of languages in the world; it no longer is. The model of reality that Jäger presents is his attempt to explain the kensho insight in such a way that it incorporates not only Christian and Buddhist perspectives but the perspective of the scientific community as well; however, it can no more purport to be a literal or exhaustive rendering of reality than any other model. Models will always require refinement and adjustment.

He starts by distinguishing between spirituality and religion and between what he identifies as the esoteric and the exoteric. These distinctions are roughly parallel.

Spirituality is a path that leads to experience or insight. Religion, on the other hand, is the formulation of dogmatic principles, the expression of obligatory beliefs and practices. Spirituality is vital and alive; religion is "instruction that has evolved into dogmatic theology."[96]

By esoteric he means practice which understands the goal of religion to be the cultivation of the experience of the divine. Exoteric practice, on the other hand, consists of ritual, scripture, and dogma. The esoteric refers to the reality that all religious activity strives to reveal; the exoteric is the cultural manifestation, the outward appearance of particular religious institutions. The exoteric is the façade; the esoteric is the significance. At the exoteric level, each of the world's religions is distinct and largely irreconcilable with other religions. At the esoteric level – at the level of mysticism – all religions are ways of experiencing the divine, and no individual religion can lay sole claim to be the one true path.

---

95   Jäger cites John 17:21: " – that they may all be one. As you, Father, are in me and I am in you, may they also be in us, so that the world may believe that you have sent me."

96   *Search for the Meaning Life*, location 1327.

He compares the various religions of the world to stained glass windows.

> They give the light that shines through them a specific structure. If
> there is no light, the windows are dull and meaningless. Thus it is
> the light that is the decisive element. But we can't see the light with
> our eyes. Light makes things visible, but is itself invisible. It only be-
> comes visible when it is divided into colors and takes on a structure.
> This is true also about religions when considering the divine. Reli-
> gions give a tangible structure to the intangible. The price religions
> pay for this is the reduction of the divine to one part of its entire
> spectrum. It would be foolish to take that part for the whole.[97]

This is not a criticism of the exoteric forms; specific cultural expressions of religion
are necessary. As Jäger puts it, a religion is no more capable of existing without those
forms of expression – including scripture, ritual, and theology – than a person can
exist without a body. The problem arises when an individual is exclusively loyal to
a particular cultural expression. An extreme example are the sects – both Christian
and otherwise – that decide that a mode of dress and technological development
from a specific era of history is to be maintained perpetually. When the cultural
manifestations of religion are taken literally – fundamentally – then they become
hindrances, focusing, as they do, on the symbols rather than what those symbols
seek to convey.

Expressed in theistic terms, the mystic element of all religions proclaims our
essential unity with God. Jäger views the universe as God's self-revelation. "Such as
we are, we are the way the Divine Reality expresses itself. We are the unique and un-
mistakable revelation of the divine life."[98] He tempers the ostensible conceit of that
statement by acknowledging that we are only one of potentially hundreds of millions
of forms of intelligent life that may have evolved throughout the universe. It is a perspective reminiscent of the assertion of the American astrophysicist, Carl Sagan, who
suggested that humankind is "a way for the cosmos to know itself."

> God and the human species are in a relationship to each other like
> gold and a ring. They are two completely different realities. The
> gold is not the ring and the ring is not the gold. But in a golden
> ring they can only appear together. They are coexistent. The gold
> needs a form to appear, and the ring needs a material to become
> visible. They are "not-two." As the gold reveals itself as ring, so

---

97   *Mysticism for Modern Times*, p. 18.
98   *Search for the Meaning of Life*, location 199.

God reveals himself as the human species. They can only appear together. This, for me, is the meaning of the Incarnation of Christ. Through that particular incarnation it should be made apparent that everything represents an incarnation of God, from quarks and leptons to purely spiritual forms that we have no idea about. We are "god-beings." I could also say: God has manifested himself in the human species.[99]

What prevents us from being aware of this self-revelation of God is ego-consciousness, our preoccupation with ourselves as unique individuals.

We think that as human beings we are on a quest for God. But we're not the ones searching for the Ultimate Reality. Rather it is the Ultimate Reality that causes the dissatisfied yearning and the search in us. God is the seeker. God awakens in us. We ourselves can't *do* anything; we can only let go so the Divine can unfold itself.[100]

Our call in life then – the meaning of our lives, the purpose of our lives – is to cultivate the capacity to be responsive to God's self-revelation, to allow the Divine to unfold within us and experience that unfolding. God is

– the sole Reality, always present in all things. We are a sport (*Spiel-form*) of the Divine. We are the God symphony. We are the dance of God the dancer, and dying is as much a part of this dance as being born.[101]

The fear of death – which is natural if one identifies solely with the individual ego – is mitigated when we identify, instead, with the stream of life pouring through us and manifesting itself in us.

– when we die we will step out of our body. Death is only a separation of our deeper identity from this physical body. Only the form dies, not the life. Life gives the billion forms of phenomenon their existence – and takes it back again. Our true existence is not static, but dynamic, and this dynamic pattern flows into increasingly new forms. Thus our true identity lies in the flow of life. We have no life

---

99   *Mysticism for Modern Times*, p. 19.

100   *Search for the Meaning of Life*, location 255.

101   Ibid., location 294.

of our own. Everything that exists is the sparkle of the Divine. We don't live our own life, but the life of God.[102]

This is not a denial of the value of the ego, just of its sense of primacy. "The ego makes us human. It creates culture and gives rise to progress and development of every sort."[103] The problem is that it also preoccupies awareness in such a way that we are not able to recognize our deeper identity as a manifestation of the Godhead, what Buddhists call "Buddha Nature."

The concept of the Divine in this formulation, while not familiar to many Christians, is that of the mystics and, in Jäger's opinion, represents a more mature understanding of the nature of God than the more common image of God as an entity which can be petitioned but which also must be feared, a father-figure who loves us when we are good and punishes us when we transgress his will. That can be an attractive image because it fulfills one's desire for security, but it is also an image that easily falls apart when challenged by the circumstances of one's life. A more mature understanding recognizes that God is wholly beyond human conception or understanding, beyond all the images we form of him. This is the significance of the first commandment which essentially states that we are not to mistake anything we think about God for the reality of God. Anything we think of or say about God is – at best – an analogy, and to cling to the elements of an analogy is to fall into "an idolatry worse than idol-worship – namely the worship of concepts and intellectual constructs of God."[104]

Even after the Second Vatican Council, elements within the Catholic hierarchy criticized Buddhism as a self-centered quest in which individuals sought personal peace of mind by separating themselves from the cares of the world. It is a perspective Jäger takes pains to refute.

In what Jäger termed the "grammar school" vision of religion, Christianity is essentially an ethical system. Our purpose in life, it posits, is to know and obey the will of God as revealed through scripture and the church. Sins, therefore, are not just human weaknesses; they are offences against God's will and merit that eternal separation from him which is damnation. In the mystic understanding, God is no longer external to and separate from his creation; he is no longer the supreme judge and arbiter of human behavior. The concept of sin as disobedience to divinely decreed laws is also dispensed with. But there remain ethical ramifications to the mystic perspective. If there is a fundamental interconnectedness – an interdependence of all being – then

---

102   Ibid., location 333.
103   Ibid., location 1140.
104   Ibid., location 397.

our actions have the potential of impacting all other beings. Recognizing this, experiencing it at a deep personal level, results in a sense of responsibility not only to other persons but to the rest of the ecosphere of our planet and beyond.

The process of evolution, in Jäger's understanding, is the unfolding of the life of the divine in creation.

> Anyone resisting this life engenders disharmony that spreads through the entire universe. Perhaps this resistance is the one real sin humans commit. Accordingly, it would probably be better to designate "God's will – karma" in a positive sense, and to call the universe not "interdependent," but "intersupported." In other words, what we have is less mutual dependency and more a shaping influence of everything on everything else. All our energy should be directed at harmonizing with the unfolding of the Divine.[105]

The Eastern concept of karma, with which Jäger identifies God's will, emphasizes human responsibility for the way in which things unfold. The term means "deed or action," and the basic concept is that actions have consequences. It is not a matter of disobeying God's will but, rather, a recognition that the choices one makes have inevitable results. Whether one's actions are "shaped by greed, hatred, and delusion or by good will, generosity, and love, we sow seeds that develop differently. We create the conditions for weal or woe."[106]

∾

The concept of God – or the Divine – is the great challenge to reconciling Eastern and Western perspectives. Buddhism and Daoism are at home in a universe where the initiating power, or energy, of Being is inherent; the process occurs naturally, without requiring a primary agent responsible for it. That is the perspective of most of the scientific community as well. The traditional Christian perspective, on the other hand, posits that creation is an act of God's will. Jäger tries to effect a reconciliation of these perspectives by re-imaging God.

> The essence of God is One. In what we call creation, the One split itself into an unlimited number of phenomenal forms that remain related to one another and yet are a quite individual expression of the whole.[107]

---

105   Ibid., location 3360.

106   Ibid., location 3364.

107   Ibid., location 3437.

There is, of course, no answer possible to the question of why this happened. Once the dissemination of Being takes place, then humankind becomes one of the means by which God operates. God "seeks the path in us … God wants to unfold through us … God's seeking is the process of evolution that manifests itself in us as this seeking."[108]

Human activity is driven by a longing to return to the lost sense of unity that resulted from the evolution of ego awareness, the sense of individuality, of being a separate agent. All pain, therefore, is to some extent the pain of being separate.

> All sin is basically nothing but being cut off from our deepest essence. It is the peculiar drive of our ego for autonomy and demarcation. Humans sense the deficit of separation more keenly than other creatures. And so the search for the part that completes us began with our becoming human.[109]

And the force that energizes this search for unity is love.

> With love there appears in creation a strong new field of energy: the metaphysical yearning for the One. This is the primal force of evolution. For the goal is not regression back into the One, but evolution, which leads forward to the One. In reality this is not a matter of going forward, but of experiencing that the unity is still there, as ever.[110]

Love is the redeeming force which frees us from the limitations of egocentricity.

Sin in this scenario is the effort of the ego to assert itself in resistance to the Love that draws us to unity. Ethical behavior, therefore, is not something imposed from without but rather something that naturally evolves from the awareness of Love. In Buddhist terms, as prajna (wisdom) deepens it naturally manifests in karuna (compassion). But prajna can only dawn if the seeker works to "uproot" the "endless blind passions" that impede awakening.[111]

---

108   Ibid., location 3436.

109   Ibid., location 3443.

110   Ibid., location 3440.

111   Cf. The Four Vows: "All beings without number, I vow to liberate. Endless blind passions, I vow to uproot. Dharma gates beyond measure, I vow to penetrate. The great way of Buddha, I vow to attain."

While many Catholics might find Jäger's model of Christianity difficult to understand or sympathize with, they would doubtless agree with him in identifying God
with Love.

In spite of his conflicts with the church hierarchy, Jäger has remained faithful to
Catholic Christianity. Although he admits he cannot identify with all aspects of the
tradition which have evolved over time, it remains his home, and, because it is his
home, he wishes to protect and support it. From his perspective, the best way to do so
is by cultivating mystic awareness more broadly. That, he believes, will be the church's
best hope for remaining relevant and valid.

CHAPTER SEVEN

Elaine MacInnes

James Ford, the founder of the Boundless Way community of Zen Centers, told me this anecdote about Sister Elaine MacInnes.[112] "When she decided she should join the American Zen Teachers Association, one of our more famous Zen teachers was assigned to interview her because she was having difficulty filling out the forms. And he said he'd never been more nervous than when having to ask her if she was *qualified*."[113]

Recognized as a peer by other American roshis, Sister Elaine does not always sound like them. For example, she defines Zen ("depending on the occasion," she is careful to qualify) as "responding to God's presence at all times, in all circumstances."[114]

She is closer to Buddhist orthodoxy when she states that "Zen practice does not start and end on our cushions. Each day should be twenty-four hours of harmonious practice." Or that "Being one with our present activity is central to Zen practice."[115]

"The secret in Zen," she adds, "is not to think, not to assume, but *to be*."[116]

When I met her, Sister Elaine did not introduce herself to me as a Zen teacher or even as a Catholic nun. "I'm a musician," she told me. And I wonder if that is a factor in the sensitivity with which she responded to Zen training.

She was born in 1924 in Moncton, New Brunswick – in the Canadian Maritimes – on the 7th of March, the feast day of St. Thomas Aquinas, something her devoutly Catholic family made note of.

---

112   Cf. McDaniel, *Cypress Trees in the Garden*, pp. 133-40, 141-42, 174, 304, 309.

113   From an interview I conducted in May 2013 for *Cypress Trees in the Garden*.

114   Elaine MacInnes, *The Flowing Bridge* (Boston: Wisdom Publications, 2007), p. 76.

115   Ibid., p. 84.

116   Ibid., p. 93.

Her mother was a musician and took care that her children were all introduced to music. Elaine was taught violin. The state of mind a performing musician needs is close to the meditative state. One cannot *think* while playing, Sister Elaine points out; one "is no longer conscious of the left hand fingering and the right hand bowing ... The artist could not possibly consciously control all these as rapidly as the composition demands."[117] Her Zen teacher, Yamada Roshi, once said, "Everyone has two hands. When we are absorbed in doing something with both hands, we are not aware of them. My two hands are in fact living my life, which is not two. From life's point of view, there are not two hands."[118]

When she was ten years old, she happened upon a book in which she found reference to Thomas Aquinas's argument for a Prime Mover. It was one of the arguments the 16th Century Jesuits had used to explain the necessity of a Supreme Being to their Japanese hosts. The Japanese had not been convinced, but the idea struck the young Elaine forcefully. "I remember being deeply affected and impressed. Incredibly, I seemed to understand. God the Prime Mover! I closed the volume quickly and believed it with my whole heart."[119]

When she was in her teens, the Second World War broke out. A number of training fields were established around Moncton for British pilots, and local residents made an effort to welcome the young men into their homes. Romances were common, and both Elaine and an older sister formed attachments to English airmen who later died in action. That was no doubt a factor in her decision to enter the convent, but it was not a step she took immediately. First, she completed a degree in music from Mount Allison University in Sackville, New Brunswick, and then did further studies at Julliard, after which she went to Alberta and performed for a while in the string section of the Calgary Symphony.

She entered religious life somewhat later than usual and was 30 before she completed her postulancy in the order of Our Lady's Missionaries. While in the novitiate, she came to reflect upon the passage from Paul's Epistle to the Galatians that (although she would not have known it) Thomas Merton believed expressed the spirit of Zen: "I live, now not I but Christ lives within me."

> I do not know or remember how I came to be attracted by that
> phrase and can only say that it seemed to be given as gift. Of course
> I desired earnestly to know it experientially, and at the same time I

117   Ibid., p. 104.

118   Ibid., p. 113.

119   Elaine MacInnes, "The Light of Buddhist Wisdom and the Three Births" in *Beside Still Waters*, ed. Harold Kaminow et al. (Boston: Wisdom Publications, 2003), pp. 174-75.

was equally determined to discover how I was going to practice it.[120]

Then she happened upon the book *One with Jesus* by a Belgian Jesuit, Paul de Jaegher, in which he writes about the significance of that passage in his own life. He also said that he experienced the Divine Indwelling not as intimacy but an identification.

> Identification! When I read that, my head-world and heart-world exploded from two to one, or – as Zen masters say – "not even one." The joy of the raindrop is to enter the ocean. Total identification. Now how to practice that?[121]

Although attracted by what she read, she was unclear what to do about it. De Jaegher did not provide directions on how to proceed, although the book was, as she put it, full of encouragement. She attempted a few experiments on her own, "but they all went through the thinking process, which I soon discovered was creating an objective twosome. I did, however, have my own inspired insight, that the secret or core of that teaching lay in the two words 'not I.'"[122]

∾

After taking final vows in 1961, she was assigned to Japan where she taught music to school children. She felt an immediate respect for the culture and immersed herself in it. During her time in Japan, she studied several traditional arts including flower arrangement, calligraphy, and the tea ceremony. She first encountered Buddhist spiritual practice when a friend introduced her to the Tendai monk, Somon Horisawa. Like other forms of Buddhism, Tendai makes use of meditation, although the practice isn't as central as it is to the Zen sect. Somon Horisawa served tea to Sister Elaine and her companion, then turned to her and inquired, "How do you pray?" When she asked what he meant, he said, "For example, what about your body position?"

"I hastily assured him that body position is not important in prayer, and he heartily disagreed. 'Body position is *very* important in prayer.'"

Her introduction to Zen came a little later. She was studying Japanese music terminology at the Jesuit University in Hiroshima where she met Hugo Enomiya-Lassalle. "As far as I can remember," she tells me, "that's the first time I heard anything about Zen. And I'm so glad I heard about it from him. The rest of my time in Japan, I met so many people who admired Lassalle. I was reading everything on spirituality then, because that was my first mission abroad. And I liked what I read about

---

120   Ibid., p. 180.

121   Ibid., p. 181.

122   Elaine MacInnes, *Zen Contemplation: A Bridge of Living Water* (Ottawa: Novalis, 2001), p. 46.

Zen, but it was when I got all of this from Father Lassalle that I had a deep inner conviction that this is okay, that this is the legitimate stuff."

But when she asked him to teach her, he demurred, telling her he wasn't qualified. "And I thought, 'Well, gracious! What's this? Here he is, a Jesuit priest, and he says he's not qualified!' And he said, 'I'll find somebody to teach you.' And I said – and I'm not sure why I said this – I said, 'I think I'd rather go to a Buddhist nun than a Buddhist priest to learn my Zen.'"

Lassalle arranged for her to attend a Zen temple in Kyoto for women, Enkoji. "So on my own, I went there and met the old roshi." This was Fukagai Gichu. "And at first she wasn't too keen on me. She looked at me. She had almost no English. Well, my Japanese wasn't too bad, but it was pretty primary." The roshi quoted the opening words of the Lord's Prayer in Japanese, then she said, "'If you think your father's in heaven, if you think that's God' – she said – 'there's no place for you in Zen.' And I said, 'Whoa!' I thought she had made quite a jump. So I said, 'There are some things you're going to have to trust me for.' And I don't know whether she liked that or not.

"They were an ascetic group, and it was terribly difficult. They said, 'Well, you'll have to come and make this sesshin, and we'll get someone to give you your orientation at that.' The rising bell for the nuns at that time was 3:00 a.m., and you had to be in the zendo, all dressed, and doing zazen at 3:05. And it was really tough going. And I didn't have the opportunity for a real dokusan, because we had no translator, and the roshi was still pretty convinced that there wasn't much hope for me because of my Christianity and my sense of God. I think I probably thought at that time that her conception of what I thought of God was wrong. I sensed that. But I had limited Japanese, and the fact is that you can't speak very much to most teachers. I never had interviews with her. I'd go in for dokusan, and she might say something. She might not. She might ask me to say something. And then I'd leave. The dokusan was less than a minute. Which was fine. Sometimes dokusans are like that. But I must have got nourishment from somewhere because I kept going back. To the end, I never got very far with her, but she kept me at this thing."

Sister Elaine sat with the Buddhist nuns of Enkoji for eight years and, under Fukagai Gichu's guidance came to learn, as Somon Horisawa had told her, that the way in which one sits is indeed important. Meditation engages one's whole being, body, mind, and breath.

By this time, Lassalle had opened Shinmeikutsu in Hiroshima, and Sister Elaine assisted him there. She told me that during one of the retreats he facilitated, "I had some kind of a little experience. And he said, 'Well, I don't know enough about that experience. I've got to get you with a real teacher.' So he took me to Yamada Roshi on the way home from the retreat."

Sister Elaine would come to refer to Koun Yamada as her "father in Zen." He was more at ease with Christians than Fukagai Gichu had been and was pleased to learn that Sister Elaine was a musician. Musicians, he told her, tended to be less "head bound."

"He never pretended to understand Christianity or just what we meant by 'God,' but he was very positive. He said, 'I don't understand it, but the church has gone on for centuries.' And he said, 'Zen belongs in the Church.' I said, 'What do you mean?' He said, 'Well, we're losing it in Japan. It's falling apart. Buddhism is failing terribly. Buddhism has failed my family,' he said. 'Not me. But my children.'"

She tells me that he expressed the hope that Zen might eventually become a "stream" within Catholicism, then added wryly that she didn't expect to see that happen in her lifetime.

The Rohatsu[123] sesshin of 1972 was her second sesshin with Yamada, and, during the first few days, she was uncomfortable about some of the things said during his Dharma talks. She spoke to Enomiya-Lassalle, who was also participating in the retreat, about her concerns, and he told her to trust Yamada. She was, he suggested, on the edge of overcoming the sense of being "separate" that is so strong in Westerners.

> That evening, *dokusan* with the roshi was uneventful, but he brought me into the concrete-me more fully. I returned to my place in the *zendo*, looked at the "me" that seemed to be ensconced in a hard shell. Suddenly, the very core of that shell burst open. Its lovely contents shot out into every part of my being. I was inundated until there was no me left. No boundaries anywhere. How beautiful and clean and pure ... born into this world of the Infinite ... belonging and fitting and home-ing! How utterly perfect.[124]

Her kensho reminded her of a time when, as a child, she had been playing with globules of mercury from a couple of broken thermometers and noticed the way they were drawn to one another. "When the raindrop enters the ocean there are no boundaries," she wrote. "There is just the ocean."[125]

"I'd been sitting for years," she told me, "so it wasn't too remarkable. When you have a real teacher, they use their Zen techniques that work. And I think I was primed for that too. I came out very, very much believing in Yamada Roshi. So much so that I just spoke to the sisters and went up to Kamakura to be where I could be close to the Roshi."

---

123 Rohatsu marks the anniversary of the Buddha's enlightenment. Traditionally, Rohatsu sesshin are the most strenuous of the year.

124 MacInnes, op. cit., p. 184.

125 Ibid., p. 181.

In 1976, the OLM closed its missions in Japan, and Sister Elaine was sent to the Philippines, although she made regular trips back to Japan to continue her koan work with Yamada. She also received Dharma transmission from him that year.

In the Philippines, she met Father Catalino Arevalo. "He was the outstanding Jesuit in the Philippines at the time. And he knew that Zen is an Oriental type of prayer. And when he heard I was there – this is before he even met me – he said, 'Good. We're Orientals here, you know.' And the Jesuits – the foreign Jesuits – were getting old, and they were turning over their community bit by bit to Filipinos, and Father Arevalo was certainly one of the most outstanding." With his encouragement, she opened her first zendo in Manila.

> By November, we had about 30 sitters and a chapel in which to sit, so we organized a formal installation of the Manila Zen Center on November 21, 1976. Father Arevalo spoke at the mass, and his opening words were: "Today is the Feast of Christ the King. Every particle of creation is filled with the beauty of Christ, the love of Christ, the truth of Christ, and the goodness of Christ." I couldn't help but think most Buddhists would feel at home with that statement.[126]

They may have, although it is unlikely their understanding of "Christ" would have been precisely the same as hers. But as she had told the abbess at Enkoji, there were things the Buddhists would have to trust her for.

It was a tense period in Philippine history. The authoritarian regime of Ferdinand Marcos had established martial law in response to the rise of the New People's Army that sought the overthrow of the government and the expulsion of US influences in the Philippines. In spite of the NPA's affiliation with the Communist Party, many priests and nuns supported the rebel cause, and as a result Government forces in Manila tended to be suspicious of the Church.

"The vast majority of people who came to me in the Philippines were anti-Marcos," she tells me. "And I had to be careful where I went because I didn't want to be put in prison too. And I learned that the government had sent somebody to join my zendo to hear what I was talking about because we sat on the floor. 'There's something wrong with those people. They sit on the floor!'"

---

126   Ibid., p. 106.

"So you were known to the authorities?" I say.

"Oh, yes. Yes. Well, every foreigner was. We had to be careful at that time."

One of the most significant figures in the revolutionary movement was Horatio "Boy" Morales, who had served for a time as a senior economist in the Marcos government. He was arrested in 1982 and held at the Bago Bantay detention centre where he and nine other political prisoners were regularly subjected to intensive interrogation and torture. While Morales was imprisoned, a visitor brought him a pamphlet put out by the Manila Zen Center. He read it with interest, then send a note to Sister Elaine asking her to visit him.

"And the authorities allowed this?" I ask.

"Yes, although some of the guards were nasty, of course. I was told more than once, 'We know what you're coming in here for. You've got full access to Boy Morales, and now you've got time alone with him, too. You're not fooling any of us.'

"He sat many hours a day," Sister Elaine tells me. "At least four hours a day. So, that's going to work, eh? But he had a lot to get over; his torture had gone on and on." He achieved kensho and was halfway through the Sanbo Kyodan koan curriculum when the revolution finally ousted Marcos. After his release, when Morales was asked how he had survived his time in detention he credited Sister Elaine and Zen practice.

"Oh, yes," she laughs. "I got phone calls from all over the world because the revolution itself was worldwide news, and he was the last person left in that particular prison. And he gave me full credit for going in. He said what a risk it was for me to go in given the prevailing conditions at the time. 'Because we were the bad guys in prison,' he said."

⌘

One of the phone calls came from Ann Wetherall of the Prison Phoenix Trust in England. "She was a judge's daughter born in India when he was on circuit there, and then back in England living in Oxford. Quite an accent! And very sincere. Lovely person. Not well. She'd been having cancer bouts for some time when I met her."

Ann was looking for someone to continue the work of the Trust when her disease would prevent her from doing so. "The Prison Phoenix Trust was a staff of two people who wrote letters to inmates and that's all they did. They didn't go into prisons. Ann asked me if I would go to England, and I was on my way to a meeting in Europe – you know how they have these international Zen meetings – so I went via England to visit her. And she told me about her cancer and about her group."

Ann asked Sister Elaine whether meditation could be taught to prisoners. Sister Elaine agreed that it could. "'But,' I said, 'you can't just do that through the written word. Teaching meditation was a face-to-face thing.' She said, 'My bouts of cancer are getting more and more problematic. And I've just got to do something about getting this better organized.' She asked if I was interested. I told her I wasn't interested in letter writing. I said, 'To me, the prison is where I want to be. It's got to be face-to-face.'"After Ann died, the board contacted Sister Elaine again and invited her to offer a meditation program in the prison system. She accepted the opportunity. The first prison they worked in was "a therapeutic prison just outside of Oxford. And the warden was Tim Newell who is a Quaker. And we became very good friends. Most of the prisoners had been in for some years and were in therapy. Almost all the staff were trained in therapy."

Newell appreciated her work, and gradually she was able to establish a network of volunteers who taught yoga and basic meditation practice in eighty-six prisons throughout Britain.

After she retired from the Phoenix Trust, Sister Elaine returned to Canada, where she was made an Officer of the Order of Canada in 2001 in recognition of her humanitarian work. Ironically, when she tried to duplicate the work she had done for the British prison system in Canada, she ran into resistance.

"I suspect because the people I was talking to didn't appreciate meditation and didn't know what it could do for human beings," she suggests.

One of her current students, Patrick Gallagher,[127] was with us during this meeting, and he added, "One of the problems in the early days was that Zen didn't fit into the slot that they were used to. It wasn't a chaplaincy. It wasn't a specifically religious thing. It didn't fit. So they didn't know what to do with it. I think that your Order of Canada helped. You'd been honored by the country, so you weren't" – he searches a moment for the proper word – "flakey."

We all laugh.

❧

Patrick is a teacher in the Sanbo Zen tradition as well, and, after my meeting with Sister Elaine, he and I retire to a nearby café. He tells me that although when Sister Elaine returned to Canada, it had ostensibly been to retire – she had been nearing 75 years of age – one of the first things she did was start a new zendo in Toronto. Patrick attended its first gathering.

"A friend of mine called me one night, and we were just chatting about this-that-and-the-other, and he said, 'By the way...' – this is what I thought he said – 'I'm going to a talk by a Catholic nun who is also a Zen master.' And I said, 'That sounds interesting. I'd like to come.' And he said, 'I'll check.' And then the conversation went on, and I thought, 'What do you have to check? Don't you just go and listen?' But by then we were in another part of the conversation. So about a week or two later, I got a call from a woman I didn't know saying, 'I'm calling on behalf of Sister Elaine

---

127   See Chapter 14 below.

MacInnes, and she'd like to meet with you.' And I remember thinking, 'Wow! She vets her audience! She must be nervous about the Vatican or something!' So I said, 'Fine.' And she gave me some different options and took the time that worked for me. And I went along to the meeting. I knocked on the door, and this older nun opened the door, and I remember thinking as I went there, 'Well, if it's crazy, it will just be an experience.' We went in and started talking, and I realized in about two minutes that we weren't talking about the public talk that she was giving, but she was vetting me to see if I would be a suitable candidate for a zendo that she was establishing. And I thought, 'What the heck! I'll go with it.' So we had this very interesting conversation about spiritual life and prayer life and these sorts of things. And she said, 'Well, why don't you come along? We're having our first meeting in …' Whatever it was. I can't remember. I biked home and thought, 'I'll give it a shot.' And that's how we met. It was kind of by accident.

"That first meeting was held in the public library basement. And I didn't know the first thing about it. She said, 'Well, we'll start off in chairs, facing the wall. And it's going to be eleven minutes. Don't move and try and keep your mind still.' I thought, 'Oh, my God! That's impossible! Eleven minutes! How can I possibly do that for eleven minutes?' It was an eternity, and I sat there thinking, 'I can't move. I'd be so embarrassed. But this is so hard!'"

The membership of that first group was almost entirely Catholic, but over the years the makeup of Sister Elaine's zendo has attracted people from a variety of backgrounds. Catholics still remain in the majority, followed by people Patrick identifies as secular humanists, "people who are not part of any recognized religious community, but many of whom have Christian backgrounds they have either rejected or just left. I think that one reason that the numbers of Catholics is so much higher than anyone else is because of Sister Elaine. I think that she gives a kind of imprimatur – this is OK for Catholics to do – that at least some people would initially want. Since she also lives in a Catholic world, it's much easier for Catholics to find out about her and what she is doing. But she has always been clear that this practice and what she offers is open to anyone."

ॐ

Sister Elaine makes a distinction between "Zen" and "Zen Buddhism." What she offers is teaching in Zen; she even denies knowing much about Buddhism. When asked if it is possible to be both a Christian and a Buddhist, she quotes the Dalai Lama's response to that question. "That would be like putting a yak's head on a sheep's body."

She naturally speaks about God and in her teishos finds parallels between some of the koans she speaks about and passages in the Bible. The koan that tells the student to "move a mountain" has an obvious similarity to Jesus's statement that "If you had faith the size of a mustard seed you could move a mountain." She compares the koan "count the stars" to the passage in Genesis in which God tells Abraham to "Look up to the heavens and count the stars if you can." And the lengthy koan "In a well that has not been dug, water is rippling from a spring that does not flow; there, someone with no shadow or form is drawing the water" can be compared with the story of Jesus's meeting with the woman at the well in the Gospel of John.

For Sister Elaine, the universe – all of Being – is the self-communication of God that we fail to recognize because of the intrusive presence of the individual ego. The goal of Zen practice is to help the ego subside in order to be receptive to that divine self-communication and then allow it to work through us as compassion. It is a Christian expression of a basic Zen formula: the practitioner first achieves samadhi (concentrated attention), which leads to prajna (wisdom), which in turn, if sufficiently developed, manifests in karuna (compassion).

Zen, she points out, is not understood intellectually but intuitively. The initial step in Zen training, therefore, is to bring the discursive intellect to a standstill so that intuition can be activated. This is the route to coming to know God. As she says in one of her teishos, "Where God is concerned, contemplation is appropriate, for God is utterly unknowable by reason, and so no thought can give us an idea of what he is."[128] She uses Saint Richard of St. Vincent's description of contemplation as an activity beyond thought – an activity in which "all thoughts, all desires and hopes, all fears, all images and all ambitions" are surrendered.

Unlike Cosme de Torres, Sister Elaine is comfortable with the Buddhist concept of the Void (*sunyata*).

> [Saint Richard's] "forget, forget, forget" is like the "*nada, nada, nada*" of John of the Cross. And it is the most natural thing in the world, to compare these texts with the Zen Masters: "Empty, empty, empty" "Mu, Mu, Mu." Where there is nothing, there is everything. What is the root-source of nothing?

> In our Zen stream spirituality, we seek the return of our Original Nature to its original spontaneity. For a while, perhaps when we begin, we see this Original Nature as an object. But soon we have to give up the attempt to make our nature an object of contemplation. We have to eliminate all symbols and all thoughts, and *allow this nature to be totally itself, pure and spontaneous.*[129]

---

128   MacInnes, *The Flowing Bridge*, p. 16.

129   Ibid., p. 17.

Kensho or awakening arises only when thought is "simplified to nothing at all, and the object of contemplation [is] sublimated out of existence."[130]

---

130   Ibid.

A Conversation with Bodhin Kjolhede

It was not only the Vatican's Congregation of the Doctrine of the Faith that had concerns about Catholic clergy experimenting with Zen. Some of the leading figures in the establishment of American Zen had reservations as well, notably Philip Kapleau. While Kapleau remains a controversial figure in the Sanbo Zen school,[131] his principle Dharma successor, Bodhin Kjolhede, has emerged as one of the most respected teachers in North America. Even people who question Philip Kapleau's credentials generally admire Bodhin's grasp of the Dharma and his skill at presenting it.

In January 2016, Bodhin and I scheduled a conversation by Skype one Monday afternoon about the matter of Catholic engagement in Zen. As his image came onto my screen, I saw one of his students standing behind him showing him how to activate the program. We began the conversation by admitting that we were both still clumsy with contemporary technology and laughed about the fact that, at times, we had to turn to much younger people for advice. When we had been talking for about an hour, I noticed that my recording device had shut down. Apparently, I had forgotten to charge the battery. Bodhin immediately suggested we re-do the conversation

---

131 There are two elements in the controversy. The first is that Kapleau had not completed his training when Hakuun Yamada ordained him and authorized him to teach. Although Yasutani supported and encouraged Kapleau's work in the United States, the two of them quarrelled about how rigidly Americans should adhere to Japanese models. Yasutani died shortly after the quarrel and the two were never reconciled. Sanbo Zen teachers point out that while Kapleau had been permitted to teach, he did not have inka, the formal acknowledgement that a student had completed training.

The second and more important issue regards whether Kapleau had the right to claim authorship of the enormously influential *Three Pillars of Zen*. They note that the book was actually the work of three people, Kapleau and two others he identifies as his "collaborators" in the Editor's Preface but whose names do not appear on the title page: Koun Yamada and Akira (Ji'un) Kubota. Yamada and Kubota succeeded Yasutani as the second and third abbots of the Sanbo Zen school.

later in the week. That, he said, would give him time to gather his thoughts. So the following Friday we tried again.

RBM: Since you've had a chance to reflect on our earlier attempt, I thought I might take a slightly different approach. You are a Buddhist priest.

BK: [*nods*]

RBM: So that was a nod.

BK: [*chuckling*] Mm-hmm. Yes.

RBM: Was that a requirement of your training or was it something you chose?

BK: Oh, I chose it. I'd been here about five years, and I was really completely sold on doing this for my whole life, so I asked to be ordained.

RBM: And Roshi Kapleau was also a priest?

BK: Yeah. He was ordained by Yasutani Roshi.

RBM: Are all of Roshi Kapleau's heirs ordained?

BK: All of his Dharma Heirs are ordained although two of my five Dharma Heirs are not ordained.

RBM: So it isn't a requirement.

BK: I think Roshi Kapleau wanted to have people ordained, but I feel if someone's qualified in every other way but have family or work they have to stay with, then I'm still okay with sanctioning them as teachers. Because in the Rochester system, to be ordained means that's your vocation. You don't sell shoes or anything else. You have to do that full-time. *If* you're able to.

RBM: Okay. So one does not need to be an ordained Buddhist priest to be a Zen teacher.

BK: Not for me they don't.

RBM: Okay. So, the issue we were discussing: Yamada Koun Roshi gave some degree of authorization to teach to twelve Catholic religious that I can identify. These were not just practicing Catholics, they are professed nuns and priests. There might be more that I'm not aware of. He was also known to have told people that he feared Zen was dying in Japan and apparently expressed the hope that it might continue on as a tradition specifically within the Catholic Church. He certainly told several of the Catholic religious he was teaching that he didn't expect them to become Buddhists, but that he thought Zen would make them better Christians.

BK: [*nods*]

RBM: And, last time, you confirmed that you had heard similar statements from Zen Masters when you were in Japan, that Zen was dying in that country.

BK: Yes, from Tangen Roshi and Harada Shodo Roshi. The first one's a Soto teacher, and the second one is a Rinzai teacher, and they both said to me

– privately – that they felt Zen was dying in Japan and being reborn in the United States.

RBM: Did you question that?

BK: You mean when these two roshis told me that?

RBM: Mm-hmm.

BK: I didn't have much exposure to Zen in Japan other than at their temples. So I didn't have a lot of knowledge about it, but I certainly had gotten whiffs of the decay of Zen in Japan. So, when they said it, it didn't surprise me.

RBM: Okay. So, when we started this conversation, you said that Roshi Kapleau was critical of the combination of Zen and Catholicism.

BK: Yes. He was. Yeah. He didn't talk a lot about it, Rick. But he was kind of suspicious of it, and I took that to mean that he felt that the Catholic priests who were putting Catholic ritual in Zen practice were somehow appropriating something... Uh... Yeah, I have to be careful because he never spelled it out. He just sort of grumbled every now and then about the phenomenon of Catholic Zen. But he did seem to think that in some way they were trying to appropriate Zen and mix it up with Catholicism. And that bothered him. He was not a big fan of mixtures. He explained to me that the Japanese, as a whole, don't like mixtures. Either you're Soto or you're Rinzai. Either you're this or you're that, and don't mix them up. And I'm similar, by the way. I think that Catholicism on its own has a great pedigree, has great tradition behind it. As does Zen, of course. But then when you mix them, you don't have more; you have less. I can't defend that. It's just sort of a gut feeling that each tradition is whole on its own, then, when you mix them, something's lost.

RBM: Did either Roshi Kapleau, or you, have any doubt about the qualifications of the Catholics Yamada Roshi authorized to teach Zen? Their Catholicism aside.

BK: If you leave the Catholicism aside, then it just becomes individual Zen teachers, and the only one I've ever met is Ruben Habito, and I have high regard for him. I don't know quite what his teaching is, but I feel fine about him.

RBM: Is Buddhism a religion in the same way that Catholicism is a religion?

BK: Well, we get into semantics. It depends upon how you define religion. If you define religion as positing a Supreme Being, an omniscient, omnipresent Supreme Being, then no. Zen isn't a religion in that sense. It's not a theistic religion. But if you understand religion as based on faith, faith in what cannot be apprehended through the senses and the intellect, a faith in what is beyond our normal faculties for knowing things, then I see Zen as a religion. It can be, but it doesn't have to be – and this gets me back to what I was saying last time – that there are people who just want to do the meditation, without the religion. And that's fine with me. They can use it as a concentration practice, and that's great. But I think that's a very limited way of practicing Zen.

RBM: One of the other things we talked about that time was the distinction between a tradition where the – let's say – the "Primal Agent," because I just don't have another term for it here ...

BK: Sure.

RBM: ... was either external to or inherent in Being. So in the Daoist tradition, it's inherent. In the Christian tradition, at least as generally put forward, that primal reality is external to creation.

BK: Yeah, but I think I would not be comfortable with seeing Daoism as positing any kind of agency. My understanding of agency is some kind of entity that can effect change.

RBM: You're right. The word "agency" is what's causing the problem here. But the distinction is that in some way, let's call it the impetus, the power, the *energy* ...

BK: Yeah.

RBM: ... is either inherent or external.

BK: Yeah. That's fair enough. That sounds all right.

RBM: So in that sense, Buddhism is on the inherent end.

BK: Depending upon the kind of Buddhism. You know, in Nichiren Buddhism they ask the Buddha for a car – a nice car – or a house or a handsome boy friend.

RBM: But as we understand the Zen tradition in North America.

BK: Yeah. Yeah.

RBM: Okay. You said last time that you don't know what, if any, the religious affiliations of the members of the Rochester Zen Center are.

BK: Yes, that's right.

RBM: So one does not need to be a Buddhist to practice Zen.

BK: Not in Rochester they don't. No.

RBM: Nor does one need to be a Buddhist to go beyond the introductory concentration process and enter into formal koan training?

BK: That's right. Well, this gets into assumptions, and you know what they say. But I assume that anyone who's working at least on subsequent koans, the koans subsequent to the break-through koan, that they probably consider themselves Buddhists. But I don't really know.

RBM: You had said earlier that Roshi Kapleau said the Japanese don't like to mix, but in fact they are probably more at home with it than we are. You can be a nominal Buddhist, be enrolled at a Buddhist temple, yet turn to Shinto for ceremonial purposes – weddings, that type of stuff – and run your household along Confucian lines. They apparently don't see any discrepancy in this. What I'm trying to get here is a sense of how someone involved in Buddhism from a Buddhist perspective – someone like you – makes sense of the way people, like Ruben, who are strong, committed teachers, can at the same time maintain an involvement with Catholicism, which – I agree with you – seems to have an irreconcilable perspective.

BK: A good way of putting it. I agree. Yeah. I don't know what they do with those. A creator God with some sort of agency, and Buddhism which denies *any* enduring entity of any kind, any sense of agency. I don't know what they do with it.

RBM: So, just trying to work this out – finding some way of articulating it – it is possible to practice Zen without being a Buddhist, formally, although perhaps as the insight deepens one becomes a Buddhist in fact without ever having taken jukai or whatever. So, can you separate Zen as a practice from Buddhism as a tradition, whether we call that tradition a religion or not?

BK: I think so. I think anyone who crosses his legs and follows his breath is practicing Zen, but they may not be a Buddhist. Is that what you mean?

RBM: So one could come to the Rochester Zen Center, be committed to one's practice, enter into koan training with you ...

BK: Mm-hmm.

RBM: Might, perhaps, flourish. But would not necessarily at any point in that process declare themselves a Buddhist per se.

BK: I think that's quite possible. I think it's unlikely. But it is possible. No where along the line would I say, "Well, you have to make a claim as to what your religion is." If you're Buddhist or not. It just isn't an issue. Rick, I think now as we talk you're helping me. I think a lot of people when they come here for the first time – we have these introductory workshops – when they come for the first time, most people would not consider themselves Buddhist. But they want to do the practice. They want to join with us in the zendo to do Zen meditation. And I suspect – and this was true for me, too – they find the principles of Buddhism, the doctrine, more and more believable, that the doctrine matches their experience the longer they go along. And they just sort of ease into being Buddhist, and maybe someday they're sitting at a job application, and they might say, "Well, I guess I am a Buddhist. I'll put that down."

RBM: It's not quite the same, though, as when you separate yoga from Hinduism. Which happens a lot. People take physical yoga and know nothing about Hinduism, don't care about it at all. But this is not that simple. It's not that separable; however, in some way, the practice of Zen is – or can be – different from the practice of Buddhism.

BK: Yeah. Or even, Rick, the practice of Zen does not necessarily mean you're a Zen Buddhist. I would say that especially newer practitioners here might consider themselves practicing Zen meditation, but that they don't consider themselves Zen Buddhists.

RBM: Which brings us to the issue of whether or not one can be a dual citizen. So having come this far, do you still feel a discomfort with someone being dually a Catholic and a Zen practitioner?

BK: I don't have much discomfort with someone practicing both – practicing Catholicism and practicing Zen meditation. What I do have more concern about – and I think I speak for Roshi Kapleau now – is among teachers, that a Catholic priest …

RBM: Ah!

BK: … or someone who considers themselves a Catholic *teaching* Zen … There's the rub, as Shakespeare said. And I'm remembering now – as we talk – Roshi Kapleau, I think he said the same thing. He said, "Fine. Let anyone who wants to practice meditation. Great." But once it's a teacher who's Catholic and practicing and *teaching* Zen, then we risk watering down the tradition, the Buddhist tradition, the Zen Buddhist tradition. Because teachers are – in a sense – the holders of the tradition. And once they introduce Catholicism, then it's something else.

RBM: Which is why, as you said last time, you feel uncomfortable with the mass, for example, being included in the sesshin format.

BK: Yeah! Exactly. Exactly. Stick with your own rituals. Let each of these be on its own. But once you start bringing that in, then I suppose someone could catastrophize and say, "Well, are we gonna lose purely Buddhist rituals and other traditions once they started getting mixed with Catholic ritual?"

RBM: So there'd be some anxiety that a Catholic Zen teacher who has authority to transmit, who can identify heirs, that perhaps the lineage descending from him would separate at some distance from more traditional Zen practice … [*pause*] … I guess that was a question.

BK: Oh, yeah. Yeah, that would be my concern. That it would lose its integrity. The Zen Buddhism taught by a Catholic priest would lose its integrity and become some other hybrid. Yeah. Lose its integrity. That's my concern.

RBM: So let's look at it another way. You know Willigis Jäger; we've talked about him before. He talks about the exoteric and the esoteric. And the exoteric is the face of the tradition, the religion, to the community. And he uses the example of a pillared dome. So you have these pillars which are each distinct, unique, separate, different history, different ritual content, different belief systems. But if you look up, you see that they've formed a dome. That they come together at the top. That somehow each of one of these – in his perspective – is an expression of the same thing, even though in Catholicism it is presented as an external deity, in Buddhism it is Emptiness and recognition of one's innate Buddha Nature. But at some level – which he would call mystical – they come together. Does that make sense to you?

BK: It does, once you get away from forms – ritual and devotions and other forms. Then that, I think, is a valid way to look at it. I'm not sure what the definition of mysticism is, but – as I said to you last time – I feel like I'm eye-to-eye with Meister Eckhart and St. John of the Cross and other Christian mystics. What they express seems very much pure Zen, except for the use of the word God. [*We both laugh.*]

RBM: And if they understand God not as this autonomous external agency that the popular church maintains… And I believe this is the case, with the European mystics for example, where they speak of God as something encountered within rather than without. Eckhart's "The eye with which I see God is the eye with which God sees me."

BK: Yes.

RBM: I'm rambling. Let me put the question this way: In your experience, can people have that insight which I – and I believe you – would identify as kensho outside of Zen practice?

BK: Oh, yes. Absolutely. Yeah. There's some very stirring accounts of that, like Flora Courtois, although I've been told that, unfortunately, her kensho account is out of print. It's not available anywhere.[132] She was a college student in Ann Arbor and had what sounds like a very deep, spontaneous realization, just through questioning – pure questioning of her own – it just bubbled up. She'd never heard of Zen; she, maybe, never heard of Buddhism. That's the most dramatic one I've heard of. There are credible suggestions that Rainer-Maria Rilke had had an awakening. William Blake. Abraham Lincoln, I even heard. But I think it's rare, very rare.

RBM: That's not exactly what I meant. Those are spontaneous, which are an interesting phenomenon in themselves. As it happens, I had one. And several of your colleagues discussed their spontaneous experiences with me when I was doing the interviews for *Cypress Trees*. My question is if you have any experience of, or knowledge of, someone taking a different practice path than Zen – say Vipassana meditation or yoga – and coming to an experience, an insight, which you would recognize as the equivalent of Zen kensho? What I'm getting at here is Jäger's argument that if you follow the practice, it will somehow come to the same place. Is there anything in your experience that

---

132   http://www.bodysoulandspirit.net/mystical_experiences/read/published_collections/flora.shtml

would validate that?

BK: That would be so much speculation on my part. I go back to… To me, an important measure of the validity of such an experience with a Catholic or with someone else is whether they have generally seen through concepts like God. I see God as a concept. And if after what they describe as a kensho or awakening, if they can say, "Yes. Fundamentally there is no God, in terms of having any substance to it," then I would be willing to think, "Okay. Maybe that was a kensho." But if they insist upon talking about God as an agent, then I have a hard time seeing how that could be a genuine awakening.

RBM: And I think the argument they might make is that what they come to is a recognition of God not being – in fact – an external agent but an inherent energy.

BK: Fair enough, and I can tell you, it wasn't many years ago that it occurred to me that these words such as Buddha Nature, True Nature, Central Mind, Original Mind – all of those synonyms that we use in Zen – that those could be seen as synonyms for God. And so, yeah, fair enough. I just am suspicious that if you cling to the word God, that there is some sense of agency there, or entity.

RBM: There's a connotation that the term itself can't shake.

BK: Yeah. Yeah, that's it. Because of our conditioning. You know? I have a different response to the word "God" than I do to "True Nature" or "Central Mind." The word "God" has a lot of freight. Because for most people – most people I've read – they use it in terms of a Creator and an agency. There is no Creator in Buddhism.

CHAPTER EIGHT

Maria Reis Habito

During my conversation with Ruben Habito, he mentioned that his wife, Maria, was now the principal teacher at a Zen center in Indiana. "Where in Indiana?" I asked.

"South Bend, near the campus of Notre Dame."

"I grew up in LaPorte, about 25 miles west of South Bend," I told him, "and certainly, when I was living there, the idea of a Zen Center in Northern Indiana would have been pretty far-fetched."

"Well, you never know where these Zen communities will mushroom up," Ruben said.

It is a basic principle of Buddhism and Zen that all things change — even, it appears, Indiana.

❧

Maria Habito works with Hsin Tao's Museum of World Religions based in Taiwan and is engaged in facilitating dialogue between faith communities. Because of the unique perspective this gives her, our conversation covered a wider range of topics — including the fundamental issue of the viability of religious institutions — than others I conducted.

We began by discussing the South Bend group, which is called the Sophia Zen Center. She tells me that it was founded by a local psychologist, Tom Petersen. I ask how large a community it is.

"On retreats we have any number between 15 and 23 or so," she tells me, "but I think not everybody's coming to retreats. So I think the sangha size is 30 to 40. It is really inspired by what we had in Kamakura, where Yamada Roshi built a zendo in his backyard. Here it is adjacent to Tom's office. But the point is that Tom and Margaret, his wife, are very involved in the sangha, like sangha parents. And that is like the example given by Yamada Roshi and his wife as well."

"You don't have an Indiana accent," I note.

She smiles and shakes her head.

"Where did you grow up?"

"I grew up in Germany. I was born in Köln and grew up in Saarbrücken which is on the French border."

"Was it a religious family?"

"My parents were Catholic, and we were quite regular church goers. My father, who was an economist, was also very much interested in philosophy and theology. So we had all these books at home."

When she was a child in the 1960s, that region of Germany was relatively prosperous. "It is a part of Germany that had belonged to France," she explains, "and was given back to Germany after the war. So conditions in that part of the country were very good because everybody was rebuilding after the war and there was a lot of spirit of optimism."

"Where did you go to school?"

"I went to the Ursulines. It was an all girls school."

"Was that a family decision?"

"No, it was normal. The major factor behind it was that I got carsick very easily, and that was the only school I could walk to."

"What was an education in an Ursuline school like at the time?"

"We would have religious education and attend mass once a week. And from primary school, I just remember the fantastic stories that the priest told us about St. Thérèse[133] and all of that. I think religious education was mainly story-telling, and I loved it. And then in high school, it was in the '70s, and there was a bit of unrest after the Second Vatican Council. We had some nuns who left, and we had lots of secular teachers, so to speak, who were not nuns. It was a very protected environment – I can say that much – and I think we got a very good education. I also think it was open because it was after the Second Vatican Council so we had some introduction to other religions. You know," she chuckles, "when you are growing up maybe you would rather not go to school than go to school. But I didn't suffer, and I didn't particularly suffocate."

"How many languages do you speak?"

"I think about six maybe. Five or six."

"So many you can't remember!" I say, laughing.

"Well, I learned Latin but don't speak it as such. We start out with German

---

133 Saint Thérèse of Lisieux was a Carmelite nun who died in 1897 at the age of 24. She became known as the Little Flower of Jesus and was venerated for the simplicity and sincerity she demonstrated throughout her life.

and then, of course, French and English. Chinese. Japanese. And now I'm learning modern Hebrew."

I ask how she came to learn Chinese and Japanese, and thereby hangs a tale:

"After I graduated from high school, my mother got to know a Chinese Catholic priest in Taiwan, Father Joseph Wang. He had invited her and my aunt to visit, and so she said as my high school graduation present she would bring me along. So I went, and I fell in love with the country and the language, and it was very easy for me to pick up everything. I had already been enrolled in the university in Saarbrücken to study sociology and philosophy, but I had always been interested in Chinese philosophy, so I decided to go to Taiwan and learn the language. And that's what happened."

"Where had the interest in Chinese philosophy come from?"

"I think maybe part was my grandfather who was sent to China to fight the Boxer Rebellion, and, whenever we went to visit my grandmother, there were those items he had brought back from China, like a teapot and a box for cookies that had those Chinese mountains and the sages and so on. And then, you know, my family name is Reis, and it means *rice* in English. So in high school if there was some report or something to do with Asia, I was always the one who was called to do that for some funny reason. And so this is how I started reading more than just about geography and so on, and I was very intrigued by the *Daodejing* at that time."

She enrolled in the Taiwan Normal University in Taipei and resided in the international students' dormitory. When she had been there a few months, one of the other residents asked if she would like to meet a Buddhist hermit. "And I said yes, and that's when I met my Buddhist master, Hsin Tao. Now he's well-known, but at the time nobody knew him. He was meditating in graveyards and lived in this little tiny tucked-away hermitage near a lake in the middle of Taiwan."

Hsin Tao was still a relatively young man of about 30 at the time, although he was already addressed as Shih-fu, or Master. "He grew up in Burma, now called Myanmar," Maria tells me. "He was born of Chinese parents in Burma in '48, and there was still some struggle going on between the Communists and the Taiwan Kuomintang. He got caught up in this. He was an orphan – he lost his mother when he was three and his father when he was about four – and he became a child soldier."

"Really!"

"Yes. At age eight. So he saw so much war, suffering, death. And as a child he had all these questions on his mind, 'What is life all about?' So when he came to Taiwan, he continued being in the army school, and actually it was not easy for him to leave. But he finally decided to become a Buddhist monk to explore these questions of 'What's the truth of life?' and 'What's suffering?' And he found that the traditional training that he received as a monk wasn't enough for him. So he decided to go on and practice on his own in the wilderness."

There were several other people at the event to which Maria had been brought. "I didn't speak Chinese then. I had just been in Taiwan for three months, and I knew a little bit but not too much. And Shih-fu was sitting on the terrace, serving tea to a handful of people. I was just contemplating the lake until I realized that they were talking about me. And then I asked the gentleman who'd brought me, 'What's going on?' And he said, 'They are all excited because the master has said there's a very deep karma between him and you.' And I said, 'Karma? What does that mean?' I wasn't even familiar with that expression. And then the Dharma Master said, 'It's a connection from a previous life.' And I thought to myself, 'What connection can there be between a Buddhist master and a German Catholic?'" It was, however, the type of statement that a young girl would naturally find intriguing.

At the end of this visit, Hsin Tao told her, "You are a tree that can bring rich fruit. Therefore I want to plant your roots in fertile ground." He invited her to come see him as often as she wished, and, although she was confident her roots were firmly planted in Christianity, she also felt drawn back to the hermitage and returned frequently.

In 1983, he told her that because she understood him better than many of his other visitors he would like her to formally become his disciple. He was planning to undertake a world tour to promote a project he was about to initiate, and he would value her assistance as a translator. When Maria explained that she felt her German-Christian heritage made her an unlikely disciple of a Buddhist master, he said that in order to open up "to truth completely, you need to learn not to make an image of yourself. Don't cling to your German 'I' and to your Christian notions. Don't make them into hindrances on your path, but let them help you instead."[134] She took refuge vows[135] and was given the Dharma name Hui-yueh (meaning "wisdom moon"). With that, she said, she became a "freshly hatched Buddhist Christian," although at first, discipleship didn't go much further than that.

"You were fairly young at the time," I remark.

"That's right. I think I'd just turned 20."

"Would you have described yourself as a devout Catholic?"

"I don't know what you understand by 'devout.' I would go to church on Sundays. But I had never been to confession, so I'm not sure."

"I'm trying to get a sense of how you reconciled your Catholicism with this interest in Buddhism."

"You know, it was difficult because the master kept asking me so many questions to really explain my Catholic faith to him. And then he would speak about 'no self'

---

134   Maria Reis Habito, "On Becoming a Buddhist Christian," in *Beside Still Waters*, ed. Harold Kaminow et al. (Boston: Wisdom Publications, 2003), p. 207.

135   One formally becomes a Buddhist by taking refuge in the Three Treasures: Buddha, Dharma [his teaching], and Sangha [the Buddhist community].

and karma, and all those other Buddhist terms, and my solution was to start reading about Buddhism. Basically I wanted to check him out and see if others also said the same things. So I started reading all these books by Buddhist scholars to figure out what was going on."

She had been attending Sunday mass at Father Wang's parish, but, when she started visiting Hsin Tao on the weekends, there was not time to do both. "I told Father Joseph that I had these meetings with a Buddhist monk. And he was very supportive. He said, 'Go as much as you want. Because for us Christians it's very important to learn from the Buddhists.'" She understood this as official permission to continue. Eventually she introduced Wang and Hsin Tao, and the two became friends.

❧

When she completed the language course in Taiwan, she returned to Germany. "I enrolled in philosophy at the Institute for Christian Weltanschauung and took most of the courses on Christian philosophers. And my professor there was a student of Heinrich Dumoulin, and he was very interested in me doing comparative topics for my papers." The professor was Eugen Biser, an early advocate of Christian-Buddhist dialogue.

She also began Zen practice after returning to Germany. "Shih-fu told me that he was very happy that I wanted to study Buddhism when I got to the university, but, unless I started practicing meditation, I wouldn't know what I would be writing about. He said, 'You will just make more books from reading other books, but you will not get the essence of what this is all about.' And I took that very seriously, so I looked for a Zen group to join and start sitting myself. It so happened that another student had applied to participate in a sesshin with Father Enomiya-Lassalle, and he said to me, 'You can have my space because I cannot go.' At the time it was very difficult to get into Father Lassalle's sesshins. They had long waiting lists because so many people wanted to participate. So through luck I got into one held at a Franciscan monastery outside of Munich, in Dietfurt."

"If you were with a group of friends, just spending an afternoon trading stories, what story would you tell of Father Lassalle?"

She doesn't need to consider. The story comes to her immediately: "Ah! When I first came to sesshin, and I asked Father Lassalle, I said, 'You know, I'm Christian, but I met this Buddhist master, and now he wants me to meditate, and do you think Jesus would mind if I did Buddhist meditation?' And he looked at me and he said, 'You know what? I wouldn't worry about that.'

"And there was another story: he had hearing-aids. He didn't hear so well. So one day I came into his dokusan, into the interview, and – I don't know – I said a lot, and

I was in trouble then, I don't recall exactly what it was about. And he looked at me and said, 'I forgot to put in my hearing-aids. Would you say all of this again?' And I just dropped it all and said, 'You know what? It's not important.'"

"So you're at Munich University, studying philosophy and Chinese religion," I recapitulate, "and you're doing Zen practice with Father Lassalle. Did you have a career plan in mind?"

"You know, when I came to Munich and I spoke to my professor at the time – he had written books on Chinese philosophy – he said to me, 'Don't expect a regular job to come out of this, but something will come out of it.' And he was asking me what I wanted to do, what other subjects I was interested in, and I said, 'Well, I want to do philosophy' – which he thought was very good – 'and English.' And he said, 'Why would you want to do English?' And I said, 'With Chinese I will probably end up as an English teacher in China.' And he said, 'Nonsense. You do Japanese instead, and you become a scholar.' Because all the important encyclopedia articles on Chinese Buddhism are written in Japanese. So I said, 'All right.' So I switched from English to Japanese and just trusted that something would come out of this."

What immediately came out of it was a scholarship from the Japanese government to continue her studies at Kyoto University. It was 1986, and she was 27 years old. She was able to re-establish contact with Enomiya-Lassalle while in Japan and attended sesshin at Shinmeikutsu. It was also during this period that she met Ruben.

"So I was doing research in a French institution housed in one of the temples there, and my boss took me along to a conference in Nagoya which was on, I think, Christian mysticism and esoteric Buddhism, some topic like that. And Ruben was one of the speakers at the conference. And we met each other, and I told him I have a Japanese Zen master, and it turned out we had the same teacher. So I said, 'Oh, I'm on my first koan!' I was so proud. And Ruben said, 'Well, I'm on my last koan,'" she says laughing. "That's how we met at first."

The koan she began with was Mu, which Enomiya-Lassalle had assigned her at the retreat house in Dietfurt. She worked with it for six years in both Germany and Japan. Finally, in 1987, "I had an experience where Father Lassalle said, 'Yes, it's a kensho experience.' But it would be good if I saw Yamada Roshi about it. And I happened to be in the same international conference in Berkeley as Yamada Roshi whom I had not met before. So I met him for the first time in this Buddhist-Christian conference in Berkeley, and he called me in for an interview and then confirmed it was a kensho experience. And he said, 'It would be good if from now on you would study with me in Kamakura.' And I said, 'Fine.'"

"Ruben was at the same conference in Berkeley," she adds. As he had, she keeps the details of their courtship private, just telling me that they proceeded cautiously. "I finished my doctorate at the University of Munich at the beginning of 1990, and then Ruben was offered this position here at the Perkins School of Theology. He came one year earlier, in '89, and was teaching for one year here, and we were keeping apart to figure out if this was really the right step to take." They determined it was and were married in 1990 in Dallas.

∾

Maria and Ruben's sons, Florian and Benjamin, were born in 1991 and 1993, so for a while, as the mother of two small boys, she had little opportunity for formal Zen practice. "I suffered from not being able to do retreats and so on, because Ruben was a professor, and he was also the Zen teacher for those Zen retreats offered in Dallas, and I took care of the children. And then someone suggested to me that it was important for me to do retreats, so I did two retreats with Jan Chozen Bays[136] in Portland in Oregon. And after that we had a Zen teachers' meeting here at our center, and one of the Philippine teachers said, 'Maria, why don't you study with your husband? He's the best teacher among our group.' And I said like, 'What?' And then I thought, 'Maybe she is right. And so I picked up my practice again with Ruben."

When her sons were older, she became re-associated with Hsin Tao and assisted him with the Museum of World Religions he was establishing in Taiwan.

"And that's your day job now?" I ask.

"That's right. Yes, I organize international conferences for them. Right now – just two days ago – I came back from Salt Lake City. I'd organized a series of Buddhist-Muslim dialogues after 9/11, so we also had two Buddhist/Muslim panels in Salt Lake. But I also translate for the Dharma master."

In 2008, she received authorization to teach Zen and began working with students in Dallas as well as in South Bend. "Students here can go to different teachers at the same time. So some of these students only come to me, and some of them also come to Ruben or one of the other teachers at the Maria Kannon Center. So it's not an exclusive group."

"At any point during your Zen training, did you ever have doubts about Catholicism?"

"No, I think that solved itself in the kensho experience. Or do you mean on a dogmatic point of view?"

"I just wonder if at any point you felt something like, 'I'm a Buddhist now; I'm not a Catholic any longer.'"

"For me I think it was important to discover the mystical tradition in Catholicism. And if you listen to St. John of the Cross or Meister Eckhart, I think it sounds like the same experience. Although I don't like to say the same or different. But you

---

136   Cf. McDaniel, *Cypress Trees in the Garden*, Chapter Fourteen.

feel at home there. So there's no need to strip yourself of that. You want to discover it more deeply. And when you get to the mystical level that is beyond language, you find that in Zen as well as in Catholicism. But it's a good point. My Buddhist master in Taiwan loves Christians, especially the Catholics because they have a monastic tradition, but he always very much emphasizes that you really have to let go of the notion of God to come to a deep realization. And so sometimes he will tell me, 'Don't think like a Christian.' And it's like kind of a banter between us almost, but I understand what he says. As long as you think of God in the dogmatic way, it's probably very difficult. But the Catholic tradition has so many ways of going beyond that. You know? So it's the language you grow up with, and it's very difficult to shed your first language. But I believe the Christian mystics agreed ultimately that God is beyond any language or thought that you can construct. Of course the Buddhists may say there is no God. But when God is beyond any language and anything you can think, then you can't even say yes or no anymore."

"You'd mentioned earlier that you'd organized some Buddhist-Muslim dialogues after 9/11. Why Buddhist-Muslim?"

"Because the majority of people in Asia are either Buddhist or Muslim. So we had those dialogues in China, Malaysia, Indonesia, and so on, and the idea was that if these two populations learn to talk to each other and to cooperate with each other, we will all be in better shape. It was a reaction that Dharma Master Hsin Tao had after 9/11, especially after the destruction of the big Buddhist statues and relics in Bamiyan by the Taliban,[137] that now it's time to speak to the Muslim world and not vilify every Muslim because of what happened."

"Is there the same tension between Islam and Buddhism as there often seems to be between Christianity and Islam?"

"Not historically. But what we see now – especially in places like Malaysia and Indonesia where relations used to be quite peaceful – is that there is a lot of this Wahhabi very conservative kind of Islam that's being imported from Saudi Arabia. I helped this interfaith organization in Indonesia organize a Buddhist-Muslim youth camp which was followed by a dialogue conference in Jakarta. And they wanted to do the same thing again the year after. And they said, 'Maria, the situation now is too dangerous because from the Muslim side it is discouraged.' The Buddhists are quite open to dialogue, but unfortunately from some of the Muslim side we see the same kind of radicalization that we see in other countries, and the Muslims who are very moderate suffer from that."

---

137   In 2001, the Taliban declared two 6th century monumental representations of the Buddha carved into the cliffside of the Bamiyan Valley in Afghanistan to be idols and destroyed them.

"Does your interfaith work go beyond the Buddhist and Muslim communities?"

"Yes. Especially our work with the Elijah Interfaith Institute.[138] We have at least six religions represented, and I had started a group ..." She pauses, then says: "I was a little bit upset this morning because right now the situation in Israel is very difficult between Israelis and Palestinians. And I have a group I meet twice a year there, which is composed of a group of Yeshiva students – very conservative Jewish students that live in a settlement – and Palestinians from south of Hebron also in the West Bank. It's just two days, one over-night, and we have been doing that for the last three years, and I was supposed to do one again two weeks from now. But I just received an email from the leader of the Palestinian group, and it said, 'Maria, right now we cannot go into Israel. So we can't do the retreat at the Dead Sea.' This is a place on the West Bank where Palestinians don't need a permit, but it's under Israeli control. And they said, 'The condition is that we bring our wives, and the condition is that we cannot have meals with the Israelis because we cannot be seen in public with Israelis.' And now I have to decide is it really worth going ahead with that, and whether Yeshiva students agree to this. That's something that I find very challenging and also very gratifying, because I really have these two groups that talk to each other and meditate, and they always leave as friends. So I can see here the transformative power of Buddhist meditation in defusing those tensions and opening people's hearts to each other."

"You did use the word 'wife' rather than 'spouse,' should I draw from that that most of the participants are male?"

"Most of the participants are male, which is very common in these kinds of settings. Yes. In Palestinian society, it takes an extra effort to have women involved. In our last meeting, we had two women involved, which was the first time."

"Does the fact that you are a woman pose any challenge?"

"I first thought so. When I met the group the first time, the person who organized couldn't be there. So this was in the old city of Jerusalem. So I'm coming there, and I'm facing these five Jewish Orthodox men and five Palestinian men, and everybody looks at me! But it went well. I think it also helps. Because I am completely beyond any category they can put me in. So it feels safe for them."

"Is there a Zen component in this interfaith dialogue?"

"Absolutely. It was in Indonesia that we started. We had so many young people there, both Buddhists and Muslims, and so my Chinese master, Hsin Tao, said, 'Would you all like a little introduction to meditation?' And the Muslims were very open to it. In all the other areas we'd done these dialogues so far, we stayed away from meditation practice because it can be a touchy issue with Muslims. They're not sure if

138   The Elijah Interfaith Institute is based in Jerusalem and with a branch office in the United States. See http://elijah-interfaith.org.

they're allowed to do this or not. But in Indonesia there is so much Sufi influence in the culture that they are more comfortable with meditation than more conservative areas.

"Now the beginning in Israel was a little bit different. I had tried to organize a Zen retreat for Israelis, and we spread the news about it through an interfaith organization that I was working with. Then I got an email from ten Palestinians saying, 'We would like to join your group.' And in the final result, five of them came, but they hadn't quite understood. They mistook 'meditation' for 'mediation.' They thought they would come for a meeting with Israelis where they mediate." In spite of the initial misunderstanding, the Muslims stayed, although they found the practice difficult. "They had a lot of struggles, but at the end they said, 'This is an excellent training for our patience, but we would like to do something like that together with Israelis where we can also have dialogue.' So I devised this new form where we combine interfaith dialogue with meditation. And it has worked very well so far."

"I understand that religion is still pretty important in Texas," I remark. "But in many other places, especially among university-educated people, it's often dismissed as something irrelevant today, something passé. So let me ask you, as someone who works for the Museum of World Religions: 'What is the value of religion in the 21st century?'"

"You know, those are traditions that go very far back, and there are still so many people that live and practice those traditions. If you are not familiar with religious texts and the language, there's all this population in the world with whom you would find difficulty in communicating or even understanding."

"But part of one's difficulty in communicating with them might be that one assumes they're caught up in an archaic mindset."

"I think that within each religion there are different stages of spiritual growth. From where you take texts very literally to where you will understand that you need to interpret the texts. And I think that most religions have scholars that are way beyond what you call the archaic stage. Maybe you are familiar that there has been this long-standing group who undertake Buddhist-Christian dialogue, and these are highly educated people that are in dialogue with each other and certainly don't consider religions archaic. So the question is who you are talking to. I find the same situation in Buddhism itself. My dissertation was on the *Great Compassion Dharani* – the *Great Compassion Mantra* – which is recited in practically all Zen Centers especially in Asia but also in many of the Western places. And you find exactly the same attitude among Buddhist populations. Some of them understand that Guanyin, the Bodhisattva of Compassion, is really describing your True Self. But for many it's a deity out there that comes to your help when you invoke her help. I am comfortable with both attitudes, because that's what the culture consists of. Now as for Christian-ity, I'm not sure with the present pope that people would think that he's representing a very archaic religion. He was very popular when he came here to the States. And he's trying to shake-up some things. Or somebody like Thomas Merton, for example. Would you say that he is an adherent of an archaic religion? I don't think so. I think it was Karen Armstrong, a very well-known scholar of religion, who said in a panel in Salt Lake City that every generation is equally distant from God, meaning that every generation has to figure out again their own approach to the ultimate. How we understand it, how we form our relationship."

"I assume that if interfaith dialogue is to be effective it needs to include people with no faith as well."

"Definitely."

"Certainly one of the things that made Zen popular in the 1950s and '60s, when the Zen boom in America took place, was the idea of a spiritual tradition without a God. Because a lot of people did find the concept of God to be, for lack of a better term, 'archaic.' And I think that feeling is even more common today. All you need to do is listen to contemporary news coverage. There is a sense that religion has be-come a cause for dissension, a cause of conflict. Fundamentalists are challenging some pretty basic human rights issues in the US; there were the scandals about the sexual abuse of children in the Catholic church. All of that has given religion a pretty nega-tive connotation. So how would you address that? How would you address someone who attended an interfaith dialogue with that perspective?"

"Of course, the corporate ego of religion is something that always gets in the way, and it has to be put aside for interfaith dialogue to be possible. There's absolutely no question about it. But people who come to spiritual practice are looking for a real-ization of what this life is all about and who they are. And often I find that people who come to Zen retreats from a Catholic background, for example, have rejected all of that kind of Catholicism they learned growing up. But they are not at peace. So they are struggling with what they had learned as children, the language, the tradi-tions, what their parents practiced. And I do think that they are looking for a way of overcoming the interior split that they're experiencing. And, to my surprise, I often find that people who come to a Zen retreat in the beginning, or even some of my students here on Monday nights, may have a very negative attitude about religion. But they gradually open up and are able to speak about it, find some other way of looking at it. Because when you look at organized religion, of course, you see all the terrible things that have happened because of it. There's no denying it. But at the same time, there are still teachings within religions – if you look at the teachings of the mystics, for example – that can help you heal that longing that most people feel inside themselves. If that longing is stilled by joining a Buddhist group and finding comfort there, there's no need to discuss it. But what I find with many people is that they need to go beyond, they still need to be in dialogue with what they learned from their childhood. That is how I would put it.

"I will just give you two examples from the Jewish tradition, somebody like Rabbi Alan Lew or Norman Fischer. Alan Lew had completely rejected everything that had to do with orthodox Judaism, but then through Zen practice he finally became an orthodox rabbi himself, teaching other rabbis how to meditate. Or Norman Fischer who published a book on the Psalms from a Zen perspective.[139] So my experience is that people tend to come back to their religious roots – rather than completely reject them – through spiritual practice, but seeing everything in a completely different light."

"Is Zen a religion?"

"If you look at Zen in Asia, you would have no question that it is a religion. But if you look at Zen in the west, it's a bit of a different story. And it's very interesting that if you look at Zen Centers as such, they don't have as many traditional Buddhists – Asian Buddhists – as the so-called Buddhist churches do. So the Zen Center seems to be something that's more appropriate to the Westerners who have rejected their own church and don't want another church. But if I see, for example, the Chinese disciples of my Buddhist master in New York, when they come together it is about prayer, rituals, it's about services, praying for the dead, exactly the same thing that you would see in Asia. If they come from Zen meditation in some other place, they would say, 'Oh, this is just one aspect, a very isolated aspect.' In Asia all of this is very integrated, but, for Westerners, they are very comfortable at the Zen Centers because some of them already have churches at home, so they do not need another setting where there are so many rituals, and they are just looking for a place for just meditation. This type of center does not exist in other places around the world; I think it's a very western creation."

"Let me rephrase the question then: Is Zen, as it's practiced in North America, a religion?"

She pauses a while before responding. "It depends on what you understand as religion. Or you can ask if it's a religion or an organized religion. You know, religion means 'connecting with.' Religion means 'binding two things together.' So if you felt religion connects to whatever you understand to be your true self, then you would say that Zen is a religion. It's something that unifies and binds together."

"From a traditional Catholic perspective, religion is what unites me with God. So can an agnostic, if not an atheist, tradition be a religion?"

---

139   Norman Fischer is Soto Zen priest in the lineage of Shunryu Suzuki and a former abbot of the San Francisco Zen center. The book is *Opening to You: Zen-Inspired Translations of the Psalms*, New York: Penguin Books, 2003.

"Agnostic, of course, is different from atheist. Our teacher, Yamada Roshi, said, 'I don't know what the kensho or satori experience means for Christians. You have to figure that out and put that in your own terms.' He didn't say you can't put that in your own terms because it so different from everything you could ever experience as a Christian."

"So we'll stick to the word 'agnostic.' Can an agnostic tradition be a religion?"

Again, she pauses before replying. "As I said, in Asia it is already a religion. It has the trappings of a religion. What is it in the west? It depends on what centers you are looking at. It's interesting, in Sanbo Zen we say in our sesshins, 'Zen is *not* a religion.' But you say that to people who come from a religious background very often, and you want to make sure that we are not there to compete or to convert any of the traditions that they may already be practicing in. So in that sense, it's always emphasized by the teachers that Zen is not a religion. But it's really how you use words. Right? When we say that, we mean Zen is not something that's competing with what you have traditionally, but it can help you deepen in that tradition. And we don't say that you have to let go of everything else."

"So, if not a religion, what is it?"

Maria is initially hesitant to categorize Zen as one thing or another but eventually she tells me:

"I find, in every sesshin I guide, I follow Father Lassalle's tradition: the first talk will always be about the basics of Zen. The meditation; why do we do Zen; the three fruits of Zen. So I start each sesshin again with the basics."

"What do you mean by the 'three fruits'?"

"The first one is concentration, concentration leading you to samadhi.[140] And then out of samadhi you can have a kensho experience, realizing your true nature, or satori, however that's described. And then the third one is integrating or embodying this experience in your daily life."

In other words, Zen is a practice through which one can first come to awakening and then learns to manifest that awakening in one's life and activities. In that bare summary, there is nothing that conflicts with living a Christian – or agnostic – life as well.

---

140   Deep meditative absorption.

CHAPTER NINE

Pat Hawk

Combining Zen practice and Catholicism is based in "the recognition in experience of a resonance between the two traditions. Many Catholics remark, after their first Zen experience, that it is what they have always been seeking." So wrote the first Catholic priest born in America to receive Dharma transmission. Patrick (always known as Pat) Hawk went on to note that what such people are seeking is "not a thing, nor even understanding, but rather a living awareness of no separation from" that Ultimate Reality that may be variously understood by different religious traditions but that is innate in everyone. This "direct, non-mediated experience has been the central focus of Zen in Buddhism and contemplation in Christianity;" therefore, the technique of Zen is able to offer a way of practice for those seeking to pursue the contemplative tradition in Christian prayer.[141]

Pat Hawk was a member of the Congregation of the Most Holy Redeemer or Redemptorists. Much of the biographical information I acquire about him comes from his biographer and student, Helen Amerongen. "He grew up in Granite City, Illinois," she tells me, "across the river from St. Louis, one of two children. He was the first child, and then he had a sister seven years later."

"Was it a devout family?"

"Yes. Very Catholic. Very standard Catholic family. Happy to have a child become a priest."

"That was a family goal?"

"It was something to be welcomed."

Pat claimed that he knew he wanted to become a priest by the time he was seven

---

141   Patrick Hawk, "Authority: The Role of the Teacher in Buddhist/Christian Formation" in *Studies in Formative Spirituality*, XIV:1, February 1993, p. 23.

years old.

"From very early in life I was attracted to Catholic ritual, the bright vestment colors, the sounds of bell and music, the smell of beeswax candles and incense. Something present inside me called to me through these things…"[142]

In the 1950s, it was common for young boys to begin training for the priesthood while still in high school; he was 13 years old when he entered St. Joseph's College, the Redemptorist minor seminary in a suburb of St. Louis.

"Had he chosen St. Joseph's because it was nearby?" I ask.

"It was partly happenstance," Helen says. "He had a friend in grade school whose mother knew a Redemptorist priest, and she was bringing her son to check out the college. Pat heard about this and said he wanted to go too. So he went and saw it and decided that was where he was going."

Three students from Hawk's grammar school class enrolled at St. Joseph's, but he was the only one to go on to ordination.

Greg Mayers entered St. Joseph's two years later, in 1958. I ask if he remembers his first meeting with Pat Hawk.

"I do. I was 12 at the time. One of the requirements in seminary, everybody had to play sports. At the time, the way the seminary was organized, it included six years of school. The last two years of the minor seminary would now be considered the first two years of college. And the student body was divided into seniors and juniors. So the first three years were juniors, and the last three years were seniors. And Pat Hawk was in his last year of being in the junior category. So we had to play sports. I wasn't very good at sports, and it was baseball. And they organized the teams as majors, minors, and… Oh, God, I've forgotten what the third one was… Rookies! Rookies. So I was in the rookies, and Pat Hawk was in the rookies. And we were all out on the diamond, and Pat Hawk was the team captain. And I was very embarrassed, 'cause I didn't know how to play. But I was smart enough to know that nobody ever hit a ball to right field. So I decided that was what I wanted, to play right field. So Pat Hawk comes out, and all these kids gather screaming about what position they wanted, and I got close enough to him to say, 'I want right field.' And he looked at me with the withering eyes of a fourteen year old and said, 'That's my position.' That was my first encounter with Pat Hawk."

"What was he like as a student?"

"Quiet. He was a very quiet person. And private."

"Introverted?"

"Introverted, yeah. Very much so."

As is common with introverted persons, Hawk was reflective, and, Helen tells me, when he was in the major seminary he had a crisis of faith.

142   Patrick Hawk, "The Pathless Path" in *The Catholic World*, May/June 1990, p. 129.

"In what way?" I ask.

"Losing his faith in God. He never doubted that he should be in the seminary or that he would be a priest. Even in spite of the crisis of faith, he did not doubt that this was where he wanted to be."

Later I came upon an article in which Pat described this period of his life:

> — the regular way of devotion and piety eventually comes to a dead end, and the path begins to take a turn that is dark and difficult. Then one cannot practice as one did before. It is a bewildering time. There is no more consolation; all is dry and seemingly unprofitable. Most people feel there is something wrong with them; although they still believe deeply, they do not know how to go on, and they get almost no help from spiritual advisors.[143]

He was only in his 20s at the time, and the Second Vatican Council was taking place, which allowed seminarians greater freedom in their reading than earlier generations had had. "He was a prodigious reader," Helen notes. He was also the assistant to the seminary's librarian and saw new books as they arrived. One by Jean-Marie Déchanet was entitled *Christian Yoga*.

> At that time the maps of the journey, the plans, even the destination outside myself disappeared. The path became pathless and began to walk the way of itself. I "found" pointers, pointers "found" me. In the beginning the pointers came in the form of books. The first was J. M. Dechanet's *Christian Yoga*, and the way of sitting and breathing became the steps on the path that was going nowhere in particular.[144]

Following the instructions provided in the book, he began a private meditation practice.

Greg and Pat's training overlapped during the four years of theological study in the major seminary prior to ordination. "We had an extremely competent Dean of Men who had started counselling and group counselling sessions with the students. And I met Pat in the group counselling sessions, and we kind of had a bonding there. Then after seminary, those of us who were in the group counselling thing would meet every summer to develop and sharpen our skills at counselling."

Hawk's first posting after ordination was to a Redemptorist Church in St. Louis. "That was what was called the 'tirocinium year,'" Helen explains. "You might call it an

---

143   Ibid.

144   Ibid.

internship. So, one year in St. Louis, then he was posted to the seminary high school in Edgerton, Wisconsin, where he taught English."

He was a popular teacher and served as one of the spiritual directors for the students, but he was still struggling personally.

☙

Greg and Pat fell out of touch for a while, although Greg knew that Pat had developed an interest in Asian spirituality. In addition to Dechanet's book, Pat read the Zen popularizer, Alan Watts – whom he recommended to Greg – as well as Shunryu Suzuki's *Zen Mind, Beginner's Mind*, which he admired. So when the Palisades Retreat Center, where Greg was on staff, sponsored a Zen retreat for Christians facilitated by Robert Aitken,[145] he informed Pat of it.

The retreat came about largely because of Aitken's involvement with the peace movement, which had brought him into contact with members of the Catholic Worker Movement. Aitken lived in Hawaii, where he'd founded the Diamond Sangha. Helen explains that in 1977 he was participating in what came to be called the Bangor Summer at the Trident Missile Base in Bangor, Washington.

"There were all these demonstrations, and the Catholic Workers of Seattle were major movers in them. And some of those Catholic Workers and some other people – who were spiritual advisees of some of the Trappists at Our Lady of Guadalupe Abbey in Lafayette, Oregon – knew each other. So one of the Catholic Workers took Robert Aitken down to meet Bernard McVeigh, the abbot of Guadalupe Abbey, and together they cooked up this idea of offering a Zen retreat 'for Christians and other travellers.' And that first retreat was at Palisades. Greg Mayers was a spiritual advisee of Bernard McVeigh. So although he was not in on the initial conversation, Greg heard about it from Abbott Bernard and invited them to use Palisades. That's my understanding."

"So after Bernard McVeigh said Bob Aitken had agreed to do sesshin for Christians," Greg tells me, "I thought, 'Oh, Pat Hawk practices Zen! He would be interested in this.' So I called him up and told him about it and said, 'Why don't you come out and attend?'" It wasn't until later that Greg learned this would be Pat's first formal Zen retreat, although, as Helen points out, he had privately continued the exercises he'd found in *Christian Yoga*.

"That solitary sitting was his steady daily practice for years before he had anything to do with specifically Zen practice," she tells me.

"Did he ever talk about what that first retreat was like?"

"He said he took to it like a duck to water. I said to him, 'Did you find it awkward?' You know, all the ritual and everything. It was not actually the full-blown

145   Cf. McDaniel, *The Third Step East*, Chapter Six.

ritual of a Zen sesshin. They did have some Zen ritual, but they modified and Christianized a lot of it. He immediately formed a relationship with Aitken. Aitken told me that he saw, right from the beginning, that Pat should be a teacher. He said he saw it at that first retreat."

Greg informs me that shortly after that retreat, Pat entered "a rehabilitation center for alcoholism for priests. After that, he came out to the retreat center I was working at and stayed with us for about six months."

"He was a patient?"

Greg nods his head. "He was an alcoholic," he says gently.

"When did that start?"

"I don't remember. He was teaching at the seminary – the minor seminary – and the other professors there did an intervention."

"Did he shake it? Did he acquire sobriety?"

"For a while, and then he had to go again. Alcoholics don't ... There are often a lot of slips in the disease." Sometime after our conversation, Greg wrote to me, adding, that "Pat was open about his alcoholism and didn't hide it from his students, nor make much about it. My understanding is that the disease is incurable, but treatable." Helen tells me that Pat went for treatment twice, after which he remained sober for the remainder of his life.

∾

The Redemptorists at Palisades hosted several sesshin conducted by Aitken, but eventually Aitken came to feel that the tone of these was growing too Christian for his comfort. "People were bringing him things that he couldn't handle," Helen explains. "Their experiences often were within a Christian framework. He had a Dharma brother, Willigis Jäger of Germany, who was also a Yamada Koun student, and he recommended Willigis to the group, and they invited him to come. So Willigis Jäger took over leading those retreats. Pat did one or two retreats with Willigis, and Willigis invited him to come to Germany. Pat got approved to do a year's sabbatical in Germany, so he did that from August '84 to August '85."

After the year with Willigis, Pat returned to the US and completed his Zen training with Aitken, who gave him transmission in May 1989.

"Willigis was not empowered to give transmission then," Helen tells me. "There was a controversy within the Sanbo Kyodan – now Sanbo Zen group – about who could give transmission. And that power, to this day, is reserved to the abbot. But Aitken was himself a Zen Master with full transmission from Yamada Koun Roshi, so he felt empowered to give transmission himself. He gave transmission to Pat and others in the Diamond Sangha, then sought to have his heirs recognized by the Sanbo Kyodan. Yamada Koun's heirs in Japan refused to do this, which led to the split of the

Diamond Sangha from the Sanbo Kyodan. It's a complicated story."

By 1986, Pat was offering Christian contemplative retreats modeled after those conducted by Jäger in Germany. The first of these, co-facilitated by Greg, took place at the Bishop DeFalco Retreat Center in Amarillo, Texas. They were not Zen retreats, but the format had clearly been influenced by Zen.

Although Pat was given permission to teach Zen in August 1988, he did not lead sesshin until after his transmission in 1989 when Jäger – who found travel between Germany and Washington State taxing – asked him to take over the Northwest group. A little later, Greg was also authorized to teach by Willigis, and he and Pat began leading sesshin in the Northwest and at the DeFalco Center where they were both now located.

"The Bishop of Amarillo at the time, Leroy Matthiesen, was very supportive," Helen tells me. "But then he retired, and Bishop John Yanta took over, and he dismissed the Redemptorists."

"The diocese owned the retreat house," Greg explains. "The Redemptorists were the ones contracted to run it. This really had nothing to do with Zen. The bishop did not like the fact that he did not have absolute control over us."

"So it wasn't an issue over the content of what was being presented?"

"He had no idea what we were doing. He reported to my provincial that the Holy Spirit told him that it was time for the diocesan priests to run the retreat center." His tone is skeptical. "So that's how we left Amarillo."

Other sources are less diplomatic, suggesting that Yanta was fundamentally opposed to the idea of the Zen and contemplation retreats. He is reported to have once said that "Cowboys don't need contemplation."

Greg returned to Palisades. Pat moved to Picture Rocks Retreat Center in Tucson, Arizona – now known as the Redemptorist Renewal Center – which would be his home until his final illness.

"Is that where you first met him?" I ask Helen, who is on the faculty of the University of Arizona in Tucson.

"No. I met him while he was still living in Amarillo. He was coming regularly to Tucson to offer sesshin for Zen Desert Sangha." Zen Desert Sangha had been established in 1982 by a group of people interested in practicing Zen, although they did not have a teacher at the time. They eventually affiliated with Aitken's Diamond Sangha, and a number of teachers – including Aitken and Nelson Foster – came to Tucson to lead sesshin. In late 1989, Hawk did so for the first time and later became the group's guiding teacher. He became increasingly in demand both as a Zen teacher and a teacher of contemplative prayer practices and regularly led retreats in Arizona, New Mexico, Ohio, California, Texas, the Pacific Northwest, Australia, and elsewhere.

Like many of Pat's students, Steve Slottow was not Catholic. He had been drawn to Zen by Philip Kapleau's (and Yamada Roshi's) *The Three Pillars of Zen*. While still a very young man, he moved from Illinois to Rochester, New York, in order to practice at Kapleau's center, although he didn't become a resident. "We weren't in the inner circle. We'd go there for sittings; we'd go there for sesshin, but we didn't have any say in the way the place was run. We didn't work there. We had a sort of outsider's status. In those days, staff were pretty much insiders, and people who weren't on staff were outsiders. They were involved, but it was almost like a monk/lay thing except that it wasn't really a monk/lay thing. It was very much an insider/outsider thing."

Kapleau had sought to duplicate the intense Japanese training style of Sogaku Harada Roshi. "People screaming Mu in chorus and very, very heavy use of the kyo-saku. So there was a lot of bushido/samurai spirit in Rochester at that time. And everyone was very young, of course, all the students. It was too bushido-ish for me."

Steve played in an Old Time music band in the Rochester area for a while and then, when the group broke up, went to the City University of New York to do graduate work in music theory. He still attended occasional sesshin at the Zen Center, now under the direction of Kapleau's principal heir, Bodhin Kjolhede. "I'm not casting aspersions on his worth as a teacher, but there has to be some rapport, and I felt that Bodhin and I were kind of talking past each other?" He makes the statement a question. "We weren't connecting very well, and, at a certain point, I stopped going to sesshin at Rochester. And I was looking for places to practice. I bounced around, and I eventually found out that Robert Aitken's heir, Nelson Foster, had a small group in New Haven, and he would go a couple of times a year and give short sesshin there. It was called the East Rock Sangha. And I had been attracted to the Diamond Sangha and to Robert Aitken for a long time because it seemed much less bushido-samurai than Rochester. Also, Aitken's lineage credentials were pretty impeccable. He was a successor of Koun Yamada. And – as we all know – Kapleau's teaching credentials were kind of cloudy."

Steve found Foster helpful. "He was very nice; he was very impressive." But he only visited New Haven periodically. At the time, Steve was also engaged in an early internet chat-line dedicated to Zen practice. One of the other members mentioned attending a sesshin with Pat Hawk. "I knew that Pat was a Dharma brother of Nelson Foster. But Nelson wasn't around that much. And Pat sounded interesting because Pat was…" He pauses to reflect, then says, "He was a curmudgeon. He was very quiet. He wasn't exactly reclusive because the order he belonged to wasn't an eremitic order, but he was as much of a recluse as he could be. He was extremely plain and down to earth. He was very understated. There was no charisma. You see? I distrusted charisma. So somehow he sounded like my type of guy. Kinda grouchy. Very quiet. Didn't care about impressing people. So I went down to Tucson, and I did a sesshin with Pat."

"Do you remember your first impression of him?"

"Pat liked to meet prospective students in a very informal setting before the sesshin started. So we just went to a little table outside. He was a very plain guy dressed in old clothes. Totally unassuming. He didn't talk very much, just asked a few questions about where I was from and what my interests were and why I was there. He was this plain, quiet, dry – extremely dry – guy. He didn't seem particularly enthusiastic. I was totally charmed. He was just this kind of desert rat. He was living in Tucson, but, of course, he wasn't *from* there. But he sort of fit into the landscape, although I'm not sure he even liked it. There were no frills, no airs. Nothing to stand out. I told him about my Rochester Zen Center experience and said that I felt a little burned-out with Rochester. And he replied, 'Well, we're used to dealing with Rochester burnouts here.'"

"If you were with a group of friends, drinking beer, trading stories, what story would you tell about Pat Hawk?"

"I would probably tell about this time Pat was traveling somewhere, Europe or Japan or somewhere, and – unusually for Pat – someone was traveling with him. The other person was very unobtrusive and hardly said anything. And Pat paid him the ultimate compliment. He said, 'Traveling with you is almost as good as traveling by myself.'"

I mention to Helen that another of Pat's students had described him as a curmudgeon.

"Yeah. He had that side. He had a curmudgeonly side, for sure. Although that's misleading too, because he was mostly a gentle soul. And he had a dry wit that could be gut-splittingly funny. But he was not into chitchat. And if you were trying to chat with him, you could feel that he was a curmudgeon. But you didn't have to be into chitchat to encounter his rough edges. He was reserved. Quiet."

"Can you describe him?"

"About 5'7". For much of his life, he was skinny. He gained weight partly because of his medication, partly because he quit smoking the last few years of his life. But most of his life, he was pretty slim. He kept a lot of hair all of his life. It turned grey. It turned pretty white by the end. He was not obviously a handsome man. In fact, he would just fade into the woodwork outside of the dokusan room. But he had a presence that made him a deeply attractive man."

I ask her to tell me a Pat Hawk story.

"Well, a student of Pat's was working with him in Santa Fe, and there was only Zen sesshin at that center. Then this person moved to the Northwest, where for a long time Pat's retreats were all Christian contemplative. He eventually offered Zen retreats up there, too, but for years it was just Christian contemplative. So this person was travelling from the Northwest to either Tucson or Santa Fe to do Zen retreats, and it was expensive. So Pat said, 'You know, you can come to the contemplative retreats.' But, as with many people, this student wasn't interested in getting involved with anything Christian. And Pat said, 'It's the same silence. You can just sit.' So the man went to the contemplative retreat. And first time going into interviews, there's Pat sitting in a chair instead of on a cushion on the floor – just one of the small differences in format between Zen and Contemplative retreats. And the man says, 'What's with the chair?' And Pat says, 'In Christianity, we have a merciful God.'"

∞

After completing his graduate work, Steve got a job at the University of Texas in Denton, which brought him closer to Arizona. He tried to attend two or three sesshin a year with Pat, and in between sesshin they kept in touch electronically. "Originally it was doku-i-chat and then turned into doku-skype."

"How would a Pat Hawk sesshin have differed from a Philip Kapleau sesshin?"

"There'd be a lot less use of the stick. The stick would come around at certain times, and you could ask for it. It wasn't administered if you didn't ask for it. I usually did ask for it because my shoulders would tighten up. But it was much more low key. At Rochester, they would give encouragement talks that would try to sort of rouse you into a frenzy. They might disagree with that, but to me that seemed to be the purpose. Arouse the spirit of struggle. Pat did encouragement talks too, but they weren't particularly meant to get you all excited, to arouse a lot of energy. There wasn't that sense of expectation. At Rochester there was the sense that if you weren't practicing with the required degree of fervor you weren't holding your end up. You know? And there was none of that. The sesshins were not loose," he hastens to add. "They were pretty taut. But there was none of this bushido-samurai thing. You weren't supposed to be any certain way. They were still difficult. But a lot of the sense of being expected to be a certain way wasn't there. And there wasn't a dokusan rush. In Rochester, there was a dokusan rush, but in Tucson you simply put your card out if you wanted to go to dokusan, and, when your turn came, the jisha[146] would tap you on the shoulder, and you'd get up and get in the dokusan line. There wasn't this fervent, fevered rush. So it was a lot more low-key, but it was still taut. Now, mind you, he also held Christian contemplative retreats."

"Did you attend any of those?"

"I ended up going to those later on because they were scheduled around the holidays, and they fit better into the academic year. And I could simply continue to work on my Zen practice during those."

The forms of the Christian retreats and the sesshin were distinct. Although Zen students were welcome to participate in the Christian retreats – and vice versa – there

---

146   The zendo monitor.

were no overt Buddhist elements in them, nor were there Christian elements in the sesshin.

"He kept them entirely separate," Steve tells me. "I compare Pat's approach with Ruben Habito's approach. Habito was sort of after a kind of fusion. Pat was after a kind of apartheid where the Christian stuff was quite different from the Zen stuff. So the Zen sesshin were Zen sesshin. The Christian stuff, there were Christian figures on the altar; instead of sutra-chanting there were readings from the Psalms. There was the mass with the Eucharist, which was optional. People who were there primarily for the Zen aspect could simply continue working on their Zen practice during these and have dokusan. In the Contemplative Intensive Retreats, the CIRs, it wasn't called dokusan; it was called 'interview,' I think."

"But it was a meditation retreat?"

"It was basically a sesshin format, but the schedule was easier. As Pat said, 'We change the idols on the altar.' And some of the people who went to them didn't follow the forms very precisely. The CIRs had forms and rules. It's just that some of the participants – the ones, I think, who were not very interested in the Zen side – were not very invested in following them precisely."

"Mostly they were both silent sitting facing the wall," Helen tells me. "But the rituals were different. The Zen retreat started a little earlier in the morning. The bells were pretty much the same, regulating standing and sitting and so on. The first thing in the morning with the Zen retreat there's a thing called kentan where the teacher walks around the room; it's a formal inspection of the zendo that's not in the contemplative retreat. In the CIR, first thing in the morning you chant *'shalom'* for five minutes. So there's a little difference there. The schedule for dokusan – the one-on-one meetings are called 'interviews' in the CIR – the schedules were a little bit different. There were a few things like that. In the CIR, there was 'conference,' which was the talk in the morning after breakfast. On the Zen side, there was teisho, and that was after lunch. The conference topic could focus on the Desert Fathers, a story from the Desert Fathers, or perhaps the Christian mystics, Eckhart, people like that. On the Zen side, most teisho began with a koan; he'd read the case and go on from there."

I ask about the specific technique used in the CIRs. "Were people assigned some sort of practice?"

"You could do any number of things. You could be told to count your breath, or you could follow a sound – in your head, not speaking it out loud – in the way of the *Cloud of Unknowing.*"

"Like a mantra?"

"It doesn't get called a mantra but a sound. A sound that has no meaning."

"Okay. Mu."

But Helen says that using Mu as an example is misleading because it's a koan. "But a sound with a long vowel. Something connected to the breath often. Occasionally you might be given a Christian koan. I never worked with a Christian koan, but there were some kicking around. What is that, at the beginning of the gospel of John: 'In the beginning was the Word'?"

"'And the Word was with God, and the Word was God,'" I continue the passage.

"Something like that. It's got a little bit of a twist on that and is very brief. That kind of thing. You could be given that as a practice. But most likely you would be started out on breath-counting or following a sound."

"To what end?" I ask.

"Sorry?"

"To what end? To what purpose?"

"To what end?"

"I've come to this Catholic retreat center, and there's this priest who tells me to sit and count my breath. It would be natural to wonder to what end."

She doesn't answer immediately. She often takes her time and considers questions before responding to them. "Why did you come to the retreat?" she asks.

"It doesn't matter really. Somebody recommended it. I'm approaching retirement and am not sure what's next in life. Mid-life crisis. Achieved most of my life goals, but I'm out of touch with my faith. Whatever. Trying to find out if there's something here, if there's anything in it."

"And the only way to find out is to try it. And *it* will tell you if there's anything in it. As you sit in silence, you will learn if there's anything in it for you. But it's not something anybody can tell you about, you have to experience it for yourself."

This refusal to define specifically what one acquires through Zen practice is something I encounter frequently throughout these interviews.

I ask Steve if he had a sense of how well Hawk was accepted by other members of the Redemptorist Congregation. "I don't know about the whole congregation, but in the part that was at Picture Rocks Retreat Center, he was very accepted. He basically ran a whole program of Zen and contemplative retreats at the center called the Pathless Path. And the order had no problem with this whatsoever. He was well-regarded, well-respected."

"The Redemptorists were supportive," Helen tells me. "And two of his Redemptorist confreres, one being Greg, went to his transmission ceremony in Hawaii. The other was Bob Curry, who at the time was Pat's superior. As far as I know, nobody opposed it on the Redemptorist side. Were there others who were kind of suspicious of this Zen thing? Yes, I think so."

The broader church hierarchy was not always sanguine about Zen. 1989, the year of Pat's transmission ceremony, was also the year that then-Cardinal Joseph Ratzinger spoke out on what he felt were the dangers attendant upon Catholics taking up Eastern meditative practices.

"Pat would allude to this sometimes," Steve says. "He was reluctant to have anything recorded. He only published two articles in rather obscure journals because he wanted to keep a very low profile. He was very straightforward about that. He didn't want to draw a lot of attention to himself."

Helen had been raised in a Catholic family in Edmonton, Alberta, one of eight children. "I mostly dropped my practice of Catholicism as soon as I was old enough to be independent. I went back for a while, exploring. I always from the time of my teens – I don't remember exactly when this started – had a natural affinity for a silent sitting practice which I did on my own for no particular reason. And when I was 23, I had an experience which led me to think, 'Oh! So that's what it's all about!' And after reading Huston Smith's *Religions of Man* I thought maybe Catholicism could give me a framework for continued practice. That was a good experience, but I came to feel the Church was not a good fit for me. Although the Catholicism that Pat presented was valuable to me. He did not hold to literal dogma. He understood his faith in the light of his own profound experience of reality, and as such his presentation resonated with the experience that is available to all of us through silent sitting."

Pat Hawk had said that " – when one meets one's true teacher there is an intuitive recognition."[147] But that recognition doesn't necessarily come immediately.

"How did you meet Pat?" I ask Helen.

"After college in Edmonton, and then postgraduate work in St. Andrews, Scotland, and Boston, I got a faculty position at the University of Arizona and moved to Tucson with my husband and young daughter. Through a friend I'd met in Tucson I heard about Pat Hawk, and that he was coming to lead a sesshin for Zen Desert Sangha. I was told, if you wanted to come to the teisho – the talk – you could show up at this time, at this place. And wear dark clothing and keep your eyes lowered. That was all the instruction I was given. And so I did go to the teisho, and I found this person – who I only saw from a distance – quite unprepossessing and the experience strange. There was all this bowing and chanting, and it felt cult-like to me. I just couldn't get out of there fast enough."

She is speaking slowly and reflectively. "Then he came back to town about a year later. This is now getting into the late 1990s. I believe that first time I saw Pat was in 1995. And then I don't think I saw him again until a little more than a year later,

147   Patrick Hawk, "Authority: The Role of the Teacher in Buddhist/Christian Formation," p. 25.

and he was doing a Dharma talk and a Q & A. And these friends were going, and I decided to go. By that time I had been sitting with a group that sat the Benedictine Monastery in Tucson, as well as on my own. And things were happening in my worldview, in the way I was seeing. Pat Hawk didn't impress me at that meeting either, but the people and the questions they were asking were my questions. I felt these were my people, that they were seeing things the way I was seeing things. So that got me sitting with Zen Desert Sangha a little bit. Soon after that, Pat Hawk was in town and offering dokusan at one of the member's homes. I went, and that was the first time I *met* Pat Hawk. I had seen him the two times before that, and I went in and…" She struggles to find the words she wants. "I… I presented to him what I was doing and just a little bit – not great detail, not a great story – just a little bit of where I was. And he offered me a few words. Something very simple and completely apt. But the experience was not so much what I said or what he said, but of his presence, his total presence, and the sense of being completely received. I don't know if I'd ever felt anything like this before. I came out of there and felt tears of gratitude for the fact there was this person in the world, and that he took it upon himself to be available to anybody who came, and that I had happened to meet up with this person. It was a very different experience from when I saw him at a distance and just felt nothing. And then I began doing sesshins with him, and after that I encountered him as much as I could for the rest of his life."

"What made him an effective Zen teacher?" I ask. She doesn't immediately reply. "You mentioned feeling totally received by him."

She nods her head slowly. "That was perhaps his greatest gift. Also, the very fact that he had his own struggles, his own demons, and that he had faced them, gave him a kind of trustworthiness. And he had a nose for guiding people. He had a good instinct for giving people what they needed at a given moment to move them along."

∾

I ask Steve, "How long did you stay with him?"

"I stayed with him till he died. When I began working with Pat he had already been diagnosed with prostate cancer, and eventually the schedule of his sesshin was lightened – you got up later, there were fewer rounds – mainly to accommodate Pat. It was hard for him. And eventually he sent a very, very short note to his fellow teachers in the Diamond Sangha, to his students as well, saying, 'I've been told I only have so long to live. I have some things to take care of. I'm retiring as of *now*. No more sesshin, no more dokusan, no more Skype. We'll figure out what to do. But that's it.' And he stopped teaching at that point. And then he got worse and worse. I talked with him a couple of days before he died. I had a short phone conversation with him. And then we got some daily bulletins from the people who were taking care of him. Then he died. I don't know how long it was after he retired. Maybe a month or two. It wasn't a long time."

Helen tells me: "He died in Liguori, Missouri, which is where the Redemptorists have a healthcare facility including hospice care. He was flown out there in mid-April 2012, and he died May 8, 2012. So he was there for about three weeks."

I ask Greg Mayers if he worked with any of Pat's students after his death.

"Very briefly. I think they were hoping somehow to revive the program that he was involved in in Tucson, and I was invited to give sesshin. But there were very few students that showed up. You can't really step in. I tried to tell them that. 'Look, this stuff gets really personal with the teacher. Nobody else can come in and step in and take that person's place.'"

Steve tells me: "When Pat announced his retirement, I knew I wanted to work with another teacher, but I cast around for a while. I went to some all day sits with Ruben Habito, who's nearby. His center is in Dallas, very close to Denton. And I went to a sesshin with Leonard Marcel, Pat's Dharma heir." In the end, he began working with James Ford[148] of Boundless Way Zen, then living in Providence, Rhode Island. "Mainly through Skype," he tells me. "Recently he retired from the Unitarian ministry and moved to Long Beach, California, where he's established the Blue Cliff Zen Sangha. Once they get up and running, I'll start doing sesshin with him there."

Pat Hawk viewed his Catholicism and his Zen practice as complementary. What tension there was between them he compared "with the tension of having two arms. With practice one becomes ambidextrous. It is just a matter of doing. Let not your right hand know what your left hand is doing and it is done."[149]

"Tell me a Pat Hawk story."

Greg takes a deep breath, then says: "We were in Amarillo, Texas, in the Redemptorist common room, and I was looking out. And it was the Fall. And I said, 'This is the first time in my life that I've ever experienced Fall.' And Pat Hawk said, 'I hate it when you do that.' I said, 'What?' 'Read my mind.'"

148   Cf. McDaniel, *Cypress Trees in the Garden*, Chapter Ten.

149   Patrick Hawk, "The Pathless Path" in *The Catholic World*, May/June 1990, p. 131.

Greg Mayers

"I was born in New Orleans, Louisiana," Greg Mayers tells me. "I was raised in Baton Rouge. Southern Louisiana is very Catholic country. So I grew up in this marinated Catholic environment."

"When did you know you wanted to be a priest?"

"Probably six months before ordination."

He's a witty man, and there is a lot of humor in the interview. "Okay," I say, trying again. "What made you think you wanted to go into the seminary in the first place?"

After a moment's reflection, he says, "The question is ill-phrased. Growing up in a Catholic parish, you're altar boys and boy scouts and all that kind of stuff, and you just kind of go along with the flow. This would be 1958 when I entered the seminary. In those days Catholic schools groomed boys for the priesthood, and a whole bunch of us altar boys just went onto the seminary after the eighth grade. There must have been about thirteen. I don't think it was any decision at all. It was just that was where the river flowed. The parish I grew up in was run by the Redemptorists. I didn't know anything else, so I went to the Redemptorist High School Seminary, which was outside St. Louis. I took my first long trip at the age of twelve on a train with a whole bunch of other kids."

"What was the seminary like?"

He shrugs. "I don't know. It was just normal to me. I didn't know anything else. I don't remember anything unusual. It was kind of scary. You were away from home, and you're in a new environment, which is a boarding school environment. Meeting a whole bunch of kids from all different parts of the Midwest. That was kind of new. Then being introduced to studies that I didn't even know existed. Ancient history. That was an adventure. And, of course, Latin; we had to take Latin, which scared me. That always frightened me. And the way they taught Latin wasn't very good. They just took the grammar and said, 'This is the grammar. Memorize it.'"

"Other people I've talked to noted that minor seminary in that era wasn't always a particularly pious environment."

"Well, it's adolescent boys. But we had to learn how to meditate. We had meditation in the morning and then mass. It was more pious than I was used to."

"What kind of meditation?"

"They would read a little something, and then you would spend about ten minutes meditating on it. This was high school kids. It was a big group thing. It was in chapel. We gathered in the chapel, we said our morning prayers, and then we had a little meditation period. The Redemptorists were big on meditating. Don't think in terms of Zen, but it was still a developed internal skill that nobody ever told you about before. It was thinking about those little readings that they had developed. And then at the end of it, you were supposed to make some kind of resolution to – you know – do good and avoid evil." He laughs. "Whatever. But it was a training. It was the beginning of training and adapted to what high school kids could deal with. So when one of these Japanese Zen guys asked me, 'When did you begin meditation?' 'Age twelve.' I didn't begin Zen at that age, but I began a meditation, an interior discipline."

"So you said you finally knew you had a vocation about six months prior to ordination."

"Well, you know, as ordination got closer it started to dawn on me, 'Gee! This is serious! Am I gonna do this the rest of my life?' And I decided, yeah, that's what I wanted to do, and I even told the Dean of Men at the time... I was out walking with him after lunch or something or supper, I don't remember, but I do remember exactly where I was. And this guy had the power to say, 'Cross this guy off the list. He just doesn't make the cut.' And I turned to him, and I said, 'I don't care what you think. I should be a priest. And if you don't ordain me, I'm going to sit on your doorstep until you do.' But that was the moment when I really made up my mind. 'Yep, this is what I'm gonna do.' I must have been 24 years old about that time."

"Are Redemptorists a missionary order?"

"Yeah. Founded by Alphonsus Liguori in the Kingdom of Naples in 1732. Founded specifically to deal with those who... The term that we use among ourselves is 'the most abandoned.' The most abandoned. There were a lot of clergy in the cities at that time, but the countryside was very neglected. Conditions were primitive. A lot of superstition. And so Alphonsus – the first modern Doctor of the Church, by the way – he saw the need and the neglect and said, 'We should dedicate ourselves to helping these people in their faith.' So that's how we got started. And then we moved up into Germany, and from there – you know, Germans being Germans, they're really organized – we followed the immigrants around the world."

Greg was ordained in 1970, and his first posting was as the librarian at the Redemptorist high school seminary in Louisiana. "Which was extremely depressing for a young, energetic priest. I only lasted there six months, then I was reassigned to a Redemptorist parish in New Orleans because a classmate was having trouble with the old fathers. He wasn't getting along with them. And for some reason they thought that by putting two of us together, it would dilute the problems. I was only there for a year or so, then I was invited to be on staff at the Palisades Retreat Center outside of Tacoma, Washington – a place called Federal Way – which is what I really wanted to do. I wanted to do retreats."

Although Greg's formal studies had come to an end after ordination, he pursued a personal interest in spiritual direction and had taken training with a Jesuit spiritual director, Armand Nigro, in Spokane, Washington. "We were studying the spiritual exercises of St. Ignatius and the rules for discernment."

"What did you understand spiritual direction to be?" I ask.

"Spiritual direction, to me, meant helping, guiding people in deepening their relationship with Jesus. Basically. I was lucky in the seminary. From very early on, from the first year I had some very good spiritual directors who were trained in pastoral counseling which was very new in the '50s. I was also trained in a form of pastoral counseling, and basically the premise behind it is everybody has what they need within themselves in order to grow as individuals."

"How very Zen." I note.

"Yes. And that was the foundation for me in my understanding of spiritual direction. Everybody has within themselves. And my task as a spiritual director was to help people respond to what the grace of God was in them – for them – and not to impose anything. The perfect image of that is husbandry. You help the garden grow; you don't make it grow. You don't determine what the plants are. You help the garden grow."

Greg admits he wasn't immediately impacted by the changes being wrought by the Second Vatican Council. "If you had seen me after ordination, and even in my training with the Jesuits, I would probably be just a good Catholic priest trying to love Jesus. If I had been categorized at the time, I probably would have been considered conservative. Uh… you are going to ask when I got into Zen, right?"

"I promise," I say, laughing. "But I still want to lay the ground work. So we got you to Washington, and you were doing retreat work."

"For about ten years I was doing retreat work there. Both in Federal Way, which is just south of Seattle, Washington, and also in Spokane, Washington, at Immaculate Heart Retreat Center, which was sort of a hub for spiritual direction and directed retreats, at least in the Northwest. I was also preaching in parish missions. And at that time, I also got involved with the Progoff Intensive Journal and became a presenter, or what they call a consultant. I got involved with it because it was a wonderful tool for myself. I thought, 'This has something to do with spiritual direction. I want to know more about it.' So I learned it well enough so I could go and teach it or facilitate it. And I figured if I could teach it, then I would know it. And that's what I wanted to do. I wanted to know it. And it fit right into what was laid early in my training, that everybody has within themselves what they need in order to grow. Progoff had that philosophy too. It's all in there. The question is, 'How do you access is? How do you get to it? How do you listen to and accommodate the active inner wisdom that is available to all of us and formulate it for each life however it's accessed?'"

"So," I summarize, "in the 1970s you're doing retreat work, you're leading missions. The focus is pretty traditional – you used the word 'conservative' – Catholic spirituality, helping individuals discover their own potential and capacity to form a relationship with Jesus. Is this pretty close?"

"Yeah."

"Okay. So, how did you find out about Zen?"

"Completely by accident." He had been on retreat at Our Lady of Guadalupe Trappist Abbey in Lafayette, Oregon. "And the abbot there was Bernard McVeigh. Abbot Bernard. And he would come and see me every day in my retreat. And somewhere along the line, he invited me to a talk about Zen with a handful of the monks there who were practicing Zen twice a day. And Bernard invited me to come and sit in Zen with them, which I had no interest in whatsoever. It was fine with me if they wanted to do it, but I'm just trying to love Jesus. Well, eventually I accepted his invitation, and I asked him what to do. And he said, 'Well, you sit like this, and you just count your breath.' That was it. So I went and sat, and, as anybody who jumps into zazen knows, the only reward is that you get through it. About the only thing you can say is, 'Wow! I made that! I did that.'"

After his first attempt, he didn't think it was something he would go back to. But a little later, he did a six week retreat with the Trappists – "Bernard wanted me to be a Trappist," Greg tells me – and during the course of it, he joined the monks who regularly sat zazen. There were six of them, out of a community of forty. In the end, Greg remained a Redemptorist, but one with a new spiritual practice. "I thought the Trappist life was really sane. It was wonderful. I really liked it. But that wasn't my vocation. I couldn't say 'yes' to it. And while I was there, of course, there was much more regular sitting, a regular experience of sitting in zazen. And somewhere along the line, Robert Aitken came to the monastery to give a talk. And I remember being in a small group with him, and I have no idea what he was talking about. I don't remember. I didn't understand what he was talking about. But I do remember very clearly looking at him and saying, 'I don't know what that man has, but I want it.' And that's really when I think I jumped into Zen."

"I'm curious how you made sense of it," I say. "You'd been trained in that carefully crafted Ignatian type of spirituality and their discernment process. And now somebody tells you to sit still and count your breaths. How did you make sense of that as a spiritual exercise?"

"That's a very good question. And it plagued me for a long time. Here I was, sitting in zazen, counting my breath, and I was plagued with this question that came somewhere down the line, 'How can it be that sitting here doing nothing is any kind of spiritual practice? How can I, a good Catholic priest, sit here and just do nothing and call that a spiritual practice?' It really did plague me. And I might have asked Bernard. I don't remember if I asked or not. I never got an answer to the question. And over the course of about a year, it just faded away. It just was a non-issue."

"So if someone you were working with today put that question to you, how would you respond? 'How is this a spiritual activity? How is this getting me closer to Jesus? How is this making me a better person? A better Catholic?'"

He pauses, purses his lips, then says, smiling, "I don't know." Again, we're both laughing. "If you don't want to do it, don't do it."

"I guess that's what it comes down to," I say.

"It really does. I don't know. I have no idea. It's all a mystery to me."

In other interviews, I had pressed the point, but it's clear that I'm not going to get much more from Greg, so I move on.

"So it just wasn't an issue any more, you said. Then what happened, after you felt at ease or felt that this was somehow a valid exercise?"

"Very shortly... and I didn't know it at the time, I had no idea until much later, because I hadn't even heard of the word, I didn't understand anything. But I was sitting by myself where the monks sat in kind of a basement room that they had set up. I was sitting there, and I had a small kensho experience. I remember exactly what it was. I heard a bird. That's all. I *heard* a bird. Maybe for the first time in my life, I heard a bird. It was vivid and fresh. But I didn't know that it was significant. I had had a previous experience, before I got into Zen, on retreat in Spokane, where I was at the edge of a parking lot there, and looked down at the grass, and I saw a blade of grass. A green blade of grass. And I had reported that to my spiritual director, who didn't consider that to be of any significance. It was just passed over. It was not remarked upon. But I was struck by it. The vividness and the freshness of that experience. I wouldn't understand that these were kensho experiences until much later when I had my own very deep kensho experience. And then I looked back and, 'Oh, my God!' They were kinda like preambles or seductions to keep on going."

"When you had the experience of hearing the bird, were you doing breath meditation at the time or shikan taza or what?"

"You're giving me far too much credit. That sounds far too noble. I think by that time it was just a great ego project, that I was determined to succeed at this very difficult inner practice. I don't think there was any genuine spiritual or dedicated Zen practice going on. It was just another of these mountains to conquer. Trying to count my breath."

"What would you have imagined success at this to have been?"

"It started out as just being able to count ten breaths. The first success was just to be able to count to ten. And then to try to do that in a sustained way. And then, somewhere along the line, Aitken told me, 'When you count one, let there only be one in the whole universe.' And I was determined to do that. That, then, became the second goal – ego goal – to accomplish. And then one day it happened. It was only 'one.' Only 'two.' 'Wow! That's what they mean!' I don't know how to do it. I don't know how to tell people to do that. But it was a great ego effort I'm sure."

In October 1978, at Abbot Bernard's urging, Aitken agreed to offer a Zen retreat for Christians, and they asked Greg if they could make use of the Palisades Center. "I went to my boss and the guy said, 'Yes.' So we got the first Zen/Christian sesshin in Federal Way, Washington. It was a ten day sesshin. And instead of having Buddhist sutras and symbols, the Trappists had come up with Christian readings and psalms, and we had mass during sesshin. Very strictly disciplined, just like a sesshin is. You know, getting up at 4:30 in the morning and start sitting at 5:00."

This was the retreat to which Greg invited Pat Hawk. "I just assumed he'd been involved with Zen. So when Bernard wanted to have this sesshin with Bob Aitken, I told Pat, 'Why don't you come out and we're going to have this sesshin – Zen sesshin – and Bob Aitken's going to do it with this Christian stuff.' And he did. And after that sesshin, sometime afterwards we were reminiscing about it, and I can't remember how the conversation went, but he told me, 'I was never involved in Zen until you invited me out to this sesshin.' And then Pat Hawk winds up being the first Catholic priest in the United States to be given inka. Transmission."

Sesshin is, of course, very different from even regular daily zazen practice. There can be more than ten hours of seated zazen a day interspersed with short periods of kinhin, formal meditative walking. For the duration of the retreat, participants refrain from speaking, except in dokusan; eyes are kept lowered, and one is instructed to maintain one's practice even during work and rest periods. Helen Amerongen had told me Pat Hawk took to it "like a duck to water." It wasn't as easy for Greg.

"How did that first sesshin go for you?" I ask.

"Awful. Absolutely awful. It was the worst experience of my life. And I walked out, and I said, 'The hell with this. This is insane.' And then we had sesshin the next year. And because I had this very strong ego to conquer, I jumped in with both feet in the second sesshin. And walked out. And it wasn't till the *third* sesshin that I determined that I was going to conquer this son-of-a-gun and made it through the whole thing. And that was the last sesshin Aitken held in the Northwest. Then he turned it over to Willigis Jäger, because Willigis had just been made a Zen teacher by Yamada Roshi. And Aitken wasn't that comfortable – at that time – with all the Christian stuff. He didn't think he really knew how to address the issues that people were bringing to him in dokusan. So Willigis took over, and when I met Willigis I met my teacher. We spoke the same language and just had a compatibility right away. He was really the one who got me going in Zen."

Jäger's first thought had been that Greg's practice should be within the Christian contemplative tradition. Jäger offered retreats in both formats but kept them distinct. "When you did Zen, you did Zen. When you did contemplation, you did contemplation. And he did not mix the two; he did not poach terminology from the two different traditions and say, 'They are equivalent.' And I didn't really want to do contemplation. I wanted to do Zen under him. I said, 'No. I want to do Zen. I want to do koan study.'"

Greg attended each of the retreats Jäger offered in the US. "He would do three retreats in a row – ten day retreats in a row – and I made all of them. He would do a contemplation retreat, then sesshin, and then another contemplation retreat. Then he started his place in Würzburg, House Saint Benedict, and I would go over there whenever I could. I would take all my vacation and retreat time and put all the time together and go over there and study with him."

Greg's kensho experience occurred during this period but not during a retreat. I ask if he's comfortable talking about it.

"Sure, but I'm …" He sighs. "Well, I'll preface this by saying it's a bit arrogant, talking about kensho experience, but it has helped other people. So I'm willing to talk about it because other people have found value in it; some of my students have become my students because I've talked about this. And they've said, 'Oh, my God, he should understand.' Outside of that, I also want to preface this by saying kensho does not make anybody good or better or perfect."

The story of the development of North American Zen in the last two decades of the 20th Century is littered with stories of philandering Zen teachers, inflated egos, and questionable financial practices. "We've certainly had enough evidence of that in recent years," I say.

"We sure do. It does not make anybody better than anybody else. It can easily be usurped by – and *will* be usurped – by ego projects. Building the self up and all that kind of stuff. None of which is contrary to what the experience is and where it is to lead.

"It was 1985. It was May. At the end of May. And I was at the Redemptorist-staffed retreat center in Amarillo, Texas. And I was standing in front of my typing desk, a little typing desk. It was before computers, and I had one of these cheap electronic typewriters. And as I was standing there." He pauses and frowns slightly. "These words don't capture it, but it was like out of nowhere, out of this complete vast darkness, out of nowhere, I heard this roar begin. It just started to begin to roar. And it got louder and louder, and it just burst open. There wasn't a visual to it. It was auditory. It just burst." He is speaking very slowly. "And this explosion of utter, complete, total joy. It happened like I never ever, ever, ever imagined. And right after that, a moment, a second after that, I said, 'Ah! This is love.' And then, a second after that, 'I am love. I'm not Greg. I'm love. All of this is love. It's not out there. It's...' And then I said, 'God is love.' I remembered from Saint John's letter. And then I said, 'I am God.' And then I said, 'That's dangerous.'"

He pauses again and purses his lips. "It was very profound, with lasting effects. The effects of that experience lasted for three years. And I saw Willigis within a few weeks. I had already planned to go over to Germany, and I saw him, and I was just irrepressible. I was irrepressible, and he was very impatient with me. And rightly so. And he was not at all pleased with my reaction. And chastised me strongly. 'You gotta come down off the mountain! You can't stay up there. You gotta get into ordinary, everyday life.' He was not pampering me at all – to the contrary – but I didn't really care. 'I don't know what this is, but it's better than any damn thing I've ever experienced.'" He smiles and chuckles lightly. "It took about three years to come down off that high."

❧

Greg continued his practice with Willigis and was eventually authorized as a teacher in the Sanbo Zen tradition. "It was Willigis's energy that was behind that," he tells me. "He kinda pushed my name with Kubota Roshi and Masamichi, Yamada's son." He shrugs. "He was pushing a lot of other names too, to get them to be teachers."

"I understand there are four ranks of teachers in the Sanbo Zen tradition."

"Yeah, that was introduced by Kubota Roshi and Masamichi. The old man, Koun Yamada, didn't seem to have this organizational stuff. 'Ah, go teach.' But now there's assistant teacher, teacher, associate roshi, and roshi."

"And where are you on that scale?"

"I'm an associate roshi. But that's in Sanbo Kyodan, Sanbo Zen. I consider my lineage comes from Willigis, and he made me a Zen teacher and also a roshi."

Currently, Greg is the Director of the East-West Meditation Program established at the Mercy Center in Burlingame, California by Thomas Hand. He tells me, however, that he had only met Hand a couple of times. "And this was after he had retired and was ill. He had cancer and was dying. I had no real interaction with him."

I ask him to tell me about the Mercy Center.

"Well, the founders – our foundresses – were Sister Suzanne Toolan and Sister Marguerite Buchanan. What is Mercy Center today had been – as was typical – built as a novitiate and was later turned into a retreat center by Suzanne and Marguerite. And then they invited Tom Hand to be on the staff, and he developed this meditation program because he had been stationed in Japan as a Jesuit and had practiced Zen with Yamada Roshi. He never really advanced or never did koan studies, but he brought what he knew and set up a meditation program. The way the Mercy Center is run today is mainly due to Sister Mary Anne Schofield who founded Spiritual Directors International as a training place for spiritual directors. And it's still a training place for spiritual directors. It's still noted for its spiritual exercises and its East-West Meditation Program. And there's a lot of other stuff that goes on, of course. That's not the only thing. Retreat Centers cannot survive without hosting a lot of other groups. But they don't have any control over it. They just provide the facilities. I do not know of any retreat center that does not have income outside of its main ministry. Facilities are money pits, and, if you do nothing, they will bankrupt you."

"How did you become involved at the Mercy Center?"

"Tom Hand had retired, and the Mercy Center director at the time was Diarmuid Rooney. He was a Benedictine monk and had been sent from Ireland, from his monastery to study at Berkeley, and he ended up leaving the Benedictines and doing everything proper and marrying one of his fellow students. But they had hired him to be the director of the Mercy Center. And when Thomas Hand retired, Diarmuid was very interested in keeping the meditation program going, and he was looking for somebody to fill Tom Hand's shoes. So my name came up on the list. And he called me and asked me about it. So first I came out and did a sesshin-type thing in the summer to see if it was okay. 'You should see what I do before we go any further. Here are my skill sets, and this is what I do. If you want me to do something different than that, then we wouldn't be able to continue this conversation.' So, I did that a couple of times, and we kind of played cat and mouse, posing all these hypotheticals. You know? He'd go, 'I'm not saying I would, but if I were to offer you the possibility to come out here, would that be worth pursuing do you think? Would that be a possibility? Not that I would do it. Which, you know…' That type of tentative stuff. My answer was always, 'Well, Diarmuid, I don't know if I'd want to do that, but if I did have the support and the blessing of my provincial…' And all that kind of stuff. Eventually it all worked out."

"Why do you think Diarmuid Rooney recruited you? What made you an attractive candidate?"

"I think what sold Diarmuid was that I was in the same Zen tradition as Tom Hand, so there would not be a disruption of the program." He smiles and lowers his voice slightly. "Besides that, there was nobody else. Don't make it sound too wonderful, because the choice of candidates was very limited. He'd asked Ruben Habito to come out there, and Ruben had said, 'I can't do that.'"

Greg offers four retreats a year at the Center. Continuing the tradition of both Jäger and Pat Hawk, two are specifically directed at Christians. The other two are more purely Zen sesshin.

"And sometimes Christians take part in the Zen retreats?" I ask.

"Anybody can take part in anything. It doesn't matter to me. It matters to others, but it doesn't matter to me."

In addition, he hosts a weekly zazen session with dokusan and a talk. "And once a month we meet for zazenkai on a Saturday, on the first Saturday of the month. And then on Sunday morning we meet for – Tom Hand had started this – a Center Day. The format doesn't change; it's the same. The practice. Doing it together. Dokusan. Getting to talk to me about your practice or your koan, those who are doing koans. And a talk usually trying to encourage them in their practice."

"A teisho."

"A teisho. Or if I've had this brilliant idea that I really think the whole world needs to know, that will unveil the great mysteries of the universe, I will expound to all lengths about that."

"I'm sorry I'm not close enough to attend one of these," I say, laughing. "I've been waiting to have those mysteries explained to me."

"It sounded good at the time. You know?"

He estimates that there are between 150 and 200 persons who regularly take part in the programs.

∾

"What does Zen have to offer Catholics that they can't get from Ignatian spirituality or Benedictine forms of prayer?"

"How to do Apophatic practice." "Apophatic" is a term I will hear several times in the course of conducting the interviews for this book, but this is the first time I encounter it.

"I don't know what that means," I admit.

"There are two great traditions in Catholic spirituality. It's really an Orthodox spirituality. Cataphatic and apophatic. Cataphatic, coming from the word 'light,' is liturgy, vocal prayer, mental prayer, mental images. It is attempting to approach the mystery of the transcendent God through the limited human capacities that human beings have. That's cataphatic. Apophatic spirituality really means emptiness, nothingness. And it is the recognition that *any* human effort or capacity has to fall short and ultimately be misleading when it comes to the Divine. To God. And so apophatic eschews, or puts aside all of those cataphatic tools, and enters into silence or emptiness or nothing. The early Christian Hesychasts were like that. Then if you read Pseudo-Dionysius, he's like that too. What Zen offered me was a 'how to.' How to do this. Very practical. 'You sit like this. You count your breath like this. You do it for this long. You enter into the apophatic by becoming Mu.' It doesn't matter if you call it God or Mu, 'cause all of that stuff is inadequate. So it was very practical.

"When I was in seminary, they talked about contemplative prayer and mysticism, but they made it sound like it was completely out of reach. That only if you were really, really, *really* good and pure would God give you the grace, the mystical graces, of this union with God. And contemplation wasn't something to be cultivated; it was a gift to be given. So basically what they were saying is, 'There's nothing you can do.' Well, that happens to be true. There is nothing you can do in order to make anything happen. That is quite true. But it's also true that they didn't understand what they were talking about, because I think it's quite available to anybody at any time. It's true you don't have any control over making anything happen. But there are things you can do which…" He taps his finger on the desk, looking for the right word.

"That predispose you?" I suggest.

"That's a very good way of putting it. Predispose you to it."

When I ask him if by "it" he means "kensho," we get into a discussion about the difficulty of defining terms when talking about spiritual matters. But eventually he tells me, "Kensho is a human event that breaks through the analytical, what's called the delusive thinking, so that the raw experience, the raw reality is presented completely and totally without interference."

But the insight that comes with kensho is not complete in itself. It is capable of refinement, of being deepened, of being more fully integrated into one's personality and life. And that is the function of koan training. "If you're going to take advantage of what koans do, you have to have the initial breakthrough," he tells me. "You can benefit from koans without that breakthrough, but you're not going to get the richness of it and the real revolutionary element in the pedagogy. You're not going to get it."

Getting back to the issue of what Zen has to offer Catholics, I say, "So the intent of the practice – whether I'm attending the retreat for Christians or the Zen sesshin – the intent is to bring me to awakening. Is that correct?"

"I still have problems with the language, but correct. But in this tradition – in my tradition – it's what do you do after kensho that's important. I can't make anybody have anything, and nobody can make themselves have anything, but those who have this breakthrough, what do you do then? And that's where the tradition blossoms."

One of the most significant developments in contemporary North American Zen is the growing emphasis on the importance of karuna. Traditional Zen training is said to cultivate two qualities – prajna (wisdom) and karuna (compassion). The first generation of Zen teachers in America focused much of their effort on helping students attain prajna – through kensho – because without that insight there was no Zen. The second generation of teachers discovered, however, that wisdom (prajna) without compassion (karuna) was of little value. Greg's point is essentially the same as that which both Maria Reis Habito and Elaine MacInnes had made. Zen training begins by cultivating wisdom/insight, then the student learns to manifest that wisdom in one's life and activities through compassion.

"I have a little plaque right in the zendo," Greg tells me. "It says, 'Compassion is the heart of enlightenment.' Here's where the Christian tradition comes in. I'm not saying compassion is not found in a Buddhist Asian tradition. But the emphasis in the Christian tradition is love. The definition of love is not a verbal definition, it's a modality, it's pouring oneself out for the other. And after kensho you get this experience of whatever you call it – No Self, vastness, anything – now it's time to love, and this means pouring yourself indiscriminately out for the other. That is the heart of life regardless of whatever experience you have. It's not being blissful; it's not being peaceful. It's not doing any of these things. It is pouring the self out for the other indiscriminately. That's the heart of the matter. That's my teaching. No! Not my teaching! That's Jesus's teaching."

"Then why is it," I ask, "that in the Zen tradition there have been so many transmitted teachers who've behaved in a variety of non-compassionate manners?"

"It's a good question. It's a very good question." He takes a deep breath. "And I've been thinking about these things. You know, one of the advantages of a well-established tradition like they have in Asia is institutions; institutions are not going to eliminate those things, but they'll give some structures where they can be caught a little better and dealt with. And human nature… Just because you have kensho doesn't mean you're perfect. As Willigis told me many times in his language, his words, 'The ego has a thousand faces to show you. Selfishness is the wolf in the house ready to jump on any visitor that comes in.'"

"Selfishness is the wolf in the house that's ready to jump on any visitor that comes in," I repeat to make sure I heard it correctly.

"That's right. And you have to be aware of it. You're not going to get rid of it. You have to be aware of it. The principle is pouring the self out for the other. It is not getting my needs met. That is not compassion; that is not love."

"Earlier I asked you what Zen had to offer Catholicism, and you said 'a way to apophatic prayer.' What does Catholicism have to offer Zen?"

"Love," he says simply. "Pouring the self out for the other."

CHAPTER ELEVEN

Robert Kennedy

Robert Kennedy's[150] Dharma name is Jinsen. His teacher, Bernie Glassman, explains that the name means "the fountain of God or that place where God springs up in the world to be a source of light and peace to all."[151] There are, Glassman points out, two paths that Zen trainees follow, and while they are usually combined they should not be confused – the path of the teacher and the path of the priest.

> The path of the Zen teacher is to fully realize, and then to transmit, the unconditional experience that is the essential core of Zen and, I believe, the core of all mystical traditions … The path of the Zen priest is the clerical or liturgical path that celebrates the essential experience of the oneness of all life.[152]

Robert Kennedy is a Zen teacher in the lineage of Koun Yamada and Taizan Mae-zumi[153] of Los Angeles and a priest in the Roman Catholic church. When I once referred to him as a Catholic Zen Teacher, he corrected me, saying that he was a Zen Teacher who happened to be Catholic. "The phrase 'Catholic Zen' can imply we are mixing Zen and Catholicism into something new." That is not his intent; he and his heirs "strive to practice Zen as it is taught by our Zen teachers, but Catholics can pay attention too."

---

150   Cf. McDaniel, *Cypress Trees in the Garden*, pp. 134, 303-10, 318-19, 468, 469.

151   Robert Kennedy, *Zen Spirit, Christian Spirit* (New York: Continuum, 1995), p. 10.

152   Ibid., p. 9.

153   Cf. McDaniel, *The Third Step East: Zen Masters of America*, Chapter Nine.

"I was born," he writes, "in an Irish Catholic ghetto in Brooklyn, New York, to a devout family, and was educated by nuns and priests. And so it will come as no surprise... that on graduating from a Jesuit high school, I immediately joined the Jesuits and vowed to stay there."[154] He describes himself as a traditional, conservative Catholic grounded in pre-Vatican II theology. When the opportunity arose to go to Japan to do missionary work while completing his training, he accepted it with enthusiasm. Then, as he puts it, "the wind of Vatican II... blew away the form of the Catholic Church as I knew it."[155] He admits resisting those changes.

> My temperament and training ... led me to cling to the only form
> of Catholic life I knew. I tried to be faithful to what I was taught,
> but finally the dike had more holes than I had fingers and the flood
> of changes in my life swept away my old religious certitudes. Most
> painfully, I lost my way in prayer.[156]

He had yet to learn, as he put it, "that faith is never to be identified with the cultural forms of any given age, and especially so when that cultural form is taken for granted and deeply loved"[157] – an insight which is as true of institutional Zen as it is of the Catholic church.

"I was in Japan for almost eight years," he tells me, "and had no interest in Zen or Buddhism at all. My interest was elsewhere. I was studying Japanese and teaching in a Jesuit high school in Kobe and doing theology in Japan. I was ordained in Japan in 1965. And then I returned to the States for graduate studies."

It was on his way back to the US that he visited the Philippines, where Ruben Habito heard him speak about the need for missionaries to bring the gospel to Japan.

His interest in Zen was piqued a few years later as he was listening to the radio while driving. It was in the early '70s, when young Americans were populating Zen centers in places like San Francisco and Rochester in surprising numbers, and the radio program was a talk by Alan Watts. "And he said, 'Have you noticed that nature is never symmetrical – or rarely symmetrical – it's more like sand thrown in the wind.' I don't know why that statement hit me with the strength that it did, but I remember that I had to stop the car and think about this extraordinary moment. I forget the purpose of the talk and everything else about it except for that one statement. Which is the way, I think, that we learn sometimes. It's like striking a match. Sometimes it lights, and sometimes it doesn't. But that made me stop and begin to sit. Now why

---

154   Kennedy, op. cit., p. 11.

155   Ibid.

156   Ibid.

157   Ibid., p. 13.

I began to sit, why that question in my mind made me sit is another thing I cannot answer.

"Of course I started reading about Zen. I felt it was a way to go. There was something in my spirit that said I had to stop doing theology and turn to experience. Turn away from theory and learn from my own doing. Because Zen isn't a thinking thing. It's 'let's do it.' And I realized I had to *do* it finally.

"It was, as Catholics say, a great grace, a great gift. Although at the time I didn't know it, I was filled with a lot of confusion. Of course, this was after the Second Vatican Council when there was a great deal of confusion in the church and some experimentation, and I was part of that generation. So I sat for a few years by myself, and then I knew I had to have a teacher."

He was teaching theology and introductory Japanese to business students at St. Peter's University in Jersey City and made use of his sabbatical year in 1976 to return to Japan. "This time not as a teacher but as a pilgrim," he tells me.

He sought out fellow Jesuits who had been working with Yamada Roshi and other Zen Masters. "How ironic it was," he wrote later, "that in my attempt to put a firm foundation under my religious life, I turned to a wisdom tradition that knew that there was no firm foundation to life and that there was nothing 'religious' about life either. What a grace that was, though I didn't know it then."[158]

One of his companions in Japan was William Johnston, who explained that Zen was not so much a religion as a way of looking at life. The two of them went to Kyoto "where we walked under a blazing sun from temple to temple, sitting with any master who would have us."[159] Their discussions with these masters, however, remained at the level of theory. They were still inquiring into the phenomenon of Zen rather than encountering Zen itself.

Looking back on that summer, Kennedy compared it to a story about Master Baso Doitsu found in two classic koan collections, the *Hekiganroku* (*Blue Cliff Record*) and the *Shoyoroku* (*The Book of Serenity*). Amplifying the originally spare narrative,[160] Kennedy applies it to his own awkward initial inquiries into Zen:

> A visitor comes to Master Baso and asks him to show directly, without theories or propositions or negations, what the meaning of Buddhism is. Baso says he is too tired for instruction and suggests

---

158 Ibid., p. 12.

159 Ibid.

160 Case 73 in the *Hekiganroku*: A monk said to Master Baso, "Abandoning the four propositions and one hundred negations, what is the meaning of Bodhidharma's coming from the West?" Baso replied, "I'm tired today, ask the monk Chizo." The monk asked Chizo, who said, "I have a headache. Go ask Kai." Brother Kai said, "Coming to this point I don't understand." The monk reported this to Baso, who said, "Chizo's head is white; Kai's head is black."

he ask the head monk. The visitor turns away from Baso (and from the very "direct pointing" he asked for) and goes to the head monk.

The head monk tells the visitor that he isn't well and is not up to instruction today and suggests that the visitor ask the cook. The visitor turns away from the head monk (and from the very "direct pointing" he asked for) and goes to the cook.

The cook says that the meaning of Buddhism is a very big question, that he knew the answer once, but over the years he has forgotten it. Now he just makes soup, but it is good soup. Would the visitor care to taste it? The visitor turns from the cook (and from the very "direct pointing" he asked for) and returns to Baso.

Baso asks the visitor, "Well, did you learn the meaning of Buddhism?" "No," said the visitor. "But your head monk is sick and your cook has stopped thinking. What a monastery!"

That night the three old friends sipped rice wine after dinner:

"Well," said the head monk, "did your visitor learn the meaning of Buddhism?"

"I don't think so," said Baso. "He seemed disappointed with us."

"And he didn't taste the soup," said the cook.

"A pity," said the head monk. "All the way here on his sabbatical and he didn't learn anything."

"Perhaps next year," said Baso. "Besides, there is another teacher on sabbatical coming here tomorrow."

"To learn the meaning of Buddhism?" asked the head monk.

"Yes," said Baso. "I'll send him around to you."

"Maybe he'll taste my soup," said the cook.[161]

The monk had the living example of Baso before him, Kennedy notes, but, instead of recognizing this, sought for an answer. Likewise the head monk and cook showed him the state of his mind, and he turned away from them as well. "I would laugh," Kennedy writes, "had I not done the same thing in Kyoto myself."[162]

Finally, he tells me, he visited Koun Yamada's zendo in Kamakura.

"I remember the first time he walked into the zendo before I met him personally. I was sitting in the back, up against the back wall. I remember vividly the way he walked in to light the incense and to begin the day of sitting. Again, I cannot explain it. The very sight of him walking into the zendo was life changing. Why? I cannot explain. He was younger than I am now, but he seemed old then. He was 68, and

161 Kennedy, op. cit., pp. 91-92.
162 Ibid.

stocky, a heavy-set man. But gentle. He was a gentleman. And educated. He knew English and German, and, of course, he kept urging us to learn Japanese and for me to improve my Japanese. And he was gracious and welcoming which was tremendous in itself. He drew many foreigners to him. He was open to foreigners, open to Christians, open to Catholic priests and nuns, and we came to him in great numbers. There must have been a dozen priests and a dozen nuns who were actively sitting.

"I remember him saying, 'I'm not trying to make you a Buddhist. I want to empty you in imitation of your lord, Jesus Christ.' And that was a wonderful, liberating experience. He swept away, in a sense, all talk about Buddhism. And this was something Maezumi – his Dharma brother – also shared in California. I remember Maezumi shouting to a student once, 'Stop talking about Buddhism! Go into the zendo and sit!' And, in a more gentle way, that is what Yamada Roshi wanted us to do. He opened his home to us; he opened the zendo to us. And truly our faith did not matter. What mattered was our capacity to pay attention. As he said, 'Some foreigners come to Japan, and their will power is strong. Some come and their will power is not so strong.' It was interesting. He focused on will power, on our ability to concentrate. He never asked about what faith we had."

"How long did you remain in Japan on this occasion?" I ask.

"It was just the spring semester of 1976. Then I came back to the States. Yamada recommended I go to Taizan Maezumi, his Dharma brother in Los Angeles, and that's what I did. I finished the year by sitting in California."

The chief administrator at the Zen Center of Los Angeles at that time was Bernie Glassman, an aeronautical engineer working for McDonnell-Douglas where he developed manuals for trajectories to send theoretical manned missions to Mars.

"When I returned to New York it was to teach full time, and at that time I was without a teacher. I went back summers to sit with Maezumi. But it was around 1980 when Glassman came to New York and set up shop as a Zen teacher there that I became his student. He became my teacher.

"He had a doctorate in mathematics from UCLA, but then he met Maezumi and gave himself completely to Zen. He said it was not easy for him. He made a sesshin before becoming a monk where he realized, 'This is my life.' But he also felt it was his vocation to work for what he called 'the hungry ghosts,' people – not just Buddhists but of all faiths – who needed help in their lives. They are the ones that he wanted to work with. And therefore there's a great social emphasis in Glassman's work. I think it came from his Jewish socialism and concern for social issues. He said a lot of people like Zen because they like to sit in a zendo where it's nice and quiet and peaceful and has a certain artistic flavor. The last time I saw him, a few weeks ago, he said to me, 'Some people like Zen clubs, where they can sit together with like-minded people, where they can be quiet together.' But he brought us out on the street, where we lived with the poor. We were without money. Just begging for money to get a cup of coffee when we needed it. And we were to experience what it's like to have nothing and to live with these disenfranchised people. And that was his main goal as a Zen teacher. To be with the poor and to work with them. He gave us that orientation."

Kennedy studied with Bernie Glassman for eleven years. "And they were wonderful years. Glassman moved around a bit. He started out in northern New York, up in the Bronx. We were given a nice home there for a zendo, but we couldn't afford to stay there, so we moved to a poorer section in Yonkers. And then we moved to a convent that we were able to buy. They were very interesting years. And, again, I didn't live there. I had my own Jesuit life. But I saw him at least once a week and attended many of the sesshins that he ran. I did the koans every week. He was very gracious to me. He always had time for me and encouraged me."

"He was open to non-Buddhists undertaking Zen practice?"

"Oh, absolutely! They all were; every Zen teacher I had – Yamada Roshi, Maezumi Roshi, Glassman Roshi – they were all very open. They knew who I was, what I was, and what I wanted."

"And how did your order feel about this?"

"The Jesuits encouraged me. They support interreligious work. Jesuits have a long history in Japan and a long history of working with Buddhists. I think in the beginning, it started out with some argument and confrontation, but that was quickly resolved and turned into respect and appreciation and cooperation."

"And the broader church?"

"Well, when you talk about the Vatican, remember there are at least twenty-six major divisions in the Vatican, and they don't speak with one voice. The past two popes – John Paul II and Pope Benedict – certainly encouraged interreligious work. They recognized that this was essential to our Catholic faith, and we had to be open to others. Now that doesn't mean that every priest in the church is equally open to it. But what the Church itself wants and what they constantly urge is interfaith cooperation, that we understand the other, that we appreciate the otherness of them. Not just where they agree with us, but to appreciate their truth that is not necessarily our truth. And finally we were urged – certainly by the Jesuits – to practice with them, to practice their truth, to walk in their shoes. Otherwise we cannot really know them. So that's what I've followed. That's not to say that all bishops are happy with this work, but the teaching of the church is consistent in that this is what should be done. And the Society is deeply involved in this. If I had not been a Jesuit, if I had not been in Japan, I probably would never have thought of Buddhism in my life. So I owe it to the Jesuits and to the church because they introduced me to Buddhism and urged me to pursue these ties, or encouraged me to pursue them."

In 1991, Kennedy completed his formal Zen studies, and Glassman gave him transmission. "I first thought I would just sit quietly by myself. I thought it was a good idea, after you become a teacher, to sit quietly for about ten years," he says laughing. "Ripen a bit, you know. But actually I couldn't sit quietly because Glassman gave me a student right away. Someone he had worked with as a teacher, and he gave her to me to finish the work, and see her through, and make her a teacher. And that was Sister Janet Richardson who's now in retirement in Florida and who is a great Zen teacher herself. Then a few people that I knew came and sat with me. And finally they convinced me that my one bedroom apartment was not suitable for a zendo, and one thing led to another, and we rented this apartment in the same building and turned it into a zendo."

This is the Morning Star Zendo.

"Right now it is an apartment owned by St. Peter's University in Jersey City, and we rent it. It's just a one bedroom apartment, but it suits us quite nicely. We have a kitchen, a little dining area, a place for a zendo, and a room for private instruction for students. No one lives there. We gather and do our Zen work there. We can sit a dozen comfortably, but on Saturday morning, when there's a big crowd, there's as many as twenty-five people there. That's crowded; it's not ideal."

His early students were all Catholic. "Now a few are not. I just made a Buddhist a teacher. The Buddhists were so good to me; the Zen community was so good to me; I'm happy to be generous with them. But most of them had some connection with the Catholic faith."

In addition to the time spent at the zendo in Jersey City, he tries to respond to requests he receives from elsewhere. "I try to say 'yes' to people who ask. You know, when people say they want me to come, I try to come. Especially if they send me a ticket, they really want me to come," he says, chuckling. "So I try to say 'yes' to everyone if I possibly can. Life has been very generous to me; I try to be generous with people too. I don't have to search them out. They come and ask, and I say, 'Yes, I will help them anyway I can.'"

"Where have these requests come from?"

"Well, just recently Mexico. There's a Zen teacher there that I've installed, Inge von Wobeser, in Mexico City. In England, Father Patrick Eastman teaches in the London area and in Ireland, in both North and South Ireland; Belfast in the North, and Dublin in the South. There are Zen groups there that are largely Christian in orientation. And, again, it doesn't matter what their faith is. I imagine it's similar to learning to play the piano or a musical instrument. When it's time to practice, you practice. You're not thinking about theology or religion, working on the violin or the piano or whatever it is. So in Zen, whatever your faith is. Stop thinking about it. Certainly stop arguing about it."

"That's an interesting thing for someone who taught theology to say," I remark.

"Well, theology has its place. Not everyone is interested in Zen or suited to Zen work. Theology has its place, just as poetry has its place, and history – the history of Zen. You can read the history of Zen, but don't stay there, don't start thinking about other people's ideas and other people's enlightenment. Develop your own. So put those thoughts aside. That's essential. We should not be arguing with one another. That's the great thing about Zen. It cuts off argument and argumentation and dispute, trying to prove your point or disprove someone else's point. I think Zen brings peace finally and an end to that type of religious confrontation that leads nowhere. I don't think anyone is ever converted by argument."

Some people, of course – he points out – are more likely to profit from Zen practice than others. "Like any other talent, some people who are tone deaf aren't going to be musicians, or if they're color blind they aren't going to be painters. People have different abilities." People who have a spiritual inclination, however, regardless of their cultural background or faith "can sit well together, profit from each other's experience, as I profited from Yamada and Maezumi. They were not Catholic. They were Buddhists. But they reached out and they helped me, and I try to do that with Buddhists and non-Buddhists. I sit with them and try to – as they say – appreciate the Great Function."

"Does that mean there is some kind of pre-discursive reality we all have access to, all have the capacity to share regardless of our cultural or religious backgrounds?"

"Well, I think I'd say there is no *thing* that we share together. There is no thing. It is an appreciation of where you are and – this phrase they use sometimes – the Great Function. The unity of it. It is not one thing." He pauses, then adds, "Once we start talking about things, it divides us. You know, dogma will divide us. We're just saying, for this time when we sit, put that aside. And that's what we share together, that common openness. We will not name the object of our devotion. We will not give a name to ourselves. We let life enter into us as things are. Things as they really are. That's a good phrase from the Dharma – you know – 'things as they are.' Not as we imagine or wish them to be."

∾

In his book, *Zen Spirit, Christian Spirit*, Kennedy states that Zen is not a competing religious doctrine to Catholicism but a cultivated perspective that can enhance one's faith, a

> way of contemplation that psychologically has much in common
> with true Christian prayer. And since as a way of contemplation,
> as Yamada Roshi and others say, it can be used without reference
> to its theological background, it can teach Christians a way to pray

that is imageless, silent, and conducive to unifying the Christian personality in a radical detachment from all things.[163]

In that detachment, one gives up one's dependence on one's beliefs, one's prejudices, one's conditioned points of view; it is a detachment from all that prevents one from seeing reality as it is, rather than as one imagines or wishes it to be. And it includes detachment from the images of God one formed as a child and often fails to move beyond. God, after all, is unknowable; therefore

> — as we do not know God, we do not know God's will. We do know that we are to serve, forgive, and be compassionate to one another, but how practically we are to do these things is only revealed to us moment by moment as the circumstances of our lives evolve. Therefore, those religious leaders who claim to know God's will and who impose that will on others are to be forgiven rather than followed … [164]

The humility of such a perspective, it strikes me, goes a long way to reconciling the challenge that theism poses to Zen.

"Yamada Roshi said to us — and to me personally — that he could believe in God, but he said that he could not believe that God would make a dualistic world," Kennedy tells me. "Well, there's no reason that Christians have to believe that God has made a dualistic world. He said, 'What Christians believe about God is that He transcends human experience, so Zen has nothing to say about that. Zen should not say Yes or No with regard to the existence of God, because the Semitic religions — the Jews, the Christians, the Muslims — believe God transcends human experience. It is a different order of being entirely about which Zen should not say anything.' I remember Glassman Roshi also said that when he first encountered Zen, he was a Jewish atheist, and then gradually he realized, 'I can't say Yes or No to this question. There's nothing in my Zen teaching or training that would have me say Yes or No to the existence of God, as Jews and Christians understand God, someone who transcends human experience.' Zen Buddhism is about human experience. They might question the legitimacy of faith in general, but if someone holds it, they would have nothing to say, they *should* have nothing to say about it."

---

163   Ibid., p. 33.
164   Ibid., p. 39.

Chapter Twelve

Janet Richardson

A lthough Sister Janet Richardson and I once spoke briefly on the phone, I have not met her either in person or by videoconference. The telephone conversation took place when friends of mine, who were wintering in the area of Florida where Janet now resides, tried to help her install Skype on her computer. They weren't successful because the machine was too old to have a built-in webcam. Consequently, she and I chose to communicate through an email exchange.

The dynamics of the written and spoken languages differ considerably. When speaking, we tend to be expansive; when writing informally, we tend to be concise. There is much that one inevitably misses in a written text – the individual's voice, their physical mannerisms and expressions – and one may try to fill in those elements mentally. As soon as that happens, one is back in the realm of imagination.

Robert Kennedy told me that Janet had been a student of Bernie Glassman who, once Kennedy had been given transmission, suggested she continue her study with him. Even such a simple declaration proves to be more complicated than it sounds. It turns out that the first Zen retreat Janet attended had been facilitated not by Glassman but by Kennedy, and it was Kennedy's opening Dharma talk that caught her attention and brought her into the practice.

In her first letter to me, she tells me that her Dharma name is Jinne, Beloved of God, and that she is a member of the Sisters of St. Joseph of Peace. I had asked if she was currently retired, and she wrote: "I don't think women religious ever retire. I am not gainfully employed now. My ministry is prayer. I continue with research and writing regarding the founder of our congregation, Mother Clare or Margaret Anna Cusack. I work at fulfilling the charism of our congregation which is 'Peace through Justice' as best I can."

And, of course, I formed an initial impression from this letter that was almost entirely inaccurate. Her life and accomplishments prove to be more complex and remarkable than I at first imagined. Even her order, the Sisters of St. Joseph of Peace, turns out to have a more intriguing history than I'd assumed. It was an order forged in social engagement and conflict with the patriarchal structure of the church hierarchy. The "justice" to which Janet refers in describing its mission was originally a matter of responding to legal and political structures in 19th century Ireland that degraded and exploited the poor and had a disproportional impact on women and children.

∾

Janet Richardson was born in Brooklyn in 1925 and grew up in the township of Millburn, New Jersey. It was a bedroom community. "Many of the fathers commuted to NYC," she writes, "and the mothers worked at home." Her parents' marriage was what, at the time, was called "mixed." Her father was Protestant and her mother Catholic. Such unions were usually only permitted on condition that the non-Catholic agreed the children would be raised in the church. It was a small family by Catholic standards. Janet's only sibling is a younger sister, Sally. "My recollection is of a happy family life."

She tells me that she would not have called her family devout – although "religion was part of our up-bringing and family life" – and she refers to her Catholicism as "a counter-cultural experience."

"None of my chums were Catholic. There were no Catholics in our neighborhood, and we lived a great distance from our parish church and school. So, my sister and I went to the nearby public school. That was a very satisfactory experience in every way. The local schools were – and are today – among the best in the state. Religious education was a family affair. Friends of my mother in a nearby town had a lay catechist, Miss Milliken, come every Friday afternoon, and we attended classes there along with several other children. I still have the candlestick she provided at First Communion."

Her father drove them to the parish church but remained in the car reading the Sunday papers while his wife and daughters attended mass. He did join them, however, for what Janet calls a form of "shared prayer" on the sun porch on Sundays. "The four of us gathered, and my parents did some reading from scripture or poetry or some other worthwhile text. I do not recall any response from my sister or me, but the warmth of the sun and of the family gathering made it a memorable experience."

Church doctrine in the 1930s could be uncompromising. The local pastor declared that parents who did not send their children to the parochial school were guilty of mortal sin, which meant they would be condemned to eternal damnation if they died without repentance. Although Janet was young, she was bright enough to dismiss the idea. "I knew my mother was the best person in the world, and my father close to her, so the pastor must be in error. Besides, the local drug store – which had a liquor department – was often seen making deliveries at the rectory. Rumor suggested that there was not that much need for aspirin. So we had some doubts about the clergy."

The Richardson family did, however, accede to the pastor's insistence that Catholic children not participate in programs at the YMCA, a Protestant organization, and, as a result, Janet and her sister were unable to take part in the swimming lessons their friends attended. "So my mother arranged for us to have horseback riding lessons instead. When it came to joining Girl Scouts, which everyone did, it seemed to me there was a bit of fudging. The meetings were in the basement of a local Protestant church, but we never actually went into the church itself. In High School, it was the Episcopalian Church which provided teen dances on Sunday evening, which was another dilemma."

Other things about being Catholic put one out of step with the rest of the community. On Holy Days of Obligation,[165] Catholics were required to attend mass. "That meant I would be late for school, would have to go to the office to get a slip to admit me to class, and then walk in late. Also, the music teacher was Catholic and always singled me out to ask the hours of mass on holy days which I found embarrassing."

Generally, however, her memories of high school are good ones. She remembers "competent, effective teachers who helped each one of us do our very best and achieve our goals." On the other hand, "It seemed remarkable that in history the 'bad guys' were always Catholic kings or leaders, but we didn't study much about Catholicism and so my ignorance was bliss."

I ask what her goals and ambitions had been.

"When I was a child I recall that when people asked, 'What do you want to be when you grow up?' my sister would always respond, 'I want to be a mommy.' My response was always something like: 'I want to climb Mount Everest or sail on the Kon Tiki raft.' Amelia Earhart was a heroine for me."

In high school, her immediate ambition was to get into college. "Which I did at New Jersey College for Women, now part of Rutgers University. I was accepted at a Catholic college, but my father thought it was too far away. After college, the goal was to get a job. I worked as a translator for a few weeks, but the commuting was unpleasant and I quit. A mother of one of my sister's friends was an adoption social worker, and she suggested I try Catholic Charities. It was a whole new world! Everyone was Catholic! Religion took on a whole new dimension in my life. The women religious I met were very impressive, and then Mother de la Salle asked me to give her ten reasons why I would not come and help her Sisters. I couldn't think of a one and so I entered!"

---

165 There were five in addition to Christmas: the Solemnity of Mary, January 8; the Feast of the Ascension of Jesus, the 40th day after Easter; the Feast of the Assumption of Mary, August 15; All Saints Day, November 1; and the Feast of the Immaculate Conception of Mary, December 8.

That condensation of events is an example of the challenges of doing an interview by correspondence.

In response to my request for more information regarding Catholic Charities, she explains that the US Conference of Catholic Bishops had set up Catholic Charities in most dioceses "to offer family services, child care services, adoption services, food aid, and other social services. I was a family caseworker for two to three years and then an institutional caseworker for about four years. The children had been placed in institutions for various reasons: parental death or illness, court placements for those in trouble with the law, family dysfunction. Today most states provide foster care, but, in those days, that was not the practice."

Janet helped place children in foster care, provided casework service during the placements, and worked with families to provide post-placement care, or – in the situations where there was no family – supervised further placements. Given the number of children in care, caseworkers were unable to spend enough time with any given child in order to establish a relationship. It was clear to Janet that the children's needs were not being adequately addressed.

"Mother de la Salle was the superior at St. Joseph's Home for Boys. She listened as I described the needs for more individual care that I saw for children in all diocesan childcare institutions, and I understood that she heard my concerns and was giving me direction to respond to my concerns. These children could have more individualized care if I added my time to that of the other Sisters allowing them, too, more time, energy, and skill for the children. That's the way I saw it."

I ask how her family reacted to her vocation.

"They were very opposed," she reports. "My aunt came with tickets for a round-trip to Europe for herself and me, but I demurred. My uncle came up from Florida, saying little but communicating great displeasure. My parents were very upset. My sense is that my mother supported whatever I wanted to do – after all I was 29 – but she feared for my health. My father said 'no' and never came to visit me although he brought my mother." As he had done when he had driven the girls and their mother to church, he remained in the parking lot.

I suspect I am more sympathetic to the concept of religious vocations than Janet's father might have been, but I can understand how he must have felt. I wrote back telling her I remained unclear why she chose the convent. She had said that Mother de la Salle had asked her to give ten reasons for not entering, but what were the reasons *for* entering? "Would you," I asked, "have described yourself as a particularly pious person?"

She writes back that my letter reminded her of Pascal's line, "The heart has reasons that reason does not know," and of the words of her postulant mistress who said that a religious vocation is a call from God. "To clarify: Piety? Pretty clothes, dates, and dancing left me little time or energy for piety. Mr. Barr in our high school guidance class taught us about integrity, 'walking the talk.' This impressed me, and so, when at college, I went to the parish church for mass and monthly confession. My college roommate and friend of many years, not a Catholic, recalled that I read the Bible each night before going to bed. My recollection is that I'd been told there was some kind of reward for this although I didn't catch what it was; but a reward for fifteen minutes of daily reading seemed a good deal to me. I tried the Newman Club, but it didn't hold my attention. Your question reminds me that sixty-plus years ago the parish confessor asked me if I had ever considered a religious vocation. My negative answer then makes me wonder now if he had heard something pious in my confession."

The first phase of convent training – the postulancy – lasted nine months, followed by a two year novitiate, which she describes as "demanding but rewarding." After taking first vows at the end of the Novitiate period, she entered the Juniorate. "The discipline of the novitiate gave way to greater personal responsibility," she tells me. "When the two years of this formation were over, we went on mission; mine was the parish school where I had been teaching."

After that she had an extensive and varied career. She began as a French teacher at Caldwell College in New Jersey. Then her superior suggested, given her language skills, that she take a job at the United Nations. "I didn't ask her why. The UN was looking for agronomists, foresters, economists, and other highly specialized people. I knew a woman lawyer who was at the Holy See Mission to the UN; she suggested I try there and so I did. Most of the staff spoke Italian, English and French; so I began Italian studies."

She served in several roles at the Mission. "I was the press officer, a member of the United Nations General Assembly Third Committee which deals with social and cultural affairs, and on the delegation to various international conferences. Once or twice, I served on the General Assembly Second Committee which deals with economic affairs. I was liaison with youth groups and so on." She remained with the Permanent Observer Mission of the Holy See to the UN from 1967 to 1980, then became executive director of the International Catholic Organizations Information Center and later was the Assistant Director, Church Affairs, for Catholic Relief Services.

∾

It was during her time with the Holy See Mission, when she was nearing 50 years of age, that she first became involved with Zen. "A colleague at Caldwell College, the chairperson of the Religious Studies department, asked me to go on a Zen retreat with her. I knew Zen from the crossword puzzle clue: 'oriental discipline.' But she needed a companion, and she was a rock of good sense so I wasn't going to get into anything weird."

The retreat was led by Robert Kennedy. He had not yet received Dharma transmission and was not authorized to see students in dokusan; otherwise the format was that of a traditional Zen sesshin.

"What was it like? The evening meeting before the retreat began sold me. The topic was Karl Rahner's work on small communities of prayer in the future of the church. I was a Rahner fan. I never completely understood him, but what I could understand I liked. Our CSJP chapter had focussed on small communities of prayer and the four of us in community at 78 Grand Street had committed ourselves to it.[166] We had organized a social development project with the audacious title, Center for Human Development, to respond to the 'signs of the times' as we saw them in our neighborhood in Jersey City: families needed food, money for diapers, homeless men came for something to eat. We gathered with groups of the mothers – mostly Latinas and a couple of African-Americans – to pray, to study Paul VI's Encyclical on 'The Progress of Peoples,'[167] and to plan activities to meet their needs as they articulated them. The Center is a fabulous story, I mention it now only to show why Bob's opening lecture on small prayer groups attracted me.

"As for the retreat itself: Well, you know how painful that first retreat is, how slow it goes. I remember that through the open windows came the sounds of people having fun at the local swimming pool. There were shouts, laughter, the sound of water splashing. The retreatants were facing the wall, and Bob was seated in the middle. It occurred to me, as I sat enduring this, that he had left and was down at the pool enjoying himself. Then the bell rang!"

She recognized that in some way Zen was "something I had been searching for. I shared the experience with the Sisters at home, and we all accepted Bob's invitation to join his sitting group at St. Peter's College." All four members of her community persisted in the practice. One of the members, Mary Byrnes, has since died. Rosalie McQuaide, who retired to Florida with Janet, is one of her Dharma heirs. The fourth sister is Sister Joan Steans, who continues to reside in New Jersey.

I ask what she meant by saying that Zen was something she had been searching for.

"Searching? Well, spiritual growth is a basic dimension of religious life, and women religious are always getting instruction, going to classes and lectures to that

166 In a later letter, Janet explained: "The house at 78 Grand was the first house Mother Clare bought when she came from England. The neighborhood was 'inner city'; some sisters didn't think it was safe to live in the neighborhood and wanted the house to be sold. A community of four was not exceptional; we came together in what we saw as a response to the Provincial Superior's suggestion that we investigate different forms of local community organization/structure; the house had been used as a vocational training program for the School for the Blind where one of our members was administrator and she made the house available."

167 *Populorum Progressio.*

end. Bob's opening teisho on Rahner was on target, and his approach was, I suspect, the compass here. He also pointed out, in a teisho, that zazen was a form of prayer."

When Kennedy's teacher, Bernie Glassman, returned to New York from California, the four sisters sat with his group in Yonkers and began dokusan with him. "Glassman was a great teacher," she tells me. "He was very welcoming and appreciative of the Sisters, making sure of our comfort and ease. He obviously knew his subject – which was very foreign to me – and made his knowledge available to us in his teisho, his interviews, and the programs he provided." She admired his commitment to social engagement, his work with marginalized populations, and the Bearing Witness retreats he sponsored among the homeless of New York and at places of genocide, such as Auschwitz.[168]

"One of his most compelling and attractive projects was the Greyston Bakery in Yonkers where unemployed homeless people received job training. It made a real contribution to the community of Yonkers and beyond."

Bernie Glassman was an example of someone who had the integrity her high school teacher had spoken of, someone who "walked the walk." Still, she had a closer rapport with Kennedy, and, when Glassman suggested she should train to become a teacher herself, he referred her back to Kennedy. "I have sat with many teachers since, but Bob has been my primary teacher."

I ask why she thinks Glassman identified her as a potential teacher, and she admits she had often wondered about that. "Divine Providence? God's loving care of me? Bernie knew that I had been teaching French, and he knew that women religious are often connected with teaching." One also assumes he discerned a level of insight in her and a capacity to help others also develop that insight, but she doesn't claim this.

∾

"My initial assignment in zazen was to count the breaths to ten and then repeat, being careful not to go beyond 10. Then letting go of the counting 'since it was a scaffolding' and just following the breath. When I was introduced to Mu, it repelled me, and I found this practice very unsatisfactory." I ask in what way unsatisfactory, and she tells me she felt it was leading her nowhere. "Perhaps that was the point, but at the time the discomfort, frustration, and unsatisfactoriness were very negative for me and indicated to me a need for some alternative. I said so to Bob, and, a short time later, he told me that Bernie also recommended another practice, shikan taza, and that has been my practice and my teaching."

Shikan taza is silent, receptive sitting without focusing the attention on any particular support. One is aware of the breath, for example, without having to concentrate on it as in the earlier exercises. It is the standard meditative practice in

---

168 Cf. McDaniel, *Cypress Trees in the Garden*, pp. 246-49.

the Soto School of Zen and is considered an advanced practice in the Sanbo Zen tradition. It is a practice which, following Kennedy, Janet identifies as a form of prayer.

"Prayer is an awareness of God. Bob taught that Zen is a form of prayer insofar as it increases awareness of God. Zen is a discovery path and each of us using the path discovers God as God reveals Herself. The stillness, the awakening to depths and dimensions of an interior life, the presence of others in the same involvement. Sesshin provides samu[169] as an opportunity to collaborate with others who are similarly involved. I remember one of my students telling me that as a Christian, Zen gave her the 'how to.' That speaks to me. Was it Yamada Roshi who promised that Zen would make you a better Christian as you emptied yourself as Jesus did? That sounds good to me."

Others I'd spoken to had also cited that passage from Paul's Epistle to the Galatians and generally concur that Zen offers Christians a methodology for accomplishing that emptying. There remains, however, an unresolved question: If Zen is a path by which each of us discovers God as She reveals Herself, why is it that Asian Buddhists don't encounter Her, or don't interpret their experience as such an encounter? I tell Janet of my conversation with Bodhin, in which he'd said that a measure of the validity of one's insight is whether one has "seen through concepts like God."

"Yesterday at Mass," she writes back, "the first reading quoted Isaiah saying that God had told him that God was making a new heaven and a new earth. So things are not finished yet. My own experience confirms that; I see now things I didn't yesterday. Maybe this is true for other people too. And I recall Bob's comment that culture makes it difficult for us to see things as others do. It's a great consolation to read in the Psalms: 'I was brought forth into a sinful world.' To answer your question, I don't know why Asian Buddhists don't find God. But I find much harmony with Bodhin saying that God is a concept. And for me, more: God in whom I live and move and have my being."

And if God is a concept, so too – as Bodhin implied – are terms like Buddha Nature, True Nature, or Original Mind.

∾

In 1989, both Janet and Rosalie McQuaide were working with Catholic Relief Services when it relocated from New York to Baltimore. They set aside a small room in their new apartment as a zendo, and there they continued regular sitting practice. "We sent a picture of our new set-up to Bob. Then a phone call came from Marge Irwin who said she had just been talking to Bob Kennedy. She had read his book and wanted to get involved in Zen practice. He told her that two members of the CSJPs were now in Baltimore near her and that she should contact us." Marge and another woman began sitting with them, then another friend joined, and another after that.

---

169 Work period.

"Soon we were too many for the small room in the apartment and then began a pilgrimage from one place to another. Rosalie made up a song that we sang as we pulled up our mats, gathered our cushions, bells, candles, incense and so on and moved to a new place: 'Along the Michinoku, everything is wonderful; but in Shiogama fishing boats pulling together are most amazing of all.'"

As membership grew, the group was incorporated as the Clare Sangha. "Rosalie and Bill O'Grady, our first president, did the incorporation papers with the help of another member's brother, who was a lawyer; we based them on Glassman's ZCNY documents adapted for Maryland law."

In 2004, Janet and Rosalie moved to Florida not – as once more I mistakenly assume – to retire, but to care for family members. "My sister's husband was dying of cancer; they lived on the east coast of Florida. Rosalie' s sister's husband had a heart condition, and, for his health, they frequently came here. Rosalie wanted to have a place where her sister could be near family as his condition became more and more challenging. My sister's husband died, and it seemed important for her to have family nearby. So to respond to those needs, we moved here and changed ministries."

They moved to Lakeland, Florida. "It is a beautiful town, especially to those from metropolitan areas like New York and Baltimore. There are reportedly 17 lakes within the town limits." The community has three Catholic parishes and "multiple other Christian churches." There is also a Hindu Temple and, not far from Janet and Rosalie's apartment, an Islamic Center, where the two have made "some peace-making efforts." But, to the best of their knowledge, they are the only two people doing any form of Buddhist practice.

As they had in Baltimore, they have a designated space in their apartment for zazen. "But the apartment here is smaller, and the space gets used in many ways at different times." They had made an effort to establish a sangha when they first arrived but, as she puts it, to no avail. She quotes the Zen maxim that "when the teacher is ready the students will come; when the students are ready the teacher will come." Interest in contemplative practices in both the east and the west has always been limited to a few.

Meanwhile, the Clare Sangha – also known as the Zen Community of Baltimore – remains active. Its current resident teacher, Bruce Blackman, studied with Elaine MacInnes before working with Janet, from whom he received Dharma transmission in 2004. When I contact him about the group, he stresses that it is a multi-faith group. "All are welcome here, including persons of no faith. There are several Catholics among us, including myself, but it is not a preferred or recommended faith in our Sangha. At the outset, our founding teachers, Sister Janet and Sister Rosalie, defined the Sangha and its purpose in these words: 'The Zen Community of Baltimore/Clare Sangha consists of people from all walks of life and various religious backgrounds who come together regularly to support and strengthen one another in their Zen practice.'"

It is an unpretentious mission statement, and the practice advocated is equally modest. According to their website, the focus of Zen training and practice at ZCB is

> – on bare attention – simple, direct, non-interfering awareness, non-judging awareness. Students who establish a Zen practice find it opens the Way for them amid their own circumstances and conditions. Practice then becomes its own reward…
>
> Learning to center one's being in the present moment leads onward to the other main benefits of a Zen life. These include awakening to the Way of wisdom and compassion (forgetting the self), then embodying the Way in one's daily life – a progressive and lifelong undertaking.

෨

"What," I ask her, "does the church have to offer Zen?"

"The church has a long history and tradition that should be helpful to Zen," she writes, "at least to the Zen experience as my limited knowledge and experience can tell." She mentions the authors of the Psalms, the Evangelist John, Gregory of Nyssa, Saint Thérèse of Lisieux, and others whose insight is evidence of the wisdom (prajna) that is one of the traditional goals of Zen training.

The other traditional goal of Zen training, of course, is karuna or compassion.

"An anecdote from the early days of the Clare Sangha comes to mind," she tells me. "During confession once, as I was recounting difficulties in prayer, I told the confessor that I was a Zen teacher. He asked, 'What do you want from the church?' My spontaneous, intuitive reply – without any thinking – was 'mercy.' He slapped his knee and said, 'That's it!'"

CHAPTER THIRTEEN

Day Star Sangha

Fr. Kevin Hunt[170]

In Lakeland, Florida, Janet Richardson and Rosalie McQuaide are authorized Zen teachers without students. In Maine, not far from where I live in New Brunswick, Canada, the first zendo constructed in America is maintained by a group of practitioners with no resident teacher.

The Morgan Bay Zendo in Surry was inaugurated in 1971 by Walter Nowick,[171] the first American authorized to teach Zen. A short walk from the zendo, there is a large glacial boulder on which a plaque proclaims: "Here lie some of the ashes of the Japanese Zen Master Goto Zuigan, my teacher. They were placed here in October 1968, with hope that his teaching will continue." Walter retired from teaching in 1985, and, when he died eighteen years later, a portion of his ashes were buried here as well.

Up and down the road on either side of the zendo are houses built by people who came to this hamlet in the 1970s in order to study Zen with Walter. He didn't make it easy for them. Prospective students waited by a tree in his yard until he took notice of them. That could take a day or two. When he at last asked what they wanted and they expressed a desire to learn Zen, he might dismiss them saying that he already had too many students and didn't want more. Presumably this was enough to discourage some inquirers; others, however, persisted, were eventually accepted, and settled in the area.

The evening before I visit the Day Star Sangha in Massachusetts, I stop in Portland, Maine, to do a reading and book signing at Dosho Port's Great Tides

---

170   Cf. McDaniel, *Cypress Trees in the Garden*, pp. 134, 303, 308, 310-320.

171   Cf. McDaniel, *The Third Step East*, Chapter 10.

Zen.[172] Dosho had moved the zendo to new quarters since I was last here, and it is now located on the second floor of an old building that used to house railroad administrative offices. The architecture reflects an era before functionality took precedence over design. There is lovely interior glass in the hallways and wood wainscoting in the elevators. Great Tides is located on the second floor in a space that had previously been a hair salon. What had been the waiting area is maintained as a study corner with a small library. A few steps down, a number of zabutons are set out in a square. There are a dozen people at the reading; there is room for more, but not many more.

There are a few largish Zen communities in North America. Bodhin Kjolhede's Rochester Zen Center had 533 members at the time of our conversation. I suspect, however, that the majority of churches in Rochester have significantly larger congregations. Most Zen communities I've visited are much more modest. Zen remains a fairly esoteric taste. As Dosho told me when I first met him, "The number of people interested in going really deep is a small group widely dispersed.

"In the early days, Zen was very competitive," he went on, referring to the time – now long past – when people were willing to stand by trees waiting to be acknowledged by a prospective teacher. "We were competitive about what our schedules were and how much we sat and how intense it was, how *difficult* our place was. Today it seems like it's the opposite. Now it's competitive about whose center is the most accommodating. I was at this workshop and there was this young guy there – cute young guy – and he's like, 'Um… what is the minimum amount of asceticism necessary in order to practice Zen?'"

Since 2013, Dosho has been experimenting with an on-line program, Vine of Obstacles, in an attempt to provide a vehicle to support that small but dispersed population.

During the reading, I tell the attendees the story of Walter Nowick and the Morgan Bay Zendo, and, afterwards, Dosho's partner and fellow teacher, Tetsugan Zummach, wonders aloud what it is that draws people to Zen practice. It's a good question.[173]

In the morning, I continue onto Massachusetts.

Often the way in which professional religious and the laity interpret their religion differs significantly, and I wonder if there is a similar discrepancy between the way Zen teachers, who may be Catholic, and Zen students, who may be Catholic, view this practice. So I have arranged to visit two predominantly Catholic sanghas, the first of which is about half an hour outside of Boston.

---

172   Cf. *Cypress Trees in the Garden*, Chapter 20 and Epilogue.

173   Shortly after my visit to Great Tides, Dosho and Tetsugan accepted an invitation to be the teachers at the Nebraska Zen Center in Omaha.

Off the Interstate, rural areas of the state are often picturesque: small towns, lovely rivers, trestle bridges, and apple orchards. This is Johnny Appleseed country. Mount St. Mary's Abbey in Wrentham is a community of 45 Trappistine nuns ranging in age from 25 to 93. The male community, St. Joseph's Abbey in nearby Spencer, has 65 monks. These are relatively large communities by contemporary standards.

Visitors to Mount St. Mary's stay at the McMahon Guest House in Franklin. It is less than a ten minute walk between the two, and I see no marker identifying where one township ends and the other begins. The Guest House is a wide, brick building with white shutters and appears to have formerly been a private dwelling. It has spacious grounds with large, old growth trees that in April are just coming into bud. Adjacent to the property is a field of solar reflectors. As one approaches the house, one is greeted by a small, white statue of Jesus, arms opened wide in welcome like the famous monument overlooking Rio de Janeiro. One can hear the sound of traffic in the distance, but it is muted, and the spring bird calls are more prominent.

Inside a sign on an easel directs people to the basement zendo. An enso[174] surrounding a simple two stroke calligraphy cross identifies the door of a long, narrow room with a marble floor. Two rows of zabutons face one another. It is a slightly larger space than the Great Tides Zendo, although not by much, and, as last night, there are twelve of us.

The teacher at the Day Star Sangha is Father Kevin Hunt, a member of the Spencer community now residing in Wrentham where he is the chaplain for the sisters. He has a shaved head and has grown a little stocky with age. I had written elsewhere that his Trappist robes suit him; he wears them well. I note that the holes of the thick leather belt holding the black hooded scapular against the white robe are stretched wide with long use.

There is a very plain figure on a low altar, less an image of the Buddha than that of a meditating monk. To the side is a smaller statue of the Sacred Heart. As the sitting begins, Father Kevin lights a stick of incense, holds it between hands closed in gassho, and brings it to his forehead before placing it in a bowl of sand in front of the meditating figure. Then he steps back onto a large Turkish-style carpet and does three full prostrations, hands cupped and raised in front of him to receive the Buddha's feet. The meditators prostrate themselves as well, although some – including me – are not flexible enough to get down and up again easily, so content themselves with making deep bows.

The 1960s and '70s – when aspirants had sought Walter Nowick out in rural Maine – had been a high tide mark for both Catholic monastic and Zen vocations. Our Lady of Gethsemane Abbey in Kentucky had to undertake extensive renovations to accommodate the unexpected numbers they received, inspired in no small measure

---

174 A free-form calligraphy circle common in Zen art.

by Thomas Merton's writings. The San Francisco Zen Center and the Zen Center of Los Angeles both purchased apartment buildings near their temples to house the young people who arrived in steady streams. Since then, both centers have divested themselves of much of their real estate holdings, and Catholic religious communities have aged and grown smaller.

When I first met Kevin Hunt, I'd mentioned that there were only a few elderly monks remaining at the Trappist community located in the francophone region of my home province in Canada. The situation was similar in other places, he told me, although he believes there has been a recent revival in vocations. "They're not experiencing it in large numbers," he admits. "They're experiencing it in small numbers." One or two of the currently eleven Trappist communities in the US may have to close and their monks relocate elsewhere, still – Kevin assures me – Catholic monasticism is not as moribund as I had assumed. But it, too, is an esoteric calling.

Kevin entered the order when he was 19 years old. He notes wryly that he isn't sure he would have been accepted under current entrance requirements. "They have to go through psychological evaluations. They come to the monastery usually over the period of two years or so for three months now and three months later and things like that. When I entered – you know – 'Does he have a strong back? Can he work?'"

The order made use of that strong back immediately. Our Lady of the Valley monastery in Rhode Island had been destroyed by fire, and construction was underway on the new abbey in Spencer. "The first thing they did was put me in a ditch with a pick and shovel. I did what was lay brothers' work at the novitiate. I entered at the end of the construction, so there were still a lot of ditches to be dug."

After St. Joseph's was completed, he was sent to Snowmass, Colorado, to help with the construction of St. Benedict's Abbey and after that to Argentina where Our Lady of the Angels was being built in Azul. It was in Argentina that he was introduced to Zen. Someone gave him – as he puts it – "a very poor Spanish translation" of Eugen Herrigel's *Zen in the Art of Archery*.

"So, anyway, I'm reading this book, and I'm interested in it. And it tells about how to sit in meditation, the first time I really paid any attention to the physical aspect of it. And, of course, one of the great problems that I experienced up to shortly before that time was that our custom was you couldn't sit down in church. You either had to stand or kneel. And so when they gave us permission to sit in church, of course, I think the most common practice was what we used to call 'nodding at the angels.'" He mimes falling asleep. "And that was my greatest difficulty. I could fall asleep at a drop of a pin. You know, you had a full day's labor, especially in Argentina where your hardest labor would be when you had your shortest sleep period. So, anyway, as I read this thing, two things impressed me. One was the way they sat. And I read it a couple of times, and I said, 'If I try sitting like that, my legs are going to be so painful I won't be able to sleep.' I never achieved full lotus, but I tried to do it a number of times. The other thing that impressed me was that he gave a koan, and that koan really struck me. The koan was, 'What face did you have before you were born?' So I said, 'Gee, I wonder what face I had before I was born? What face did I have? I should keep that in the back of my mind.' Hmm? And so for six or seven years, I got several blankets together – or course, I didn't have cushions or anything – folded them up, sat on them, and for those six or seven years that's what I did."

His practice marked him as "singular."

"Because I was the only one doing that. And in the tradition of the Trappists at the time, to be 'singular' was not a good thing. But one thing that our tradition has always had and that was we've always had great liberty of spirit to follow our way of prayer. The local superiors thought I was crazy, and they said, 'We don't want you sitting cross-legged in our chapel.' So I said, 'Okay. I'll find another place to do it.' And we had a small infirmary, and our infirmaries always have a little chapel in them. And at that time I was the infirmarian, so I was able to arrange things the way I wanted up there. So there I am, sitting on the blankets. As I said, probably six or seven years passed. And I had no teacher. I didn't know what I was doing right, what I was doing wrong, or anything else, and nothing was happening.

"So I'm up in this little chapel one morning, and I'm thinking to myself, 'Well, you've worked hard at this, Hunt. And you've given it time; you've given it effort. And people haven't bothered you too much about it. They think you're crazy, but they think I'm crazy on a lot of points, so that's all right.' So at that point, I said to myself, 'Okay, I give up.' Now, I'm sitting cross-legged. And I stood up." He pauses. "And, in the motion of standing up, I saw the face I had before I was born." He pauses a little longer. "I hadn't the slightest idea what it was. Hmm? All I knew was that something had happened. So I continued for a couple more years, and then I returned to Spencer."

That was in 1969, and the abbot at the time was Thomas Keating, a noted advocate for Christian meditation. Keating supported Kevin's experiments in Zen and was happy to host Joshu Sasaki of Los Angeles at the monastery. "And so Sasaki Roshi came up. And we had him in choir, and he had a room in the monastery itself, so he participated; he ate in our dining room. He gave a couple of talks to the community.

"There was quite a lot of interest in what he said. Basically he spoke of his experience in meditation and the Zen way of doing meditation. And you know, a novice master had once said to me, 'If there's any rule in prayer it is that it will always become more simple. Less verbal.' And so he addressed that aspect, that in Zen there's no talking. That to speak a word in Zen is already a betrayal. And that was something that we could identify with because we had a rule of silence, and silence is very, very important in our practice. And he loved it, so somebody said to him something about coming back sometime and giving a weekend sesshin. And so he said, 'Yes. I come back next year.'

"Now he had spoken about koan practice and how it was used. And he said: 'I give a koan. To everybody. Same koan to everybody.' And he had noticed when we start our chanting, we make the sign of the cross. And he said: 'Hmm. Hmm. Good practice. Oh, that's a good practice. That's a good practice.' His English was not very good. So he said: 'Koan. Mmm.' He leaned over to me, 'What do you call that, brother?' I said, 'That's the sign of the cross.' 'Ah! Sign cross. Mmm. Good practice. *Strong* practice. Mmm. Koan: How do you realize God sign cross? Meditate on that until I come back.' So I did." Sasaki returned to St. Joseph's regularly for the next ten years. Not all the monks attended these retreats, but there were regularly between 25 and 30 participants. And, over time, people from outside the monastic community joined them. "One of the things that he insisted on," Kevin tells me, "was, 'I'm not here to make you Zen Buddhist monks. I'm here to make you Zen Christian monks.' Hmm?"

When Keating resigned his abbacy, his successor was not as comfortable with Zen as he had been, and Sasaki's visits to Spencer were suspended. Kevin, however, continued study with the Korean Zen Master, Seung Sahn, in Rhode Island. Then he met Robert Kennedy at an inter-religious event sponsored by the Insight Meditation Center in Barre, Massachusetts. Kevin told Kennedy about his own efforts at Zen, and Kennedy invited him to attend a five day sesshin he was scheduled to conduct at St. Benedict's in Snowmass.

At the end of that retreat, Kevin asked to be accepted formally as a student and committed himself to attend as many sesshin as possible. "And finally, I would say around 2001 or 2002, I told my abbot I had reached a point in my Zen practice where I thought I had to do an intensive period of koan practice, and I couldn't do that by seeing Bob two or three times a year. So I asked if I could go down and spend a year or so with him in his Jesuit community in Jersey City. And I spent two years there."

In 2004, Kevin received Dharma Transmission from Kennedy and was authorized to begin working with his own students. He is the principal teacher of two small Zen communities, the Day Star Sangha and the Transfiguration Zendo in Southbury, Connecticut.

∾

There has been an emergence of various forms of Christian meditation since people like Hugo Lassalle and Thomas Hand first explored the possibility of using Zen techniques in a Christian context. The Jesuit Anthony deMello adapted a wide range of Asian spiritual practices as aids to prayer; Kevin Hunt's former abbot, Thomas Keating, was a proponent of the technique known as Centering Prayer; and John Main, a British Benedictine, advocated a form of Christian mantra practice that has become the basis of a global ecumenical network known as the World Community for Christian Meditation.

But what, to paraphrase Tetsugan, draws people already engaged in their faith to this type of practice and how do they understand it?

Instead of the final round of zazen scheduled on the day I join them, the Day Star sangha members come upstairs, and we sit around a large dining table to chat. More than half tell me they are practicing Catholics. One of the men admits he was raised Catholic but feels uncomfortable with labels so no longer identifies himself as such. One of the women is actively involved with the Episcopalian Church.

It is obvious that their Zen practice is something deeply felt by the members of this community, but it is also clear that they have difficulty speaking about it. There is no immediate answer when I ask what drew them to this practice. Instead, people glance around the table as if waiting for someone else to begin. Finally the woman who helped coordinate my visit, Cindy, says, "It's my lifeline."

"What do you mean by that?"

"I can't describe it. But without my practice, I wouldn't be who I am." There are some murmurs of agreement, and someone else says, "Yes, it's hard to put in words."

"Well, let's suppose I were your daughter," I suggest, "and I was at the time of life when young people are questioning things, trying to find their way. And I know you attend this group, so I ask you why. Are you saying the best you could do is tell me that it's hard to put into words?"

"It centers me," Cindy says cautiously. "It helps me to realize I'm not just this body, that I'm connected to something larger than this. But I wouldn't want to put thoughts and ideas into her mind either."

Dave, one of the bolder members of the group, adds, "I just find that the more that I quiet my mind, the closer I get to the source."

"'The more you quiet your mind, the closer you get to the source,'" I say repeating his words. "So, I'm your son, and I give you one of those looks and say, 'What does that mean?'"

"Well, if you can quiet your mind, you can realize more of a God-nature in things, and you might find some comfort in that."

"It's a spiritual journey. Right?" the Episcopalian, Patricia, says. "I feel like somewhere along the line I got on a spiritual journey which at one time was more closely defined by the Episcopal Church. Then, about four years ago, I began this Christian Zen approach, and it's another step on the spiritual journey. Like Cindy said, it's hard to put into words, but there is something here that I wasn't experiencing previously.

It has something to do with the quietening of the mind, taking things in without words. Maybe that's why it's so hard to put into words."

Robert, who had said he was uncomfortable with labels, adds that one needs to make a distinction between religion and spirituality. "I think the essence of spirituality transcends all the religious traditions. And if a friend asked why I do this, I'd tell them, 'I'm reconnecting to spirit – my true self – when I meditate.' It's an expansiveness that's lacking elsewhere for me; Zen gets right down to the heart of the matter. It strips everything down to what is essential and true – absolute quiet, stillness, and spaciousness – that which is eternally present and unchanging, that which transcends the dualistic mind."

Madeleine, a sister in the Dominican Order, points out that if someone were to ask her about Zen, she'd invite them to try sitting before she spoke to them about it. "And we'll talk after. Because the more we talk about it, the more there will be expectations about what should or should not happen. But after you've sat, your questions are based on some experiential knowledge."

Cecilia (the "c"s in her name pronounced in the Italian manner as "ch,") states, "I believe that there is a God-essence in all faiths. And I come here for method and practice. To reach that God-center that I *feel* as well as believe. The tradition of centering or the tradition of stillness or the tradition of 'tuning-in' is not well taught anywhere except in Buddhism or Hinduism, the actual process of reaching the Deity. I come here because I need a place where I can really touch that God, whether I call him Buddha or Christ or one of the Hindu names. Coming here allows me to still myself enough within the method to find that core and go forth from it."

"So what you find here is a supportive environment that allows that centering to take place?" I ask.

"Yes, within the community. But method too."

"So it's the environment and methodology, the technique?"

"Yes. It's the connection. I could go out and try to get it on my own, but I think there needs to be a nurturing, which I also happen to find in the church. But a specific, particular place, a particular presence. I think that the solitude we have here assists in that." Several heads nod in agreement. "This is an ideal place for that."

"So what is the technique?" I ask.

Again there is a pause before anyone speaks, then Patricia laughs and says, "Breathe in, breathe out."

One of the men, Sean, says, "Absolutely nothing."

"How do you do nothing?" I ask.

"It's hard." There is laughter and expressions of agreement. "It's enormously hard. We're surrounded by noise. Internal noise. External noise. We're bombarded with stimulae. So it's so nice to be with nothing."

"I usually tell people to sit down, to be quiet," Madeleine says. "Be still. And to listen. And that's it. And it sounds simple, but it means you have to carve time out of your day. You have to still your mind. And you have to really listen. And that's the hard part."

"Of course, in the old Asian monasteries the instructions often amounted to: 'That's where you sit.' Everything else you had to figure out on your own. So what about here?" I ask, addressing Kevin. "If I show up for the first time is that how you would introduce me to the practice? Just tell me to sit down and shut up?"

"With great emphasis," he says, prompting more laughter. "You know, the actual physical aspect of practice is easy. You simply sit straight so that the body supports itself and quietly inhale and quietly exhale and quietly inhale and watch the breath go in and the breath go out and the breath go in and the breath go out." He explains that in our usual state the mind is constantly flooded with thoughts. "A thought comes in, and we chase that one. And then another thought comes in, and I chase that one. And so I am continually chasing back and forth. You know? Now the basic thing is, you don't fight thoughts. You don't even try to calm thoughts. The image I generally use is, 'Sniff one of the flowers.' And let your breath out. Sniff the flower and let the breath out. After a while, you're not smelling any more of the perfume of the flower. Now that's a physiological reaction. But it is that you stop paying attention to all of this junk that goes on in our heads. And when you stop paying attention to all the junk that is going continually on in our heads, you become aware. And the next question you're going to ask is, 'Become aware of what?'"

"I knew you were a wise man," I say.

"So you haven't got the slightest idea of what you're aware of. Even to call it 'something' is to give it a name, which doesn't work. So, the longer that you sit simply being aware, you become aware of something that's greater than yourself. Greater than everybody in the room with you. But at the same time, you become more aware of yourself, of who and what you truly are. And as you become more aware of who and what you truly are, you become more accepting of who and what you are."

❧

When I ask if they are practicing Buddhism, they make a distinction between Buddhism as a system of belief and Zen as a practice derived from that system of belief.

"Zen is the process," Cecilia says. "Buddhism is a faith. A set of tenets that I can learn, that I can repeat, that I can take in, a body of knowledge. Zen is finding the way to make that contact with something greater than one's self."

"But the rituals are Buddhist," I insist. "The incense, the prostrations."

Sean speaks up a little hesitantly. "I think of orthodoxy and ortho-praxis. I think for me, orthodoxy would be 'right thoughts.' When I'm practicing, that's not my interest. You know, we're always struggling with what's right, what's wrong, what makes sense, what's good, what's bad. So if I bow to the Buddha – and it's nice to have Jesus there too – that's what I'm doing. I'm not thinking, as I go down, am I doing a right thing, having the right thoughts? It's the practice."

"Prostrations can be easily misunderstood by people as a worship," Dave admits. "I understand that. A lot of people have that idea that you're worshipping Buddha. 'Why do you worship Buddha?' I'm not actually worshipping Buddha. I'm helping create a sacred space where I can do my meditation. I'm lessening the self. I'm saying, 'Self, you're not as important as you think you are.' And then I pay homage to the Buddhas, Jesus, and I lessen the self again. That helps to create a sense of meditation, and you can start lowering your self-mind in that quietening process."

"Yes," Cecilia agrees. "The prostration is a lessening of self. I have to get down, get my hands on that floor. And it's not me with all of my energy present. It's, like, quietening. It's like letting go some of the stuff of self, kind of surrendering to that other place in the bow."

Madeleine also dismisses the prostrations as an act of worship. "It's an expression of being grateful for the teaching of how to get your act together. That's what we're here for. So it's not a worship kind of thing, although it can look like that to some-body who's new. For me, what Zen has done is create a container for the journey. And one of my favorite things – which probably came out of Chan rather than Zen – are the Ox Herding pictures.[175] You can't stay in so-called 'bliss'; you've got to get your act together and go out into the world. You can't hold onto your experience, because it was the experience for this day at this time. And the next time you sit, you're going to want to go back to that experience, so you miss the present that you're in. I spent some time at Zen Mountain Monastery where I heard Shugen[176] say that it doesn't do any good to sit unless there's what educators call a 'transfer of learning' to your daily life. And that's also part of our Dominican tradition. Meister Eckhart says that. That as you are in the choir, so should you be in the world. And I think that's the thing that's hard. That there's nothing particularly holy about it, but it's to live life as a whole person, without all that garbage that we've collected along the way. And that's difficult because it's nice to sit and look pious and all of that, but if we're not like that outside – in the world – then it's a kind of a waste of time."

"You said that this path is not particularly holy," I note. "I wonder, do you consider zazen a form of prayer or is it something different?"

"Oh, it's a form of prayer," Cindy responds immediately. "Our lives are a form of prayer. Our practice is not just sitting on the cushion; our practice is our life, therefore our life should be a prayer."

---

175   A series of ten pictures portraying the stages of development in Zen practice.

176   Geoffrey Shugen Arnold, the current abbot at ZMM.

"The question is too ambiguous," Dave objects. "First you have to define prayer. There are so many forms of prayer."

"It is for me," Charlie says. He has that Eastern Seaboard accent in which final Rs are pronounced softly; "for" comes out something like "fah." "For me, I'm opening my heart when I sit. And going back to the bow, to me it's kind of like what David said – I'm making my space sacred. That's my holy spot. I'm doing the full bow, a touching the earth bow, attesting to all, and saying, 'Okay. Here I am. Please awaken my heart and my mind.' There isn't anything else that you can say about prayer. I don't look at prayer like, 'Oh, I hope tomorrow goes good.' Or 'I want a new Cadillac.' That's not prayer. That's petitioning and is something different from prayer. To me, prayer is opening the tuna can. Opening it up. Opening myself up."

"Well, there can be intentionality in prayer," Patricia points out, "when you know people who are ill and so forth and you project a good outcome or pray for something for yourself or others who are in need. But meditation seems to be about emptying yourself so that you become more aware of the presence of the Spirit, the mystical. I guess that's letting go of your own ego and allowing the spirit to reside. And then there's no need to say, 'I want this.' Or, 'Give me that.' Or, 'Solve this problem.' Or whatever. That breathing in and breathing out is the prayer."

"If I'm praying, that means I have a voice in my head that's saying something and I'm entertaining some thought," Dave objects. "But if I'm doing zazen, I'm trying to reduce the frequency of that voice. That's why I think there's a difference."

"Is that necessarily so?" I ask. "Can there be prayer without words?"

"Of course," Kevin says. "In fact, both in the European and Orthodox traditions you start off with a lot of words, but then you come to quiet." He pauses, then repeats. "You've got to come to quiet. There's a famous drawing by John of the Cross, the ascent of Mount Carmel. There are three gates or three ways. The one on the left and the one on the right are very, very wide and comfortable. The one in the center is very, very narrow. The one in the center goes straight up the mountain, and at the side of that road, it starts off with small letters. N. A. D. A.[177] And the letters get larger. And at the top of the mountain, N. A. D. A. But people go in different ways. Some people have to start off with a great deal of verbiage, a great deal of thinking. I think one of the reasons why people come to Zen is that they're tired of talking and they're tired of thinking. So the difficulty is, when we use the word 'prayer' we identify it with a lot of verbiage. And that is not prayer. Prayer is what Charles was describing. The opening of your heart and mind. And when you open it, God, Buddha-nature, the Absolute dives right in."

<hr>

177   *Nada* is the Spanish word for "nothing."

I notice that the group is often careful to avoid using the term "God." Madeleine pointed out that at Zen Mountain Monastery, its founder – John Daido Loori[178] – had noted that God was not an issue that the Buddha dealt with. At another point in the conversation, however, she suggests that the Zen experience of enlightenment and the Christian mystical experience might be the same. "But the tradition that they come out of frames them," she adds.

"What do you mean by enlightenment?" I ask. The question provokes another long pause.

"No one can tell anyone else that," Cindy says.

"Really?" I say. "It's right there in the Bodhidharma poem: a special transmission outside the scriptures, not dependent on words and letters, direct pointing to the mind, and attainment of enlightenment. So what is it?"

After another pause, Robert says, "I think the term 'enlightenment' is dangerous and means different things to different people. My understanding of Zen is that's it's not about attaining anything, including enlightenment."

"Sister Madeleine, you equated it with the mystical experience."

She nods her head. "Yes. I think the experience is the same in both traditions."

"So what is that experience?"

"I'll tell you a little story about something that really happened. I think it was a meeting of Buddhists and Trappists monastics getting together. And the story is that the monks were getting along wonderfully well" … (dramatic pause) … "until the theologians showed up."

Kevin smiles and nods his head in agreement.

"And I think that's it," she continues. "Our world that we live in is like a box that's made up of time and space and mass and energy, and, if something doesn't fit in that box, it doesn't exist. And it's a very small box. And so there seems to be a yearning, a desire built into who we are as humans, to transcend that box. Not to throw it out and say it's wrong or bad, but to say that it's only a very small part of who we are and what are our… I want to say 'capabilities.' But if we could make the box porous, then it would be all right. But the world that we live in doesn't allow that. If you can't measure it and count it and do all those things, then it doesn't exist. Yet we have something within ourselves that says, 'There's more than that. There's more than what's inside that little box.' And if you sit down and chase something specific – like enlightenment – you're not going to recognize what's really there because you already have in your mind what it should be. For me, Zen is letting go of all that and seeing things as they are rather than as I want them to be. And that's a life-long task, because just when we get rid of one concept, something else pops up."

"Is what one encounters in Zen practice the same as encountering God?" I ask.

---

178   Cf. McDaniel, *Cypress Trees in the Garden*, Chapter 13.

"I think the term 'God' would limit our conversation," Cindy says. "When you're brought up in a certain tradition, you think of God in a certain way. And when you come to Zen, you drop all those ideas. We can say 'God,' but it's so much more than the word. So, the source, the mystery … I like the word 'mystery' because it's so much more than the word 'God.'"

Cornelia, who is seated to my immediate left, is a little hard of hearing and until now has not joined the conversation. "'God' is a word we use to refer to a mystery. As a child I knew exactly who God was, but as an adult I realize that my understanding of God keeps changing because the term is so inadequate it just crumbles before me. I think that's why we avoid using the word. I think it requires a very spiritually mature person to accept that they will never in this life know God, but we will continue until the end of our life on this Earth seeking a better but still inadequate understanding of this Mystery."

I had been told that the sangha ends its day of sitting with a celebration of the mass, and, after the conversation draws to an end, pew cards are passed out and Kevin puts on his vestments. It is probably three years since I've attended mass, and that would have been during a visit to Mexico and so in Spanish. But the responses are familiar, and the actions – such as making the sign of the cross with one's thumb on forehead, lips, and breast before the reading of the gospel – come naturally. I feel at home here. Or do so until we come to the Nicene Creed, which states without quibble that "I believe in one God, the Father almighty, maker of heaven and earth, of all things visible and invisible." For some reason the boldness of that assertion strikes with unusual force. After all, here is a group of people who had just told me, in effect, that one needs to have an open mind – what one might call an agnostic attitude – in order to practice Zen, and now they are proclaiming, without reservation, their belief in a God who created Heaven and Earth and whose only begotten son became incarnate for us and our salvation.

I have to get back to Boston so I can't accept the invitation to stay and share lasagna with the community, and I don't have an opportunity to ask them how they reconcile the unequivocal statements of the creed with the need to "drop ideas" which they had considered so necessary, but it is a question that remains with me as I reflect back on our meeting.

CHAPTER FOURTEEN

Oak Tree in the Garden

PATRICK GALLAGHER[179]

1

The following month on our way to Toronto, my son and I stop in Quebec for what may well be my last visit to the Montreal Zen Center. It is late spring, and the garden is in full bloom. The tall tulips have yet to shed their first petals. The various flowering shrubs and trees are at their peak; lilacs perfume the yard.

Albert Low had died at the end of the previous January without leaving an heir, so – as in Surry, Maine – his students have committed to maintaining the center without a resident teacher. The situation is complicated by the fact that if they did recruit a teacher they would want one who was fluent in French.

I take my son to the zendo, which is never locked. Downstairs I notice three fresh granny smith apples placed as an offering in a bowl by the statue of Kannon. Upstairs, the zafus are stood on edge – as Albert had liked – in the middle of the zabutons.

The aspiration Walter Nowick expressed on the memorial plaque at Morgan Bay was that the teachings of Goto Zuigan would continue. As much as I admire what the volunteers there have done, I wonder if that hope will be realized.

The size of a sangha really isn't very important. The old lore from China and Japan is rife with tales of Zen Masters who had only a single student, as well as stories of abandoned temples where there was no one to continue the teaching. The essential thing has always been for a teacher to have at least one heir to continue his presentation of the Dharma. In Oregon, Jan Chozen Bays Roshi called this "the prime directive in Zen ... 'Do not let this die out.'"[180] Dosho Port said almost exactly the

---

179   McDaniel, *Cypress Trees in the Garden*, pp. 134, 140-45.

180   Ibid., p. 281.

same thing: "Keeping this way alive is hugely important for the future."[181] By which he meant both the practice and the tradition that maintains it.

These things are precarious. As Elaine MacInnes and others I'd spoken to noted, Catholicism had had its own rich mystical heritage that has since faded.

The Sanbo Zen tradition founded by Koun Yamada – who had expressed the hope that Zen might find a home in the Catholic Church – has devised an enviably effective process for ensuring its continuity. It is the order rather than the individual teacher who identifies the successors. So Patrick Gallagher studied with Sister Elaine but it was the current Sanbo Zen abbot, Ryoun Yamada, who authorized him to teach.

Patrick's zendo is simply called Oak Tree in the Garden and is located in a storefront on Vaughan Road in Toronto. There are several ethnic restaurants nearby – Thai, West Indian, Peruvian – and a large Dollarama across the street. The zendo windows are blocked by white screens and the only signage are two 8½ x 11 framed sheets of paper set on stools. On the left side of the door, the sign has an enso under which there is the query: "Interested in sitting zazen?" An email address is provided for those who want more information. The zendo has been open for nine months, and Patrick has had twenty inquiries.

The other sign, on the right of the door, changes periodically. Currently it reads:

> A monk introduced himself to Master Gensha, saying:
> "I have just entered this monastery. Please show me where to enter
> the Way."
> "Do you hear the sound of the traffic on Vaughan Road?"
> "Yes," said the monk.
> "Enter there."

Patrick and I go to the Peruvian restaurant for a light meal before the evening sit. As we eat, he tells me that the space the zendo occupies had been his wife's studio for a time. "Her work took a different direction, and she didn't need a studio as much," he explains. "And we thought, it's such a wonderful space, we'll open a store selling art and crafts and things like that. So we did a lot of work changing it from a studio into a space suitable for a store. And we were at this for some months; we were a few months away from a projected opening date. Then there was a terrible tragedy in our family. My son's wife was hit and killed by a drunk driver. So he came home to live with us, not in great shape. And we just put everything on hold and did our best to be around and to be present to him and as helpful as we could. And that lasted for a long time, about a year.

---

181   Ibid., p. 476.

"And then we started rethinking: 'Okay, did we want to go back and do that again? The store.' And we decided that that moment had come and gone. We'd had the emotional stuffing knocked out of us by Zoe's death and the ensuing year. And we thought, 'We don't have it in us to do this.' And during that time, another teacher came back, Nenates Pineda, who had previously been at the Toronto Zendo and had gone to California. So she came back to Toronto after five years away, and we just had too many teachers. So I thought I'd like to go independent, I'd like to do things the way I'd like to do things. So, we adjusted the renovations, did a lot of work. And we were finished over the summer with a huge push. My son helped. And we opened it up, put a sign in the window, and waited to see what would happen."

ॐ

"It seems to me that we are the kinds of creatures that need to have meaning," Patrick reflects after listening to the description of my visit to the Day Star Sangha. He is an active member of his own parish and a lector.[182] "That's just the kind of creatures that we are. And we look for that meaning in many ways. And there's a long tradition in the West of Christianity being an expression of this longing for meaning, this need for meaning. And I think of Buddhism and Hinduism and all religions really as attempts to express what cannot be expressed. And yet we feel a need to try to express it anyway because that's the kind of beings we are. So I think of the Nicene Creed as poetry." He pauses a moment, then admits, "Although maybe it's a stretch to call it poetry."

"I think it would be," I say. "The Creed – the Profession of Faith – is what defines membership in the Church, isn't it? When the congregation stands and recites it, the intent – at least – is to say these are the things that unite us. Failure to share these beliefs used to make one a heretic."

"In the Middle Ages."

"So today it no longer has that force? Instead of being a definition of identity – we are a group of people who affirm these beliefs – it has become something different?"

He considers my question a moment, then clears his throat before answering. "I can only say what I think it means. I can't say what other people might say, a local bishop might say."

"Who, if he were speaking as a bishop, might feel obliged to spout the party line regardless of what he actually felt."

"Right. But that's between him and his conscience. But when someone says, for example, 'I believe in the resurrection of the body,'[183] I'm not even sure I know what

---

182   During the mass, lectors read the day's passages from the Bible to the congregation.

183   While earlier translations of the Creed spoke of the "resurrection of the body," contemporary translations speak, instead, of the "resurrection of the dead": "We believe in one holy catholic and apostolic Church. We acknowledge one baptism for the forgiveness of sins. We look for the resurrection of the dead, and the life of the world to come."

that means exactly. Does that mean the resuscitation of a corpse? I'm not sure that's what it meant even back then, when the Nicene Creed was formulated, let alone now. So, then, what is it to say, 'The resurrection of the body'? I'm not sure anybody could actually say, 'It means this,' the way you could say, 'This is how an internal combustion engine works.' And that's what I mean by saying it's a kind of poetry. It's expressed as a statement of fact, but I find that when you push these things they get very slippery. So, like poetry, they're another kind of truth. It's not an explanation of how a car works. It's not an explanation at all. It's an expression of human longing. The resurrection of the body and all of those kinds of theological statements are us trying to say in this completely inadequate way, 'There's more to this, more to life, than meets the eye.'"

∾

"I remember when I first met you, when I was interviewing Sister Elaine almost three years ago now, she made reference to the 46th Psalm. 'Be still and know that I am God.'"

"That's right."

"Which implies that there is at least the possibility that if one enters into silence one might encounter something that one could recognize as Divinity."

"Yeah," Patrick says. "I'm a bit stuck on the word 'Divinity' – what that means, actually."

"A lot of people probably wonder about that," I say, and we both laugh. As we continue the discussion, we agree that it is unlikely a Buddhist practicing in Japan, entering silence, would encounter what in the West might be identified as God. Both Christians and Buddhists can have experiences that are acknowledged as kensho and yet interpret them differently. At this point, I am merely thinking aloud. "I believe Willigis Jäger would suggest that it's not so much the awakening experience itself but the interpretation of it that is culturally determined. Is it possible to have a culturally-neutral religious or spiritual experience?"

"I don't think so," Patrick says. "I don't think it's possible to have a culturally-neutral any kind of experience. Because we're in a place, at a time, in this particular formulation of flesh and bone. It's impossible not to be that. So a particular constellation of atoms forming a particular person at a moment in history in a particular place that has this longing for more, longing for meaning, articulates it in language from that place and time and that body.

"But let me pursue my use of the term 'poetry.' Sometimes poetry really has a lot of resonance and speaks to people, and sometimes it doesn't. For some people, the poetry of Christianity – its attempt to express the inexpressible in its dogma – is not a poem that resonates any longer. It does for some. So to me, I respond to the impulse in people to do this – to express their spiritual longing – rather than to any particular formulation of that longing, which is conditioned by a time and a place. Not only this time and place; the time of the Nicene Creed, the ascendance of Greek philosophy, the political issues Christian leaders were trying to deal with by calling that council. The words of the Nicene Creed are all conditioned by its moment in time."

And what are the characteristics of *this* current moment in time? It is a point we will come back to.

2

At the zendo, Patrick changes into a high-buttoned black Chinese tunic and loose black trousers. As people come in for the sit, they are also wearing black. Patrick suggests it is perhaps happenstance that all but one attending tonight are Catholic by heritage if not in practice. The one exception, Brenda, is a member of the Church of England which puts her – as he says – "right next door." He is quick to emphasize, however, that this is "most definitely not a Catholic Zen group, but a Zen group with lots of Catholics in it." It is an important distinction. "There are certainly people who come who are not and never were Catholics or even Christians. One fellow I'm almost sure is Jewish, although it has never come up; and there are some others who as far as I can tell have no religious affiliation." But he had used the word "lots" to describe the number of Catholic members, and at least one of them is a clergyman.

Roger Brennan, a priest in the Scarboro Mission Society, is among the attendees this evening. Almost a year prior, Patrick had advised me to interview Roger who belongs to the same generation as Pat Hawk and Greg Mayers, representatives of a time when Catholic seminaries were filled to capacity by young men aspiring to the priesthood. Those days have passed and in the late summer of 2015 Roger told me that, "like all other religious orders" the Scarboro Fathers are "a dying order. We're in our last gasp, although we still try to be as active as we're able. We just had an ordination three months ago, but that will be our last one. There are still a few of us who are able to be active, so we try to support lay people in mission. But we're in the process of selling our property and gradually closing things down."

Roger spent much of his career in the Philippines and China, but, although he was in Asia, he was not immediately drawn to contemplative practice.

"I grew up in a typical Catholic ambiance. Went to Catholic schools; had nuns for teachers. So we got a lot of stories of the saints and even as a very young person, I was intrigued by these. And although I wouldn't have known to describe it in this way at that time, I would say the mystics particularly intrigued me, that people could have these experiences. Growing up, I can remember that there was this curiosity, but when I went to Jesuit high school I never really took to Jesuit spirituality, the Ignatian exercises. We certainly got them," he said with a chuckle. "But it never clicked with me. It was just not my spirituality. Then in the novitiate we studied this book by a priest named Tanqueray.[184] It was quite a thick book; it was considered a classic in mystical theology at that time. It gave a very, very detailed analysis of the road to perfection, and I kind of realized I was not on that road and figured I was never going to get on that road. It was not a very appealing road. It seemed to be something for people who were somehow extraordinary. It wasn't me at any rate. And that kind of allowed me to let go of that type of spirituality. It was something I couldn't do and didn't particularly want to do. So I just said my prayers and received the sacraments, and that was sort of it."

His first posting was to the Philippines, a country he came to love. Then in the mid-'70s, his superiors called him back to Canada to do a course of study on scripture. "And I was not interested. I mean, absolutely I was interested in scripture. I loved scripture. But I was not interested in teaching in the seminary, which is what it would have become."

But he complied with the directive and enrolled at St. Paul's University in Ottawa. One spring day he was in the library. "Ottawa can be beautiful in the spring, and it was one of those days when you would really like to be anywhere but in a library, and I would have given anything to be anywhere else but in that stack room. And I was just flipping through the books looking for the one I wanted and came across this thing a little bigger than a pamphlet on Eastern religions. And because it had nothing to do with scripture, I picked it up and just started flipping through it, looking at the index, looking to see what was in there. I can't even remember if it was about Buddhism in general or Zen. I suspect it might have been on Zen. And I started reading it. Well, then I forgot about the book I was looking for. I took the book and sat down and read through it. And it reawakened in me all the interest I had had years before with the saints and the mystics and that sort of thing. It looked at that reality or that possibility from a completely different perspective. It was no longer something for extraordinary people in certain circumstances. *This* was saying, 'You can experience the transcendent. Anybody can. You don't have to be a special kind of person.'

"So that really tweaked me; however, I still had to get my paper finished. So I put it back. Got the scripture book, finished my paper, decided not to continue, and got permission to go back to the Philippines. In the meantime, I was talking with some of Our Lady's Missionary sisters that I worked with, and I was telling them I was going back to the Philippines. And they said, 'Oh, isn't that great. One of our sisters who's been in Japan for years and has been studying Zen has been assigned not just to the Philippines but to Hinunangan,' which is the town that I was working in."

184   Adolphe Tanqueray (Society of St. Sulpice), *The Spiritual Life: A Treatise on Ascetical and Mystical Theology.*

The sister was Elaine MacInnes, and, in Hinunangan, she introduced Roger to formal Zen practice. Shortly after this, she moved to Manila, where he occasionally went to attend sesshin. After this initial training, however, he did not have direct access to a Zen teacher for long periods of time and had to practice on his own – although he made use of sabbaticals to do brief stays with Koun Yamada in Japan and Willigis Jäger in Germany – until he retired to Toronto in 2009 and resumed practice with Sister Elaine.

While discussing his practice, he mentioned that he had worked with the koan Mu for a long while. I asked if he resolved it, and he laughed gently. "Now there's an interesting question. I'd say 'No,' but my teachers say I have."

"Then your teachers would say that you've had kensho."

"In fact, it's funny you asked that because I was recently discussing it with a teacher who had been with our group several years ago, Nenates Pineda, and has recently returned to Toronto, and because she was starting up again, we were sort of touching base. So she asked me if I was doing koans; I said yes. And, 'What koan are you doing?' And then it came up, 'Well I feel I've not had kensho.' And she said, 'Well, I've been told by other teachers that you do very well in dokusan and so you must have had kensho.' And I said, 'Well, if I had kensho, I must've been asleep and missed it.'"

I admit to him that at times I also felt I had the response to a koan without actually having any insight. "I don't think you can answer the first koan without having some kind of insight, but after a while you get a feel for it."

"You feel it," Roger repeated. "That's exactly what I think. I figure I've been doing it for so long and listening to the Zen language and listening to the teishos and everything. It seems to me that all I've done is figure out how you answer them."

Or perhaps that feeling is the insight.

3

After two rounds of zazen, Patrick leads the participants in chanting the Four Vows, although the formula they use is somewhat different from others with which I'm familiar:

> Creations are innumerable; I resolve to free them all.
> Delusions are inexhaustible; I resolve to extinguish them all.
> The aspects of truth are countless; I resolve to learn and master them all.
> The way of enlightenment is peerless; I resolve to accomplish it.

Then everyone does three full prostrations before an altar bearing a small statue of

Kannon, a framed bodhi leaf,[185] an incense bowl, and a sprig of lilac. After this, people relax on their mats, and we talk about their practice.

If it is not a Catholic Zen group, I wonder if the members consider it a Buddhist group. I put the question to them as I had to the Day Star Sangha, specifically referring to the prostrations they had just made before the altar. Patrick cocks his head and says that he'd also be interested to know if the group considered their practice Buddhist.

One of the sitters, Carolyn – who had done a degree at the Jesuit Theological school attached to the University of Toronto – notes, "We say it comes from Zen Buddhism, so I don't deny that there is a Buddhist aspect to it. The original teachers, before Sister Elaine, were Japanese Zen Buddhist teachers, and we say – quite often – that we're part of that tradition in some of the prayers we say at the sesshins. And I have no discomfort with that. In fact that gives me – I don't know – a sense of continuity? Tradition?"

Roger, on the other hand, quibbles: "You'd have to tell me first, what do you mean by Buddhism?"

"Well, let's say I was a member of your family," I suggest, "maybe a nephew, and I'm curious about what you're doing. I might not have a very clear understanding of what Buddhism is, and that would be partly why I was curious."

"So, if you're my nephew, and you don't know anything about Buddhism, and you're asking me if it's Buddhism, I'd say, 'No.'"

"So all that ritual isn't Buddhist?"

"Well, what do you mean by Buddhist?"

"I don't know. I'm just this 17 year old nephew…"

"Then, for me, it's not. But if you would tell me what you think Buddhism is, I would be willing to say it's coming out of a Buddhist tradition. And when I do the prostrations, I'm respecting the tradition out of which it comes. But depending upon how you want to describe Buddhism, then that will depend on whether or not I'm willing to say I'm a Buddhist. I'm willing to say I respect the Buddhist tradition. I can go that far."

"And you don't see any contradiction between doing that and being a Catholic priest?"

"I don't, no."

"And if your nephew pressed the point and asked you why not?"

"Well, what I see is a tradition in which people have come to a deep quietening of their inner self and have worked out a methodology for doing that. And that methodology is helpful for me in my Christian prayer. So I follow that methodology. And when I'm with a group of people who are also following that methodology – and

---

185   The heart-shaped leaf of the *Ficus religiosa*. Tradition has it that the Buddha was seated under such a tree at the time of his enlightenment.

who may have many, many different ways of looking at that methodology – I, with them, offer respect and gratitude for those who have worked out this methodology and for those who continue to carry it on. So for me, those gestures are an act of solidarity with the group."

"With this group rather than the tradition?" Carolyn asks.

"This group. Or if I was in Kamakura, with the group who are there, realizing that while – for me – I follow this practice for my own reasons and because it helps me in a certain way, I realize that there are other people who have their reasons and follow it for their ways. And part of their way of practicing would be to remember and show respect for the tradition and those who hand it on. Which is fine for me. And so, in solidarity with them, I also offer those gestures of respect."

"Is zazen a form of prayer?" I ask.

Several people reply at once that it is. One participant, Gail, notes, "It's the most effective form of prayer that I've ever experienced."

Another, Heather, adds, "I think 'experience' is the key word. I think when we go to church, we bring our faith. But when we sit, we experience. You experience something. And if you sit long enough and just keep practicing, you experience changes. Life becomes different for you. And you experience this connection. No separation. The oneness of things."

∿

This group is less reluctant to use the word "God" than the Day Star Sangha had been, and some of them appear to suggest that the practice is a means of encountering God. I tell them of my earlier conversation with Patrick and then ask them the question I had also put to Janet Richardson:

"If zazen – as you've said – is a practice similar to prayer through which one might encounter God, why is it that however many generations of Chan and Zen Buddhists in China and Japan did not do so?"

"Didn't do what?" someone asks.

"Didn't encounter God. Certainly when the Jesuits arrived in Japan, one of the difficulties they had was that they couldn't find anything comparable to their concept of God in Japanese culture and religion."

"Well, not the Catholic God or the Christian God," another participant, Arlindo, says.

"When they tried to discuss the idea of an external creator with the Buddhists they met, the Buddhists dismissed the concept and spoke, instead, about what the Jesuits interpreted as a 'Great Nothingnesss.'"

"That's because they're using concepts," Arlindo insists. "The experience is the same. If a monastic person has had this experience, he might interpret it differently because all through life he's been given this idea of God that he carries with him. So when he has this experience, he sees it in the light of his background."

Several people nod their heads in agreement.

"To carry on from what Arlindo is saying," Roger adds. "We just celebrated Trinity Sunday, and how do you explain that? The Trinity. We have all these words, and all these explanations, and all this theology, but we have to finally come to the fact that we don't know what we're talking about." There is gentle laughter and murmurs of agreement from the others. "We don't. I often like to say in groups when I'm talking to them – sometimes from a Zen perspective or whatever – but I say to them, 'God is nothing.' And then I'll write it on the board. 'God is no thing.' Things are creations. Things come from God. But Zen is trying to get rid of all the concepts so that when you have the experience it's pure. I wouldn't necessarily say this to a 17 year old nephew, but talking here, I can say that God is not a thing. Things are creations. God is not a creation. God is beyond creation. So God is nothing. I have no problem with that nothing. The problem is with the concepts. We carry around in our little heads all these concepts. The more theology you study, the more of them you've got. I think the important thing to remember is that God is not a thing."

I mention that earlier Patrick and I had discussed whether it was possible to have any kind of experience – spiritual or otherwise – that wasn't culturally conditioned. "It seems to me," I go on, "that you're suggesting that whatever it is that one encounters through Zen is inevitably interpreted in light of the individual's cultural background, but isn't one of the things Zen attempts to do is get beyond cultural conditioning?"

Brenda, who speaks with a soft South African accent, says, "I don't know. I don't have the answer to that question. But I think what I'm hearing is that it's a starting point. It's a starting point with language to try and articulate something that is totally inarticulable. We call it Emptiness; we call it Vastness. We use these words in an attempt to articulate something that is beyond articulation. So cultural heritage gives us a starting point, but then – as C. G. Jung says – all we'll come up with is a God-image or an image of what is. The reality will always be more than our thought, but in experience we know that we know that we know. And what it is that we know we can't articulate."

Heather comes back to the point she had made earlier about the primacy of experience. "I think what we sit for is that experience, to get beyond. And I think that's at the heart of every great religion. So I agree totally, we get caught up in different concepts of God – or God or not-God, God or no-God. The heart of our practice is what's at the heart of Catholicism too. The church tries to express it in words and images, and we do it without words."

༈

I am struck, as I had been in Massachusetts, that these are people who take their spiritual practice seriously. These are not passive members of a congregation. And, like the Day Star Sangha, the members of Oak Tree in the Garden see Zen as something that enhances the practice of their Catholic faith; it remains, however, something they would not necessarily advise someone else to take up. Zen, they suggest, is something people should come to out of their own sense of need. In particular, they tell me, they would not advise a teenager – like my fictional nephew – to take up the practice. It is not a practice for the young.

"Certainly it was at one time," I object. "The Zen boom of the '60s and '70s – of which I was a part – was largely made up of young people, and many of the contemporary teachers in America today came out of that milieu."

"There was a cultural moment," Patrick agrees. "In the '60s, there was a cultural moment, which has come and gone. There are exceptions, but – in my observation over the years – people tend to be older now. Middle-aged or thereabouts. And they come because something is not aright in their lives. It can be something major or it can be just a sense that my life is not what I want it to be. A sense of unease. But usually it's something that happened. And I think for many people it's that what they thought they were going to get out of life, they didn't get. And now they're looking. So Zen is a possibility. That seems – to me – common for many people. It isn't that they're profoundly and deeply unhappy. But something isn't quite right. So they try to sit. And some will find that they're called to it and will stick with it and others won't."

"Nobody ever said, 'Everything was perfect, so I went into meditation,'" Arlindo points out and the group laughs heartily.

Nor is it a practice to be taken up lightly. Patrick's wife, Nikki, who has not yet said anything, speaks in a slow and reflective manner:

"I come from a background of learning to draw, trying to draw. Which I did for many years before I did any Zen. So if I'm talking to someone who wants to learn to draw, I tell them, 'That's great! But you know this is something you're going to have to do for your life – right? You know that you have to do this forever. You're going to be continuing with this. That's how you learn. And eventually you even give up your expectations that you *will* learn.' The great Japanese painter, Hokusai, said – when he was dying at the age 89 or something – he said, 'If heaven will grant me just five more years, then I could become a real painter.' And pretty well anybody who tries to draw will tell you the same thing, that it's for your life.

"Well, Zen is like that. I used to say, 'Oh, that's great for Patrick. That's good. I'll support him. Whatever. But I'm too fidgety. I'll never be able to sit. I'll never be able to sit for 25 minutes. That's crazy! And for a day or five days? Forget it. I'll never do it!' And then somebody died. And it was just …" She gives a prolonged exhalation as of exhaustion and loss. "And it was like, 'Okay. That's it. I'm going to the mat. I'm going to sit. I'm going to sit every day until I die.' I just knew that. I knew that's how it was going to be. I just knew that that was what I had to do. It was time for me to do that. And it wasn't even in terms of helping. It was more like, 'Somehow I have to incorporate this. I have to digest it. Somehow I have to deal with this. And I'm not going to deal with it by all of the other things that you usually do. Running around or even crying or any of those things. I'm just going to have to deal with it.' It was like I was just up against this ultimate reality, and that's what it is when you're on the mat. You're up against an ultimate reality.

"So you can sit and think about, 'Oh, I have to do this tomorrow. I have to do that.' And then you can feel guilty later. 'Oh, I shouldn't have been thinking like that.' But your teacher is nice" – heads nod and people laugh gently – "and says, 'Don't judge the sit.'" The laughter increases and interrupts her for a moment. "But you know it's for your life. There's going to be another time when that sit is going to be very profound. And it is. So to me it's always in terms of an ultimate reality. But when you're talking to someone else, basically what you have to say is, 'I sympathize. I understand your plight. Whatever you do – if you're serious about it – you know you're going to be doing this for the rest of your life don't you?' That's it. It's every day. And some of them will try. Some of them will. Or some of them will take it up for a while then they'll lose it. And maybe they'll come back later."

Finale in Oaxaca

When speaking to Christian students like Thomas Hand, Koun Yamada Roshi made a distinction between "strict Buddhist Zen" – in which one follows "all the Buddhist teaching and everything" – and what he called "just pure Zen," Zen essentially as a practice. It is a distinction the members of the Oak Tree in the Garden and Day Star sanghas also made during their conversations with me.

Considered as a practice, Zen is a fairly simple technique – although a difficult one in which to persist – which evolved within the context of East Asian Buddhism. The teaching is to sit in silence – mental and physical – without expectation. It is an experiment, and for centuries those who undertook it in China, Japan, Korea, and Vietnam often discovered that by doing so they attained wisdom and insight which, when ripened, manifested in empathy and compassionate behavior. The practice has the capacity, in effect, to reset the default state of mind. Instead of the usual continuous interior monologue in which one rehearses and maintains one's conditioned perspective, one is able to achieve a receptive interior silence which allows one to respond freshly and spontaneously. A variety of upayas – skillful means such as koans – developed over time to assist individuals in the practice.

Similar experiments have taken place in other traditions. As William Johnston notes, the 14th century text, *The Cloud of Unknowing*, to some extent mirrors Zen instruction. The issue then becomes whether if the spiritual experiment is carried out in various contexts it will have the same results. Is the experiment replicable?

∽

North American Catholics talk of celebrating the mass or celebrating the sacraments, but those celebrations can be very tepid affairs compared to the vibrancy of religious practices in places like Oaxaca, Mexico.

Mexico is a Catholic nation. That is not to say there aren't sceptics in the country or that there isn't a fair amount of anti-clericalism. Nor is it to overlook the evangelical

Protestant sects and other religious traditions that have established themselves there. There are even a handful of Buddhists in the country, and, in the desk drawer of my hotel room, I find a copy of *La Enseñaza de Buda*, *The Teachings of the Buddha*, placed there by the Bukkyo Dendo Kyokai or Society for the Promotion of Buddhism, a Japanese equivalent of the Gideon Society that had ensured that a *Nuevo Testamento* was also in the drawer. Still, Catholicism permeates Mexican culture.

This visit coincides with the feast of Candlemas, also known as the Celebration of the Presentation in the Temple or the Purification of the Virgin. It marks the occasion when, forty days after the birth of Jesus, Mary and Joseph brought their child to the Temple in Jerusalem as required by Jewish law. The temple visit also completed Mary's ritual purification following childbirth.

On the evening of Candlemas, we have a table on the balcony of a restaurant overlooking the city square, or Zócalo. Immediately adjacent to the Zócalo is a second square, the Alameda de León, in front of the Cathedral. The Zócalo is crowded, as usual, with musicians, street vendors, lovers, a living statue of an angel, who – if addressed – offers a box containing printed "special messages;" there are food stands competing with the terrace restaurants, children shooting five-foot long balloons into the air, even a political protest camped out in front of the Palacio de Gobierno. All of this is part of the usual evening fare, but tonight in addition there are fireworks and a parade of twirling 10 foot tall papier-mâché figures. Streams of people carry elaborately robed dolls representing the Christ child, which they are bringing to the cathedral to be blessed. Men in business suits, women, children, whole families – each member with their own doll – couples holding hands as they proceed, all make their way to the church. Later these dolls will be enthroned in homes and venerated with flowers and candles. Cynics could dismiss this all as naïve, but they would miss the point. The atmosphere here is festive. People are having fun; they are enjoying this.

Fun isn't a term I would associate much with Christianity – or, for that matter, Buddhism – as it is normally practiced in the north, where it is often presented primarily as an ethical system, what Willigis Jäger called "grammar school religion." The perspective is not much different from that of Francis Xavier and the early Jesuit missionaries to the East: Life is a test. God has prescribed a law he expects humankind to abide by, and there will be an accounting. Islam and Judaism can be understood equally simplistically.

In the fifth century CE, the Emperor Wu of China viewed Buddhism as an ethical system. When he learned that a monk from India – the land of the Buddha's birth – was travelling in his empire, he invited Bodhidharma to his court. The emperor believed in karma and was concerned about the misdeeds of his youth – some of which were responsible for bringing him to the throne. He had since tried to compensate for them through a variety of pious acts. He had sponsored the translation of Buddhist texts, supported large numbers of monks and nuns, and assumed the cost of building temples. Eager to be assured that his religious activities balanced his previous behavior, he described all he had done to promote Buddhism in his country then asked Bodhidharma, "What is your opinion? What merit have I accumulated as a result of these deeds?"

"No merit whatsoever," Bodhidharma replied.

"What then, according to your understanding, is the first principle of Buddhism?" the emperor demanded.

"Vast emptiness and not a thing that can be called holy," Bodhidharma replied at once.

Wu spluttered: "What does that mean? And who are you who now stands before me?"

To which Bodhidharma replied, "I don't know," and left the court. According to tradition, he then retired to the Shaolin Monastery where he practiced zazen facing a cave wall for nine years.

The perspectives of Zen and Catholicism, as Thomas Merton wrote, are so different that "as *structures*, as *systems*, and as *religions*" they "don't mix any better than oil and water." But then perhaps that is why they can be practiced simultaneously. As Robert Kennedy put it, he is not a Catholic Zen teacher but rather a Zen teacher who happens to be Catholic.

❧

One of the distinctive differences between Catholicism and other forms of Christianity is the veneration it pays to the Virgin Mary. The Virgin of Guadalupe, her representation in the guise of an Aztec maiden, is ubiquitous in Mexico, but here in Oaxaca there is a more popular devotion.

About five blocks west of the Alameda is the Plaza de la Danza which is bordered on the north by the Basilica of the city's patroness, the black gowned Nuestra Señora de la Soledad, Our Lady of Solitude. It is Mary as the Lady of Gethsemane, to whom Thomas Merton's abbey in Kentucky is dedicated, the Stabat Mater at the foot of the cross whom Ruben Habito identified with Maria-Kannon, Mary "bearing the wounds of her own son who bears the wounds of the world."

Another distinctly Catholic tradition one finds in the churches of Oaxaca are gruesomely realistic representations of the tortured Christ either crucified or as a deposed corpse laid out in a glass coffin. It is hard to imagine a more graphic representation of the reality of suffering, the inevitability of suffering. That, of course, is the Buddha's first noble truth: suffering is inherent in the nature of existence. To be is necessarily to suffer.

What strikes me is the way in which the images of the tortured Christ and the serene Madonna balance one another. Viewed that way, the fundamental insights of Catholic Christianity and Buddhism are not that far apart. As Pat Hawk put it, we just change the idols on the altar. There is suffering; there is compassion. The Maria-Kannon figure assures the worshipper that in spite of the pain and suffering of life, at some deep and profound level – to quote the Christian mystic Dame Julian of Norwich, as Albert Low often did – "all shall be well, and all shall be well, and all manner of things shall be well."

Although the statue of La Soledad, with its diamond studded gold crown, is very different from the simple wooden figures of Kannon frequent in Zen centers, their significance is much the same. They represent that pouring out of the self for benefit of others which Greg Mayers identified as the heart of both Catholic and Zen teaching.

ভ

One of the reasons Koun Yamada Roshi thought that Zen might find a home in Catholicism is that both Catholicism and Buddhism have contemplative traditions, although the number of people drawn to these practices is relatively small. There will always be more people engaged in devotional Buddhism and Christianity than will be interested in meditation or contemplation. So while there are three Catholic parishes in Lakeland, Florida, Janet Richardson and Rosalie McQuaide are alone in their practice of Zen.

Thomas Merton suspected that monastics even from such disparate traditions as Christianity and Buddhism might have more in common with each other than they have with their co-religionists. Contemplatives like Willigis Jäger argue that Buddhism and Christianity share a fundamental insight that is then culturally expressed. It is the cultural expressions, Jäger insisted, rather than the insight, that differ.

Like Yamada Roshi, Robert Kennedy emphasized that Zen is less a doctrine than an upaya. "Zen is a practical way of doing Buddhism," he told me. "It was put together by the Chinese around the 6th Century. As Buddhism came from India, it was rather academic. And the Chinese were practical. 'How do you do this? How do you put this into life?' And that was the beginning of Zen with Bodhidharma and the Chinese Patriarchs. 'How do you practically do this?' So that was the question. And that was how Zen was formulated."

Zen asserts that through the practice one is able to attain the same insight that Siddhartha Gautama had and as a result of which he became the Buddha, or "awakened one." By transcending one's limited ego identity, one discovers or encounters one's Buddha Nature. That experience transcends language, but inevitably, when trying to describe it, the awakened person makes use of the language and cultural imagery with which they are familiar. When Koun Yamada achieved awakening, he declared: "Shakyamuni and the Patriarchs haven't deceived me!" A Christian having the same experience might easily associate it with the oft-quoted passage from Galatians, "I live, now not I but Christ lives within me."

With kensho, both Buddhists and Christians, as Merton wrote, discover that underlying "the subjective experience of the individual self there is an immediate experience of Being." The Buddhist does not feel the need to identify that experience with the divine; the East, as Thomas Hand put it, chooses "not to conceptualize the absolute." The Christian does so naturally, but the God so encountered, as Hand discovered, is a God beyond all categories, a God beyond anything the human imagination can conceive. And, in the end, that is probably the only God worth believing in. Whatever can be encompassed by human thought must necessarily fall short of the reality to which the term "God" is applied.

Ultimately when confronting what is termed "mystery" in Catholic parlance, one can only turn on one's heel like Bodhidharma, admit with humility, "I don't know," and return to one's cushions.

Acknowledgements

Many people generously assisted in the preparation of this book. I am grateful to each of them:

- Nikki Abraham
- Gail Allatt
- Helen Amerongen
- Heather Bennett
- Mitra Bishop Roshi
- Bruce Blackman
- Harry Bolan
- Fr. Roger Brennan
- Arlindo Candido
- Patricia Centofanti
- Sr. Pascaline Coff
- Cecilia Dohrmann
- Richard Donovan
- Patrick Gallagher
- Maria Reis Habito
- Ruben Habito
- Fr. Kevin Hunt
- Dana Jagla
- Fr. John Jennings
- Fr. Robert Kennedy; I am also grateful to Father Kennedy for permission to quote material from his *Zen Spirit, Christian Spirit* (New York: Continuum, 1995).
- Bodhin Kjolhede
- Sr. Elaine MacInnes; I am also grateful to Sister Elaine for permission to quote material from her *The Flowing Bridge* (Boston: Wisdom Publications, 2007);

from *Zen Contemplation: A Bridge of Living Water* (Toronto: Novalis, 2001); and from the essay entitled "The Light of Buddhist Wisdom and the Three Births" found in *Beside Still Waters* ed. by Harold Kaminow et alli, (Boston: Wisdom Publications, 2003).

- Mary Main
- Sean Manchester
- Fr. Greg Mayers
- Madeline McDaniel (my in-house editor)
- Carolyn Murray
- Dave Nelson
- Charlie Norton
- Dosho Port
- Sr. Janet Richardson
- Robert Rosa
- Stephen Slottow
- Brenda Stephenson
- Patricia St. Onge
- Cornelia Sullivan
- Cynthia Taberner
- Sr. Madeleine Tacy
- Anna Wilby
- Tetsugan Zummach

Glossary

Anatta – "No self" – The Buddist teaching that there is no permanent underlying self or soul. Rather, human beings are compounded of five elements (skandhas) which are in a constant state of change. These are enumerated in the *Heart Sutra* as form, feeling, thought, choice, and consciousness.

Apophatic – "To deny" – A school of theology which stresses that nothing can be said about God because God is wholly beyond human conception. The closest one can come to describing God is through negative language, stating what God is not. Apophatic theology is contrasted with Cataphatic theology, which see.

Awakening – One of several terms referring to achieving insight into the basic interconnectedness of all of Being. See also "kensho" and "satori."

Bodhidharma – Legendary Indian figure who brought Zen to China. Bodhidharma is considered the 28th patriarch of Indian Buddhism and the first patriarch of Chinese Zen.

Bodhi Leaf – A leaf from the *ficus religiosa*, the type of the tree under which, traditionally, the Buddha was believed to be seated when he attained awakening.

Bodhisattva – An enlightened (Bodhi) being (sattva). Certain historical or legendary Bodhisattvas function much the same as saints in the Christian tradition.

Bonze – Portuguese term, derived from the Japanese *bonso*, for a Buddhist monk.

Buddha – Literally, "The Awakened One." When used with a capital B, it usually refers to the historic Buddha, Siddhartha Gautama. With a lower case b, it refers to any enlightened being.

Buddha Nature – The capacity, shared by all sentient being, to attain Buddhahood or awakening; one's essential nature.

Buppo – Japanese term referring to varying expressions of Buddhist doctrine.

Cataphatic – A theological approach, contrasted with Apophatic theology, which seeks ways to use language and imagery to describe and understand God.

Chan – Chinese term which the Japanese pronounced as "Zen," meaning meditation.

CIR – Christian Intensive Retreats

Contemplative Prayer – In the Catholic mystical tradition, contemplative prayer is prayer without an object, a form of prayer that arises only when the individual will comes to rest.

Daimyo – A Japanese feudal lord in the period of the Shogunate.

Dainichi – Japanese name for Vairocana Buddha, which see.

Dao – Formerly "Tao." The "way." In Daoism (Taoism) the term refers to the fundamental nature of reality.

Daoism – The teaching regarding the nature of the Dao.

Desert Fathers – A group of ascetic Christian hermits who lived in the Egyptian desert during the third century, noted for their mystical approach to spirituality.

Dharani – A repetitive phrase, similar to a mantra, which encapsulates the significance of a sutra. The "great dharani" of the *Heart Sutra* is "*Gate, gate, paragate, parasamgate, bodhi, sva-ha!*" [Gone, gone, gone beyond, gone far beyond, full awakening, rejoice!]

Dharma – A term with multiple meanings but generally refers to the teachings of Buddhism.

Dharma Heir – The heir of a Zen teacher whose understanding of the Dharma qualifies him/her to be a teacher as well.

Dokusan – Private interview between student and teacher. Also referred to as sanzen.

Dukkha – The first noble truth of Buddhism. The term means "off-center" and is usually translated as "suffering." Perhaps more appropriately it should be considered as "dissatisfaction."

Eightfold Path – The fourth noble truth of Buddhism. The way to relieve suffering [dukkha] is by overcoming desire. This can be achieved by following the eightfold path which consists of right view, right intention, right speech, right action, right livelihood, right effort, right mindfulness, and right meditation.

Emptiness – See Sunyata

Enso – A free-form calligraphic circle which symbolizes Emptiness or Sunyata.

Exclaustration – The official process of leaving a religious order – leaving the cloister.

Five Mountains – The term "mountain" in this instance refers to a temple, specifically the five principal Rinzai temples in Kyoto or Kamakura.

Four Noble Truths – The most basic of Buddhist teachings: 1) All of existence is characterized by suffering [*dukkha*]; 2) Suffering is caused by craving; 3) Suffering can be ameliorated by overcoming craving; 4) Craving can be overcome by following the Noble Eightfold path, which consists of right view, right intention, right speech, right action, right livelihood, right effort, right mindfulness, and right meditation.

Four Vows – 1) To save (liberate) all beings; 2) to eliminate endless blind passions; 3) to pass innumerable Dharma Gates; 4) to achieve the great way of Buddha.

Gassho – Placing the hands palm to palm, usually with a bow.

Guanyin – Chinese name of the Bodhisattva of Compassion, known in Japanese as Kannon, which see.

Haiku – A Japanese poetic form consisting of three lines of 5, 7, and 5 syllables respectively.

Heart Sutra – A short sutra on "emptiness" frequently chanted in Zen monasteries and temples.

Hekiganroku – A classic collection of 100 koans, also known as the *Blue Cliff Record*.

Hesychasm – An Eastern Orthodox Christian prayer practice in which inner silence is cultivated to promote union with God on a level beyond images, concepts and language.

Holy Days of Obligation – Special Feast Days on which Catholics are required to attend mass. The list of Holy Days of Obligation has changed over time. Currently the feasts include the Solemnity of Mary (January 8), the Ascension of Jesus (on the 40th day following Easter), the Assumption of Mary (August 15), All Saints Day (November 1), the Immaculate Conception (December 8), and Christmas (December 25).

Inka (*inka shomei*) – "Authorized seal proving attainment." Official transmission, especially in the Rinzai School. It is the recognition by a teacher that the student has completed training and is ready to teach independently.

-ji – A suffix meaning "temple."

Jisha – The monk who monitors meditators during formal zazen practice.

Jukai – Formally accepting the Precepts and becoming a Buddhist.

Kami – A spirit or representation of natural phenomenon in Shinto practice.

Kannon – "Guanyin" in Chinese. The female Bodhisattva of Compassion.

Karma – Literally "action." The concept in Asian thought that actions have consequences. Popularly viewed as one's past actions, in this or previous lives, resulting in one's current situation.

Karuna – Compassion.

Kensho – Seeing into one's true nature, or awakening. Although in Catholic writing on Zen the terms *kensho* and *satori* are sometimes treated interchangeably, there is usually a distinction made between *kensho*, the initial experience of awakening, and *satori*, the deeper and more profound awakening to which kensho leads.

Kentan – Formal inspection of the posture of meditators during zazen by the teacher or monitor.

Kinhin – Walking meditation.

Kirishtan – Japanese pronunciation of "Christian."

Koan – (The plural of "koan" is "koan.") Usually an anecdote from the lives of the Zen masters of the past – primarily those in Tang Dynasty China – often expressed in the form of a question. The question or situation described becomes the focus of a Zen student's meditative practice and helps the student attain insight. While koan cannot be resolved through reasoning, an understanding of them can be achieved through intuition. Individual koan are referred to as "cases" in the sense of legal precedences in jurisprudence.

Kyosaku – "The Encouragement Stick." A long stick flattened at one end, used by monitors during zazen to encourage (or wake up) meditators.

Laozi – Formerly Lao Tzu or Lao Tze. The legendary author of the *Daodejing* or *Tao Te Ching*.

Lector – Individual who assists in the formal readings during the early part of the Catholic mass, the Liturgy of the Word.

Mantra – A word, phrase, or short prayer which is repeated as a focus of meditation.

Maria-Kannon – Japanese figures in which the Virgin Mary is identified with Kannon, the Bodhisattva of Compassion.

Mu – "Wu" in Chinese. Meaning, "No, not, nothing." Usually refers to the opening koan in the *Mumonkan*: A student of the way asked Joshu in all seriousness, "Does a dog have Buddha-nature?" Joshu replied, "Mu!"

Mystical Experience – In Catholicism, generally considered a direct experience of or encounter with God.

Mysticism – In Catholicism, any of a number of practices aimed at bringing about unitive knowledge of God.

Nichiren – A Japanese form of Buddhism based on the teachings of a 13th century monk of the same name.

Nihil Obstat – "No Obstruction." An official Catholic declaration that a book or article contains nothing harmful to the faith or morals of the reader.

Nirvana – To "blow out," as a candle flame is "blown out." In early Buddhist thought, it is the goal of spiritual endeavor. It is not a destination, like Heaven, but rather personal extinction and freedom from the endless cycle of birth-and-death or *samsara*.

Prajna – Wisdom.

Precepts – The ethical code to which individuals professing Buddhism commit themselves. When declaring oneself a Buddhist, one makes the formal act of "taking the precepts" in a ceremony known as Jukai.

Pure Land – In some forms of Buddhism, a celestial destination for individuals of good merit. It is not an eternal state, however, and once the merit is exhausted the individual returns to the cycle of birth-and-death (*samsara*) until they achieve final release in *nirvana*.

Refuge Vows – "I take refuge in the Buddha; I take refuge in the Dharma; I take refuge in the Sangha."

Regency – The stage of Jesuit training prior to ordination.

Rinzai – The School of Zen practice derived from Linji Yixuan, characterized by koan study.

Rohatsu – The anniversary of the Buddha's enlightenment in December. The sesshin associated with this anniversary is considered the most daunting of the year.

Roshi – Literally, "Old Teacher." In North American Zen, it has come to mean a fully qualified Zen teacher.

Sacred Heart – A portrayal of Jesus with an exposed heart crowned by flames and circled by the crown of thorns.

Samadhi – The state of concentration or absorption.

Samsara – The repeated cycle of rebirth, life, and death.

Samu – Work period.

Samurai – Warrior class in feudal Japan.

Sanbo Kyodan – See Sanbo Zen.

Sanbo Zen – Formerly, Sanbo Kyodan. The school of Zen established by Hakuun Yasutani combining elements from both the Rinzai and Soto traditions.

Sangha – The Buddhist community.

Satori – Seeing into one's true nature, or awakening. Although in Catholic writing on Zen the terms *kensho* and *satori* are sometimes treated interchangeably, there is usually a distinction made between *kensho*, the initial experience of awakening, and *satori*, the deeper and more profound awakening to which kensho leads.

Scholastic – The second stage of Jesuit formation, following the novitiate. Scholastics, unlike novices, take initial vows of poverty, chastity, and obedience.

Sesshin – (The plural of "sesshin" is "sesshin.") A Zen retreat, traditionally seven days long.

Shaka – An abbreviated form of the title "Shakyamuni," which see.

Shakyamuni – A traditional title for the Buddha meaning "the sage of the Shakya clan."

Shikan Taza – Simple awareness as a meditation practice. In shikan taza, the meditator does not have a particular focus, such as the breath or a koan.

Shingon – A Buddhist sect brought to Japan from China by Kobo Daishi.

Shinmeikutsu – "Cave of Divine Darkness." A zendo for Christians founded in Hiroshima by Hugo Enomiya-Lassalle.

Shinto – Indigenous religion of Japan. It focuses on rituals to retain a connection between contemporary society and traditional values.

Shogunate – Period of Japanese history from 709 CE until 1867, during which actual power in the country rested not with the Emperor but a series of military commanders or Shogun.

Shoken – First formal dokusan, or interview, between teacher and student.

Shoyoroku – A classic collection of 100 koans, also known as the *Book of Serenity.*

Siddhartha Gautama – The given and family names of the Buddha.

Soto – The School of Zen descending from Sozan Honjaku and Tozan Ryokai.

Sunyata – The void, an easily misunderstood term. Essentially, it refers to that which is beyond all possibility of human conception, beyond all duality (including the duality of being or non-being); it is that from which all things arise and to which they return.

Sutra – In Buddhism, scriptural writings usually, but not always, attributed to the Buddha.

Tamashii – "Eternal spirit." Japanese term used by early missionaries to refer to "soul."

Tan – A platform in a zendo on which meditators sit.

Teisho – A formal talk given by a Zen teacher.

Tendai – A Japanese Buddhist Sect derived from the Chinese Tiantai, or Lotus Sutra, Sect.

Tengu – "Heavenly dog." Demonic figures from Japanese folklore.

Tenjiku – 16th century Japanese term for India.

Tertianship – A period of continued training after ordination in the Jesuit order.

Three Treasures – Also referred to as the Three Gems or Jewels: The Buddha, the Dharma, and the Sangha.

Tirocinium – In some religious orders, the first year of priesthood after ordination.

Transmission – Formal recognition that an individual has completed their training and may become a teacher of Zen.

True Nature – Another term for Buddha Nature.

Upaya – Skillful means. The variety of techniques used by a teacher to assist a student to come to awakening.

Vairocana Buddha – A Primordial Buddha and figure of worship in devotional forms of Buddhism.

Void – See Sunyata

Wato – A single word or image taken from a koan and used as a focus in meditation. "Mu" is a wato.

Zabuton – The mat on which a meditation cushion (zafu) is placed.

Zafu – "Buddha" (fu) "seat" (za). A meditation cushion.

Zazen – Seated (za) meditation (zen).

Zen – Literally, "meditation." Zen Buddhism is the meditation school of Buddhism.

Zendo – A meditation hall. A space reserved for the practice of zazen.

CPSIA information can be obtained
at www.ICGtesting.com
Printed in the USA
BVOW03s1502180917
495177BV00004B/23/P